AMERICAN ACADEMY OF RELIGION
ACADEMY SERIES

SERIES EDITOR
Kimberly Rae Connor, University of San Francisco

A Publication Series of
The American Academy of Religion
and Oxford University Press

ENERGIES OF THE SPIRIT
Trinitarian Models in Eastern Orthodox
and Western Theology
Duncan Reid

THE GODDESS LAKSMI
The Divine Consort in South Indian
Vaisnava Tradition
P. Pratap Kumar

CREATIVE DWELLING
Empathy and Clarity in God and Self
Lucinda A. Stark Huffaker

HOSPITALITY TO STRANGERS
Empathy and the Physician–Patient
Relationship
Dorothy M. Owens

THE BONDS OF FREEDOM
Feminist Theology and Christian
Realism
Rebekah L. Miles

THE SPECTER OF SPECIESISM
Buddhist and Christian Views of Animals
Paul Waldau

INCARNATION AND PHYSICS
Natural Science in the Theology of
Thomas F. Torrance
Tapio Luoma

OF BORDERS AND MARGINS
Hispanic Disciples in Texas, 1888–1945
Daisy L. Machado

YVES CONGAR'S THEOLOGY OF THE
HOLY SPIRIT
Elizabeth Teresa Groppe

HSIEH LIANG-TSO AND THE
ANALECTS OF CONFUCIUS
Humane Learning as a Religious Quest
Thomas W. Selover

GREGORY OF NYSSA AND THE
CONCEPT OF DIVINE PERSONS
Lucian Turcescu

GRAHAM GREENE'S CATHOLIC
IMAGINATION
Mark Bosco, S.J.

COMING TO THE EDGE OF THE
CIRCLE
A Wiccan Initiation Ritual
Nikki Bado-Fralick

THE ETHICS OF ANIMAL
EXPERIMENTATION
A Critical Analysis and Constructive
Christian Proposal
Donna Yarri

AMERICAN ACADEMY OF RELIGION

Paul in Israel's Story

Self and Community at the Cross

JOHN L. MEECH

UNIVERSITY PRESS

2006

OXFORD
UNIVERSITY PRESS

Oxford University Press, Inc., publishes works that further
Oxford University's objective of excellence
in research, scholarship, and education.

Oxford   New York
Auckland   Cape Town   Dar es Salaam   Hong Kong   Karachi
Kuala Lumpur   Madrid   Melbourne   Mexico City   Nairobi
New Delhi   Shanghai   Taipei   Toronto

With offices in
Argentina   Austria   Brazil   Chile   Czech Republic   France   Greece
Guatemala   Hungary   Italy   Japan   Poland   Portugal   Singapore
South Korea   Switzerland   Thailand   Turkey   Ukraine   Vietnam

Copyright © 2006 by The American Academy of Religion

Published by Oxford University Press, Inc.
198 Madison Avenue, New York, New York 10016

www.oup.com

Oxford is a registered trademark of Oxford University Press

Scripture taken from the *New American Standard Bible*®, Copyright © 1960,
1962, 1963, 1968, 1971, 1972, 1973, 1975, 1977, 1995
by The Lockman Foundation. Used by permission.

Library of Congress Cataloging-in-Publication Data
Meech, John L.
Paul in Israel's story : self and community at the Cross / John L. Meech.
p.   cm.—(American Academy of Religion academy series)
Includes bibliographical references and index.
ISBN-13 978-0-19-530694-1
ISBN 0-19-530694-5
1. Bible. N.T. Epistles of Paul—Psychology.
2. Self—Biblical teaching.   I. Title.   II. Series.
BS2655.P88M44 2006
227'.06—dc22   2005035997

9 8 7 6 5 4 3 2 1

Printed in the United States of America
on acid-free paper

For Cathy

Acknowledgments

I want to acknowledge the many friends and colleagues who have made this intellectual journey less lonely. Brad Hinze has been a guide and companion along the way. His thoughtful responses to various parts of the manuscript were an encouragement and a motivation to carry on. I am deeply grateful for his guidance, humor, and collegiality. Pol Vandevelde and the Seminar on Phenomenology and Hermeneutics fed a need to remain in dialogue during the often lonely process of writing. My many conversations with Pol are reflected in this book in more ways than I can say—perhaps more than I am consciously aware of. Carol Stockhausen's class on the shorter Paulines was the setting where I first articulated the questions that led to this book, and she has generously made space for our continuing conversation. I hope that these pages echo in a small way Carol's passion for engaging scholarship and questioning it rigorously on the basis of the Pauline texts. Garwood Anderson's unflagging commitment to staying current with the massive literature on the new perspective has kept me honest, if exhausted. Woody has shown me by example how to approach Scripture with an attitude of faith seeking understanding. Our conversations have been a gift. David Koukal, Brad Morrison, Denis Naylor, Ellen Naylor, and Harold Stone have all read and commented on parts of the manuscript, and suggestions from each of them have found their way into the book. When asked "Was it difficult to get your book published?" I reply "I don't know, you'd have to ask Kimberly Connor." As editor of the

American Academy of Religion Academy Series, Kim shepherded the original manuscript and, in the process, helped me become a better scholar and author. Julia TerMaat at Oxford University Press patiently answered my questions and worked with me on various aspects of the manuscript. My assistant, Hilary Bussell, proofread the manuscript and created the index. My wife and lifelong friend, Cathy Guzolek, cheerfully read the manuscript while I grumbled about this and that. She has always looked for me to reemerge beyond any momentary discouragement. To all of you I say, "Thank you." I have encountered my community in your gaze, and when I look into my own self, I meet you there.

Contents

Paul in Israel's Story

I

Introduction

Our identity in Christ is not a foundation but a risk. On the road to Damascus, Saul of Tarsus was about to encounter that risk when he could find no words to express what confronted him. A "crucified" Christ simply could not be said in his tradition as he understood it. So he retold his community's story so that the crucified and resurrected Christ could be put into words. The retelling so profoundly challenged his former self-understanding that he would later say, "I have been crucified with Christ" and "Christ lives in me." To embrace Paul in his difference from us (indeed, wherever we seek to embrace another, unlike us, in one community), we, too, may be challenged to risk our formerly reliable understandings of self and community. As a community, we are called to know only Christ crucified and the other in Christ.

Is it possible, though, that this strong tie between Paul's understanding of self, community, and the community's story is something we should bracket or, as Rudolf Bultmann says, demythologize? Rather, in writing this book, I have wagered that two conversations in philosophy and theology can mutually contribute to our own understanding of the self in community: Paul Ricoeur's investigation of the postmodern problem of the self, and a conversation in biblical studies about the meaning of law, works, faith and justification in St. Paul's letters. I refer, of course, to what J. D. G. Dunn has called the "new perspective on Paul" (building especially on E. P. Sanders's influential *Paul and Palestinian Judaism*), but I also mean the lively conversation the new perspective has engendered among its supporters and critics alike.[1] This conversation centers around four major aims: to locate our interpretations of Paul in a history of interpretation; to provide contextual theologies that will let our interpretations address the church; to let Paul speak again to the church about its relation to Judaism; and, most important, to embrace Paul in one community as another whose concerns sometimes differ from ours. As a systematic theologian working across the disciplines, I have appealed (albeit critically) to respected biblical scholarship—both to become educated in reading the biblical texts and to let these scholars supply crucial background for my own exegesis. In reading and re-reading Paul's letters (especially Romans and Galatians), and in puzzling over many of the studies published since *Paul and Palestinian Judaism,* I hope I have to some extent encountered Paul as another. The story I tell in chapter 2 reflects that encounter. Douglas Harink's *Paul among the Postliberals* looks for continuities between the apocalyptic Paul and the theologies of Karl Barth, Stanley Hauerwas, John Howard Yoder, and others.[2] I look for continuity within discontinuity between Paul's story of Israel and the theologies of Rudolf Bultmann, Robert Jenson, and Jürgen Moltmann. Traveling with St. Paul and Ricoeur, continuity within discontinuity guides the journey from start to finish.

In his hermeneutics of the self, Ricoeur executes a series of detours to the self through several ingenious accounts of selfhood (accounts from linguistics, action theory, narrative theory, fand ethics).[3] Yet he doggedly refuses to grant the last word to any one of these accounts alone; rather, he puts them all into play at once in a journey led by the question Who?—Who speaks? Who acts (and who suffers)? Who tells her story? and Who is responsible? At the end of this journey, Ricoeur constructs a multilayered ontology of the self whose fragmented nature reflects the halting path of the itinerary. Ricoeur's "broken" ontology is consistent with the kind of speculation that, as Luther says, starts from a sober gaze on the cross.[4] My own contribution to this fragmented itinerary starts from the observation that along the way Ricoeur never asks the following question: Who (speaks, acts, tells her story, is responsible) *in what community?* That is, Ricoeur never takes as an explicit theme the stories that identify communities where the self and other meet. Herein lies the link with Pauline scholarship. Paul says, "I have been crucified with Christ, Christ lives in me," and in one breath he retells Israel's story and his own life story in that great drama. Yet the implications of the new perspective for an understanding of self in community are still somewhat unexplored. For example, the tenor of the question as to whether "righteousness" refers first and foremost to the self or to the community shifts when the self and community are at stake in the same ontology. In the present study I take Paul's communal self-understanding as an occasion to explore the role of community in an ontology of the self; at the same time, I use this reconfigured ontology of the self in community to better reappropriate Paul's claim: "I have been crucified with Christ, Christ lives in me."

The fulcrum of the argument, occupying a middle point between St. Paul's communal self-understanding and Ricoeur's hermeneutics of the self, is a critical engagement with Rudolf Bultmann's interpretation of Paul. Bultmann's work has been taken as paradigmatic in the new perspective debates as an example of the "Lutheran" Paul, yet to date no critical study of Bultmann's theological anthropology has clarified what is at stake theologically and philosophically in pitting the new perspective against this "Lutheran" reading. Bultmann's work has a seductive appeal in its quick, clean path to Paul's intent: Shared transcendental conditions are laid bare through demythologizing. It is certainly a less arduous route than Ricoeur's itinerary of detours. Yet the central problem with Bultmann's reading is that it sets out from a mistaken assumption about Paul's intent: It takes the kerygma as the story of the human-being-in-general, not as first and foremost the story of a community—Israel. But by giving both self and community their due, I escape the stark either/or that sometimes characterizes the new perspective's critique of Bultmann. In the end, I am quite happy to identify myself as a Bultmannian, provided that demythologizing is understood as part of an ongoing conversation in our community about how to embrace the other from out of our past. For Paul to speak to us again, we cannot appeal to shared transcendental structures of selfhood, but we can risk retelling our community's story to narrate the continuities and discontinuities between our corresponding structures of selfhood.

This book concludes with a theological framework from which to proclaim Paul's kerygma in our context. I correlate Bultmann's fundamental structure of human existence with Ricoeur's ontology of the self, thereby offering more communal interpretations of Bultmann's *soma, pneuma,* and *syneidesis*—interpretations that have been informed by this engagement with Paul but also reflect our historical distance from him. Because I find compelling N. T. Wright's evidence that Paul's "in Christ" language refers to a people included in its king, I engage Moltmann's account of the church as the community of the living and dead in Christ.[5] I do not, however, share Wright's confidence that the analogy of Christ as king can adequately serve people in Western democracies (as it once served Paul) to relate self and community. I focus, rather, on Christ as the one anointed with the divine Spirit, linking the self and community to Robert Jenson's notion of the spirit in a community.[6] This contextual framework opens the ontology of self in community to contemporary discussions in theology, including interreligious and ecumenical dialogue, ecclesiology, and pneumatology. In these dialogues, as in our embrace of Paul, we may be called on to risk our own understanding of self and community to embrace the other as other in one community.

1.1 Engaging Perspectives on Paul

Putting these reflections into book form has given me occasion to come to terms with my own relationship to the new perspective studies. I first encountered the new perspective in the writings of Terence Donaldson, Wright, and Dunn. At the time, I was familiar with Stephen Westerholm's first book, *Israel's Law and the Church's Faith* (1988), but did not study it closely until much later.[7] Then, as I was preparing this book for publication, Westerholm released a new book, *Perspectives Old and New on Paul: The "Lutheran" Paul and his Critics* (2004). I had known that my reading of Paul differed from the new perspective studies in some important respects, but Westerholm has forced me to rearticulate these differences more carefully.

The new perspective encompasses a diverse set of scholars who agree, at a minimum, on two propositions. First, something like Sanders's covenantal nomism captures the normal pattern of Jewish worship in the Second Temple period, and thus the first-century Judaism that birthed Jesus and Paul should not be characterized as a religion of works righteousness in the classic Protestant sense. Sanders, synthesizing the work of a number of predecessors, characterizes covenantal nomism this way:

> (1) God has chosen Israel and (2) given the law. The law implies both (3) God's promise to maintain the election and (4) the requirement to obey. (5) God rewards obedience and punishes transgression. (6) The law provides for means of atonement, and atonement results in (7) maintenance or reestablishment of the covenantal relationship. (8) All those who are maintained in the covenant by obedience, atonement and God's mercy belong to the group which will be saved. An important interpretation of the first and last points is that election and ultimately salvation are considered to be by God's mercy rather than human achievement.[8]

Second, Paul's letters should be read against a background of covenantal nomism. Beyond these two propositions, paths diverge. Some, like Heiki Räisänen, argue that Paul's faith–works distinction is a distortion of covenantal nomism.[9] Others, like Sanders, argue that the tradition has been mistaken in reading Paul. Recently, a number of scholars have mounted integrated critiques of both of the propositions that characterize the new perspective.[10]

By "works of the law," Sanders says, Paul indicates the covenantal nomist position, which he contrasts with his own soteriology (based on mystical participation in Christ) indicated by the phrase "justification by faith." Donaldson, Dunn, and Wright (with variations) each understand Paul's faith–works distinction as designating alternative boundary markers of the community of the elect: "Faith," Wright says, "is the badge of covenant membership."[11] Westerholm characterizes the new perspective as a certain kind of response to the second proposition, namely, "that Paul's rejection of the works of the law had nothing to do with opposition to a role for human activity in justification."[12] Standing outside the new perspective thus understood, Westherholm accepts a qualified covenantal nomism while still offering a reading of Paul's faith–works distinction that is more consistent with the Protestant tradition (Westerholm, *Perspectives* 445). Paul is not unaware of grace in the Jewish tradition, and yet his strong faith–works distinction arises out of an extraordinarily pessimistic evaluation of the human being's ability to live by moral precepts. This evaluation, attested in fragments in the tradition before Paul, only comes to fullness in Paul's confrontation with the crucified Christ (Westerholm, *Perspectives* 421).

Readers already familiar with the new perspective will know that the growing collection of books in this many-sided debate could now fill a small library room. I do not pretend to have decided any of these important issues here. Yet my deepest conviction is that theology has to start from Scripture, and so I must risk my own claim as to Paul's meaning. This task is both necessary and possible because reading Scripture belongs to the Church as well as to the academy.[13] So the reader may judge how I relate to my dialogue partners in biblical studies, I want to briefly anticipate in this introduction how I work with several key elements of Paul's story and offer points of comparison between my interpretations and those of some biblical scholars who have most informed my reading. I hope to illustrate that my reading of the text draws on the new perspective studies, is responsive to its critics, and, most important, is responsible to the Pauline texts. In the next chapter I argue fully for conclusions that I only anticipate here.

At the heart of Paul's story is the claim that Israel as a community dies and rises in its King, Jesus the Christ (Rom. 6–8; Gal. 3:10–14). In reconstructing Paul's story, I appeal to a narrative element shared by the new perspective writers and its critics alike, namely, that sin is dealt with in the death of Israel's Christ (Rom. 4:25; Rom. 8:3). This dealing with sin tends to be explained by an appeal to the image of Christ as sacrifice, an image I situate in the community's story: Sacrifice symbolizes and anticipates an Israel that passes through death into resurrection. How does Israel's death in Christ deal with sin? When the "I" in Rom. 7 is taken in all its communal import, the death of Israel in Christ comes into view as the catastrophe at the end of the road for sin in the flesh. This death is both the consequence of sin in the flesh and God's eschatological judgment (the wrath of God in its double aspect). To be sure, God's judgment falls on all those "in Adam," but the judgment has this all-encompassing scope only in first passing through the death of Israel in its Christ. Rom. 7 thus presupposes some very concrete consequences of sin in the flesh: Paul accepts personal culpability for persecuting the Church, and recognizes this persecution as continuous with the crucifixion; Christ (who is, of course, not the agent of his own death) accepts culpability on Israel's behalf for its part in the disastrous death of its own Messiah. This is not to say that Paul portrays the Jewish people as a whole as complicit in the crucifixion. It is the "rulers of this age" who crucify Christ, and the real perpetrator, Paul says, is sin in the flesh (1 Cor. 2:8; Rom. 7:11). Yet Paul stands with Christ who, as King of Israel, accepts responsibility for the whole people: some who were unwittingly complicit in persecuting Jesus; some who sighted Israel's hoped for death and resurrection in Jesus; and some who, under Torah, still wait and hope like Abraham for the deliverer (Rom. 11:26). At the cross, Christ is set forth publicly as the righteous community in the world—a community that dies to bring an end to sin in the flesh and rises, enlivened by the divine Spirit, to make God present in the world (Rom. 3:21–26; Rom. 8:4–25). Cursed by Torah and crucified by the Romans, Christ brings an end to the walk according to flesh and inaugurates the walk in Spirit (Gal. 3:10–14; Gal. 5), fulfilling Israel's hope to die and rise to new life (Rom. 4; Rom. 8:32).

In this story, "works of the law" does not refer to human achievement per se but to Paul's former expectation that God's grace would bring about a righteous community in the Torah observant. In retrospect, Paul recognizes that sin is so deeply entwined in human experience (the flesh) that the only way out is the death of the sinner (Rom. 8:3). Torah, Paul now sees, was never the means by which God would bring about the righteous community but was the means by which God would judge sin and destroy it (Rom. 7). By "justification by faith," Paul refers to the shape of the faith of Abraham, who trusts God to provide a perfect sacrifice so that Israel may die to rise again (Rom. 4; Rom. 8:32). In "justification by faith," Paul thus sights a more original understanding of his community than "works of the law" (Gen. 15:6).

Unlike Wright, who understands works of the law as "the badges of Jewish membership (Sabbath, dietary laws, circumcision) which kept Jews separate from Gentiles," my interpretation more closely follows Dunn's formulation that works of the law "is the Pauline term for 'covenantal nomism.' "[14] Yet I diverge from Dunn where he interprets Israel's stumbling as clinging to works of law after Torah's time had passed.[15] First I assert that works of the law was always a mistaken understanding of Torah (at least for Israel in bondage to sin), and that the proper shape of Israel's hope was always justification by faith (Abraham's faith that God would provide a perfect sacrifice). Second, the climactic act of sin in the flesh is not Israel's ongoing life under Torah but the whole sequence of events that leads to the crucifixion of Israel's Christ.

This reading of works of the law is consistent with covenantal nomism insofar as it depends on God's gracious election, atonement, and empowering presence. Yet like Frank Thielman, I argue that those who practice works of the law fail to grasp the depth of Israel's plight as flesh in bondage to sin.[16] Covenantal nomism, however, is not limited to what Paul calls works of the law because it also encompasses Jews who, like Abraham, hope for God's perfect sacrifice and yet do not acknowledge Jesus as the fulfillment of that hope. Thielman suggests that after the Christ event, to observe Torah without recognizing its fulfillment in Christ begins to take on the hallmarks of an overdependence on Torah (Thielman 239). I take a cue, rather, from Dunn's observation that the anonymity of the deliverer in Rom. 11:26 is deliberate: Paul exhorts those in Christ to await the deliverer together with those of the faith of Abraham.[17] I do not mean that Paul thinks separate covenants apply to Jews and Gentiles, because he clearly believes that the hopes of all peoples (and ethnic Israel's specifically) are fulfilled in Christ (Gal. 3:14; Phil. 2:10–11; compare Rom. 9:1–5).[18] Yet despite the fact that there is only one covenant, those in Christ somehow share one eschatological community with ethnic Israel, albeit a community divided in present practice.

Though I accept (with Wright and Dunn) that righteousness conveys in one sense a boundary marker of the community, I also want to stress (with Westerholm) that righteousness says something substantive about the righteous individual.[19] When Christ goes to the cross, he is the righteous community acting righteously (Rom. 3:21–26, 5:18), and righteousness thus encompasses God's judgment on what this community is and does. The traditional interpretation of "Christ is our righteousness" (1 Cor. 1:30) is not wrong if the individual's righteousness is understood as something shared in the community in Christ. I can thus agree with Westerholm that righteousness in its ordinary, moral sense is present in Rom. 2. Before Christ, there is no community in the world that acts righteously, and to act righteously is integral to what it means to be the righteous community (compare Rom. 3:23 and 5:18). But I disagree that covenant and community are absent in what Westerholm calls "extraordinary righteousness" (righteousness attributed to the ungodly).[20] God's righteousness enters the world in Christ, who is the righteous community acting righteously. How do we, the ungodly, become righteous? We are members of the righteous community in Christ, and the covenant hope is fulfilled in us (Ezek. 36; Gal. 5). If Westerholm submerges this communal and covenantal aspect of righteousness, Wright invites an opposite misunderstanding when he says that righteous is "primarily forensic/covenantal and only secondarily (what we would call) 'ethical.' "[21] God's judgment that Christ is the righteous community presupposes Christ's righteous act (Rom. 5:18). From that perspective, acting righteously precedes the forensic/covenantal aspect of righteousness. But why should either aspect be primary? Wright is in danger of privileging the communal aspect to the exclusion of the individual, and Westerholm is in danger of privileging the individual to the exclusion of the communal. For Paul, however, there is no conflict between the righteousness of the community and the righteousness of the individual. Paul is righteous in Christ.

On the much-disputed issue of whether *pistis Christou* (and similar phrases) should be rendered "faith in" or "faith of" Christ, I am largely persuaded by the reading "faith of Christ" but grant that the issue has to be decided on a case-by-case basis according to context. The position that *pistis Christou* should be rendered "faith of Christ" was propounded and defended in Richard Hays in *The Faith of Jesus Christ*.[22] The only Pauline passage of significance to the present argument is Rom. 3:21–26, where even Dunn grants that the case is stronger.[23] Nevertheless, Dunn concludes that the reading "faith of Christ" cannot be supported even in this passage. In my interpretation of Rom. 3:21–26 in the next chapter, I follow Sam Williams and Wright in reading "faithfulness of Christ" in v. 22 and 25, arguing that this reading fits better with the theme of the passage as a whole, namely, that Christ is God's righteous community at the cross.[24]

I find the wealth of interpretations described by Westerholm something to celebrate insofar as each interpretation brings theological and practical commitments forward within a history of interpretation. In reading Paul's letters, I have attempted to be guided by what these diverse interpreters have noticed. Yet interpretation must aim at the author's original intent. I am optimistic about this aim not because I think we'll ever reach it but because we all share it: We all seek to embrace Paul, in his genuine difference from us, in one community. Moreover, all sides recognize that concerns about theology, history of interpretation, and interreligious and ecumenical dialogue cannot be allowed to prevent this embrace. Still, I agree with Bultmann that some of what Paul says cannot be applied directly in our context (for example, that a people is included in its king). Therefore we must, according to the best standards available to us, let Paul be who he is (a hermeneutic circle not without presuppositions) and then risk our own understanding of self and community in dialogue with Paul as another who is different from us. My reappropriation of Bultmann's project asserts that recognizing Paul as another still comports with the claim that God is revealed when the Church reads and proclaims the words Paul wrote.

To keep the project within bounds I have not taken Luther's interpretation of Paul as an explicit theme, despite the fact that mulling over Luther's writings has greatly informed my thinking about Paul. It seems appropriate, then, in this introduction, to at least offer some indication of how Luther has affected my thinking about Paul and the new perspective.

Luther's background story for the work of Christ, as I understand it, is that in a world presently under God's wrath, a community now proclaims God's story, lives under grace, and makes God present in the world for its salvation. The work of Christ is a kind of eschatological bridge that opens a way for God to be present in a world under wrath through the joyous exchange: Everything of mine (my sin and my curse) is Christ's, and everything of his (his righteousness and his blessing) is mine. For Luther, justification is neither forensic nor imputed but flows from the presence of Christ in the believer. Faith, as a marriage to Christ, "unites the soul with Christ as a bride is united with her bridegroom," and the neighbor encounters Christ in the believer ("be Christs to one another," Luther exhorts).[25] In "Two Kinds of Righteousness" the phrase "alien righteousness" is sometimes taken (incorrectly, in my view) to convey a forensic or imputed righteousness.[26] Yet the context of alien righteousness remains the believer's marriage to Christ and does not convey an objectifying relation to Christ's righteousness.[27] It is not a radically individualized self but the whole person in relation to Christ whom God regards as righteousness.

Yet there must be a dimension of satisfaction and payment for the sinner, which is the work of Christ. It may seem puzzling, then, that in "Two Kinds of Righteousness" Luther can say that the wronged believer who forgoes recourse to law is prepared to "make satisfaction" and "pay the penalty" for the offender.[28] What holds together the work of Christ and the believer's satisfaction for another? It is what Luther calls the joyous exchange. In expounding Gal. 3:13 Luther offers a narrative summary of the work of Christ.[29] Christ intends to bring about the blessing promised to the nations (Gen. 12:3). But he cannot do so through the law, because law only deepens our predicament. So what does Christ do? Here Luther makes the remarkable claim that Christ "attached" himself to us, making satisfaction for sin in us. "By this fortunate exchange," Luther says, Christ "took upon Himself our sinful person and granted us His innocent and victorious person" (Luther, *Galatians—1535* 284). What is the effect of Christ's satisfaction in us? In his exposition of the Magnificat, Luther observes that in this world, God is present in seeming forsakenness. The evil only encounter God in the creature; those who are saved encounter God directly, but in a hidden way known only to faith.[30] Satisfaction of the law performs the same function, namely, it brings the creature into a direct relation with the creator. That the law is satisfied brings about just this: Christ bridges the distance between God's grace and a world under wrath. Speaking metaphorically, at the cross Christ molds himself into the proper shape to bring God's grace to a world under wrath, that is, to a people under the curse. Thus the historical element in the work of Christ is that at the cross, Christ becomes the one person who can let grace erupt into a world under wrath. Yet that historical accomplishment lives in the present through the Word and Sacrament:

> Thus Christ has ordained that when we come together each one
> shall take of the bread and the cup, and afterwards preach of him.
> Why? For we are to give this [bread and cup] to no one except those
> who are Christians and who have heard Christ preached beforehand.
> But the preaching or proclamation is intended for everyone in gen-
> eral, even for those who are not yet Christians. The Christians alone
> are to partake of the sacrament, but at the same time they are to
> take thought that their number may increase. . . . Once we have the
> gift, we are then to proclaim it, so that we may bring other persons
> to it also.[31]

God is present to the world in a community, and that community is God's utter gift to the world. This story stands behind Luther's distinction between justification by faith and justification by works, each of which embodies a different understanding of this community. Justification by works is a misunderstanding of the community: It takes the works of law as directed to righteousness rather than simply to keep the peace in the earthly kingdom.[32] Justification by faith is the only proper understanding of the community: It recognizes that the law condemns and that righteousness is God's gracious gift in Christ.[33] Reading Luther's faith–works distinction against this background lessens the tension with the new perspective studies that pose faith-works as boundary markers. For Luther, the boundary of the eschatological community is inclusion in Christ, expressed in the joyous exchange. Justification by faith alone lets God be God, for it alone regards the presence of the eschatological community in the world as God's gracious gift. So Luther moves seamlessly from the experience of the believer to the reality of the church: "I believe in the holy church. . . . I believe that there is no sin and no death in the church. For believers in Christ are not sinners and are not sentenced to death but are altogether holy and righteous."[34] Thus for Luther, as for Paul, there is no real conflict between the righteousness of the community and the righteousness of the individual.

It is not so clear, however, that the same can be said in our context. When righteousness, faith, and works are taken as boundary markers, we still share two key insights with Paul, namely, the inability of human beings to act righteously and faith as utter dependence on God's gift of righteousness. Yet this interpretation transforms these insights in an unexpected way: The frame widens from the individual's plight and its solution to include the community's plight and its solution. My engagement with Ricoeur aims to show that in our context, like Paul's, the self is righteous in the righteous community.

1.2 Ricoeur and the Postmodern Problem of Selfhood

In the postmodern context, "the self" names a problem.[35] As an example of the most radical sort of critique of the self from a theological perspective, Fergus Kerr contends that the Cartesian autonomous self haunts contemporary theology, affecting theologians as diverse as Karl Rahner, Hans Küng, Don Cupitt, Schubert Ogden, and Gordon Kaufmann.[36] Kerr worries that focus on the autonomous self draws a veil over the communities and traditions that give rise to subjectivity in the first place (Kerr 8). In a similar vein, Stanley Hauerwas has said that "the self but names our attempt at agency to name the play of the languages that speak through us."[37]

Does recognizing that the Cartesian cogito is disclosed in a particular horizon automatically imply that selfhood is a fiction—that the self is an epiphenomenon of community or discourse? If my identity is expressed in a story, am I nothing more than my story? Finally, is it possible in a postmodern context to speak across communities and cultures about structures of selfhood that are at least in some sense universal? I am sympathetic to the impulse in Kerr and Hauerwas to give priority to community and narrative, but I doubt that all ontological accounts of selfhood compromise this priority. David Tracy, for one, admits that although we are ambiguous selves with commitments to plural plausibility structures, responsible praxis demands that we correlate these structures.[38] Ricoeur argues that the self, although not a foundation in the sense of the Cartesian cogito, can still be glimpsed in retrospect at the end of an itinerary of detours. "Who is telling his or her story?" is susceptible of an answer, even if only through detours.

But talk of an ontology of the self might justly raise suspicion. Is it an appeal to a variant of the transcendental subject in the tradition running from Descartes through Edmund Husserl? In an essay that predates *Oneself as Another*, Ricoeur characterizes his method of hermeneutical phenomenology as carrying on the interrogation of Being proposed by Heidegger in *Being and Time*.[39] Ricoeur's method is phenomenological (in the tradition of Husserl) because he insists that the appearances or phenomena we analyze are always constituted as a meaning for an ego (or, in Ricoeur's later usage, a meaning for a self).[40] Ricoeur's method is hermeneutical, though, because he recognizes that philosophy has no privileged access to this ego or self. Rather, the self is only ever glimpsed in retrospect and must come into discourse in some interpretation.[41] Yet Ricoeur argues that his hermeneutical phenomenology is heir not only to the later Heidegger (after the so-called turn to language, or *Kehre*) but also to the early Heidegger (the analytic of Dasein).[42] Thus, if to be postmodern means to have taken the turn away from the cogito as first truth to the interrogation of language, then Ricoeur is a postmodern. But even after that turn, Ricoeur claims, the "I am" of the "I think, therefore I am" can still be glimpsed, not as a first truth but at the end of a hermeneutics. Thus, if to be postmodern means to utterly repudiate the cogito in the manner of Nietzsche, then Ricoeur is not a postmodern.[43] But then, Ricoeur counters, not even the later Heidegger is a postmodern in that sense.[44]

Are we moderns (or postmoderns, if you prefer) really the sort of beings who can make sense of Paul's "I have been crucified with Christ?" The proper starting point of inquiry (if we accept Heidegger's lesson) should not be inner reflection but analyses of everyday life (signified by the term *lifeworld*).[45] We may hope to catch glimpses of the sort of being we are in the limits or aporias exposed in an itinerary of detours: In linguistics, who speaks? In pragmatics, who acts? In narrative, who tells his or her story? In ethics, who is responsible?[46]

Ricoeur's title, "Soi-même comme un Autre," adumbrates three major themes that run through the work. First, reflection has to precede positing the self as subject (*soi* is a reflexive pronoun). I can, in retrospect, notice the "I" present in all my actions. Yet "the first truth—I am, I think—remains as abstract and empty as it is invincible; it has to be 'mediated' by the ideas, actions, works, institutions, and monuments that objectify it."[47] The self is thus encountered only at the end of the itinerary—a hermeneutics of the self. Second, two major philosophical meanings of identity correspond to two meanings of the word *same* (*même*). Ricoeur stipulates by *ipse* (or selfhood) the temporal projection of self-constancy and by *idem* (or sameness) the permanence through time of a core self. Ipse-identity and idem-identity relate to one another dialectically, and this dialectic constitutes narrative identity. Third, selfhood implies otherness "to such an intimate degree that one cannot be thought without the other."[48] The other is not just other-than-self but self and other dialectically constitute "the self" as a meaning.

Does one entity respond to the diverse "who" questions in this itinerary? Two considerations prevent Ricoeur's ontology of the self from becoming a foundation in the sense of Husserl's transcendental ego.[49] The first concerns the sort of certainty appropriate to a hermeneutics of the self, a certainty Ricoeur names *attestation*. Attestation is a kind of belief linked not to *doxa* (I believe that) but testimony (I believe in).[50] Attestation is the certainty that the aporias revealed along the itinerary testify to the self. The opposite of attestation is not falsity but suspicion. Yet suspicion has no a priori precedence over attestation, because attestation and suspicion both have to enter discourse in some interpretation of the lifeworld. The second consideration concerns the ineluctable role of the other in the constitution of selfhood. The self cannot ground truth in the manner of the transcendental ego because to say "I am" (I am an object spoken about, I am the speaker, I am the one who acts, I am the one who tells my story, I am responsible) always presupposes the copresence of self and other in a shared world. Appeal to a transcendental ego, therefore, could never trump the ongoing dialogue in a community about what is the best interpretation.

The philosophical component of my own project is a clarification and extension of Ricoeur's project, namely, to bring the ontology of the self within the scope of the community and self as correlates.[51] That the community and self are correlates means that the self is not the condition of community, nor community the condition of the self, but that each is mutually the condition of the other. What has ontological weight (and resists interpretation otherwise) is not the community or the self alone but the self in community, a community of selves. In the concluding chapter, I correlate Paul's understanding of selfhood with ours to reappropriate Paul's "I have been crucified with Christ" in our context. In the context of the argument, there should be little cause to confuse the self and community as *correlates* (a term borrowed from Husserl's *Cartesian Meditations*) with the theological method of *correlation* (or other verb forms of "to correlate") that seeks to relate concepts across diverse discourses or historical horizons (a method borrowed from Tracy).[52]

I must acknowledge a danger, though, that I might impose an ontology of the self on St. Paul's writings by fiat in much the same way that Bultmann

uses a transcendental structure of selfhood to connect then and now. Ultimately, what is called for is a genealogy of selfhood that narrates the historical
shift from Paul's understanding of selfhood to ours.[53] Until such a genealogy
is on offer, though, one could suspect that any correlation of Paul's self and
ours is just one more imposition of the present on the past. Yet if, as I suspect,
a genealogy can confirm this correlation, then the present project narrates one
episode in that larger story. At any rate, the opposing claim (that Paul's I is
somehow radically other than our contemporary understanding of the self and
cannot be connected with it) would also have to be won in some other itinerary
of detours through analysis. My itinerary begins, then, with Paul's risk in retelling Israel's story.

2

Paul as Another in Israel's Story

St. Paul's use of the pronoun *I* is communal in a sense that is somewhat difficult for the modern person to grasp. To reconstruct the kind of self presupposed in Paul's letters, I explore the relation between Paul's self-understanding and the story he tells to identify his community. On the way, I critically engage a range of biblical scholarship to identify the background to Paul's use of law, sacrifice, divine Spirit, human spirit, and conscience. My contribution, in conversation with these biblical scholars, is to interpret Rom. 3:21–26, Rom. 7, and Gal. 3:10–14 from the perspective of the community that dies and rises in Christ. In conclusion, I reflect back on the kind of self disclosed in that story. To what extent Paul's understanding of selfhood should confront our own self-understanding is the focus of the remaining chapters.

2.1 Torah and Israel's Hope

Paul's story trades on a common Jewish pattern that N. T. Wright identifies as retelling Adam's story as a story about Israel.[1] In these stories, Israel, the family of Abraham, is God's true humanity, and Israel's enemies are God's enemies. These Jews envisioned that Israel, enlightened by Torah and the divine wisdom, would rule the nations and bring about true justice (Wright, *Climax* 110). God's righteousness, then, is God's faithfulness to the covenant and culminates in God's vindication when He rules the world through Israel, his true humanity (Wright, *Climax* 24). As the eschatological marker of membership in the community that awaits God's rule, Torah demarcates Israel as a people (Deut. 6:20–25).[2]

Yet in demarcating Israel as a people, Torah also helps constitute the self-understanding of the individual Jew. Bruce Malina argues that first-century human beings are dyadic persons, referring to their strong sense of existing in relation to another (hence, dyad). "Such a group-embedded, dyadic person-ality is one who simply needs another continually in order to know who he or she really is."[3] Malina proposes a three-zone model of such a personality: the zone of emotion-fused thought (eyes-heart), the zone of self-expressive speech (mouth-ears), and the zone of purposeful action (hands-feet) (Malina 74–75). All three of these zones are implied in the description of Torah given in Deut. 30:11–14: This commandment "is very near you, in your mouth [self-expressive speech] and in your heart [emotion-fused thought], that you may observe it [purposeful action]." Torah thus not only demarcates the elect community (Deut. 6:20–25) but also helps constitute the person on all three levels of per-sonal reality: heart, mouth, hands, and feet. Torah relates the Israelite to her neighbor, to the community in her neighbor, and to the covenanting God (Deut. 6:4–5; Lev. 19:18). Thus Torah is intimately tied to the perception of who is my proper other, that is, who co-constitutes me in a dyad. Consequently Torah is a relational or even anthropological category if anthropology can be stretched to include that which mediates the relation to the other who coconstitutes me as a dyad.

The God-ward side of this relation could be expressed by the association of Torah with the divine wisdom and Spirit. Wisdom, God's companion in creation (Prov. 8:22–31), reveals and empowers the true human existence God planned for Adam.[4] Therefore in the Jew's experience, Torah was not just a law code but, as Wright observes, the "breath of the living God, identified . . . with that Wisdom who was with the creator, acting as his agent, from the beginning of the world."[5] The association of Torah and wisdom thus places Torah at the center of the Jewish understanding of the world—in modern theological parlance, Torah is the center of Israel's ontology.

A second way of expressing the God-ward side of the relation of Israel to its covenanting God is Spirit. After Paul's time, the rabbis believed that God's Shekinah presence accompanied and empowered the study of Torah and that Torah observance made one worthy to receive the Spirit.[6] Indeed, the Scriptures themselves affirm that God's Spirit empowers Torah observance, not only es-chatologically (e.g., Ezek. 36:27) but also in the present age (e.g., Psalms 51:

10–12). Even where the psalmist demands God's favorable judgment based on Torah observance ("revive me" for "I have done justice and righteousness," Psalms 119:25, 40, 121), he still petitions God to empower that Torah observance, for example, "teach me" (v. 26), "make me understand" (v. 27), "strengthen me" (v. 28), and "remove the false way from me" (v. 29). Of course, the exact relationship between Torah and Spirit in the first century is not known, but there are some indications that this same pattern held. Some first-century documents, for example, attest to the individual's spirit as the presence of the Holy Spirit.[7] Also, at Qumran, the *Community Rule* says that the Holy Spirit cleanses the devout of sin, and the *Hodayot* says that the Spirit gives knowledge of God and empowers seeking after God.[8] It is plausible, then, that a Jew like Paul would have understood Torah observance as doubly related to God's Spirit: On one hand, God's Spirit empowered Torah observance; on the other hand, Torah observance made one worthy of God's Spirit, that is, worthy to receive life.[9] Indeed, Paul himself may give evidence for such a tradition in the first century when he says that the Spirit guides his reading of Scripture (2 Cor. 3:1–4:6).[10]

Finally, Torah also expresses soteriological meaning because it makes provision for unintended sin (atonement), it is the standard by which the nations will be judged, and it is the boundary marker of the community Gentiles must enter to be saved. Thus even before Paul retold Israel's story, Torah belonged to a universalistic structure of salvation.[11] In sum, Torah demarcates the righteous community that in the present age, all must enter to be saved (soteriology); it is the heart of Israel's identity as a community, and the identity of individual Jews (community and anthropology); in relation to wisdom it constitutes Israel's world (ontology); and in relation to Spirit it empowers Israel's life (pneumatology).

Although Torah is a relational, soteriological, and even ontological category within first-century Judaism, it is not personal in the same sense as the Messiah. Where the Messiah appears in retellings of Israel's story, he can include the whole people in his person: the destiny of the Messiah is identically the destiny of the Jewish people.[12] To claim that one is "in the Messiah" is not to make a metaphysical or mystical claim; rather, it is to identify oneself as belonging to God's covenant people included in the Messiah (Wright, *Climax* 46). Whatever degree of importance various Jewish sects might have attached to the person of the Messiah, before Paul there is no tension between the categories Torah and Messiah. Torah demarcates the community, and the Messiah, where he figures in the story, is the agent of its salvation.[13] How is it, then, that Paul came to see a conflict between Christ and Torah?

2.2 Paul the Pharisee: Torah and Not Christ

Terence Donaldson argues that Paul's conflict between Christ and Torah can be traced to a conviction that predates his encounter with the risen Christ. To identify that conviction, however, calls for some speculation about Paul's commitments before his encounter. That speculation can be well founded if two sets of public data are correlated: documents attesting to a range of options in first-century Jewish attitudes to Gentile converts, and convictions attested in Paul's letters. Based on this evidence, Donaldson concludes that Paul probably belonged to a Pharisaic sect that enjoined strict Torah observance and zeal in its maintenance (Phil. 3:6; Gal. 1:13–14).[14] "Zeal was more than just a fervent commitment to the Torah; it denoted a willingness to use violence against any—Jews, Gentiles, or the wicked in general—who were contravening, opposing, or subverting the Torah."[15] Zeal operated on two levels: to bring the wrongdoer to repentance through punishment and to restore the righteousness of the community by atoning for sins. Zeal did not oppose itself to just any threat but specifically to threats to the righteous status of the Torah-observant community. How, then, did the claim that the crucified Jesus was the Christ come into conflict with Paul's zeal?

Donaldson rejects the hypothesis that Paul's Torah–Christ conflict was based simply on the Deuteronomic curse against someone hung on a tree (Deut. 21:22–23) (Donaldson 171). Rather, he hypothesizes that Paul's conflict arose out of a prior understanding of proselytism that stood behind his subsequent mission to the Gentiles. Specifically, the convictions underneath Paul's letters parallel an attitude to Gentiles that Donaldson calls "the proselyte model."[16] The proselyte model required Gentile converts to devote themselves exclusively to the God of Israel, be incorporated into the people of Israel as full members of the family of Abraham, and adopt strict Torah observance (especially the circumcision of males). At least some Jews who took this proselytizing attitude understood it to be limited to the present age, that is, that Gentiles could only enter Israel through Torah observance until the advent of the Messiah (Donaldson 69, 224–26).

With this model in Paul's background, two aspects of the Christian proclamation constitute the kind of threat to Torah observance that would have provoked his zeal. First, "the Christian community included in its fellowship those whom the Torah would declare to be unrighteous; therefore the Torah was *not necessary*" (Donaldson 291). Second, "Christian preaching declared that to be part of the community destined for salvation, everyone—even those whom the Torah would declare to be 'righteous'; even . . . one zealous for the law like Paul himself—needed to believe in Jesus; therefore the Torah was *not sufficient*" (Donaldson 291). Yet the situation of the Jew who does not confess "Jesus is Lord" is more complex than Donaldson allows. I agree that Paul's assertion "we would receive the promise of the Spirit through faith" (Gal. 3: 14) means that Paul and his interlocutor (both Jews) received the promised Spirit through faith, not Torah observance. But from Paul's perspective after Damascus, Jews of the faith of Abraham and Jews and Gentiles "in Christ" together constitute one eschatological community that awaits the deliverer out of Zion (Rom. 11:26).[17] In present practice, of course, this community is divided. But to assert that a Jew with faith like Abraham's has to believe that Jesus is the Christ "to be part of the community destined for salvation" reasserts a deadly in and out mentality of the sort that goaded Paul's zeal. Gal. 3:14 certainly does indicate that Torah is insufficient in some respect, and (pre-Damascus) that would indeed have exercised Paul's zeal. Yet to see what is at stake for Paul in rearticulating his community calls for a closer look at his original encounter with Christ.

2.3 Paul's Encounter with Christ: Christ and Not Torah

What can we know from Paul's letters about the event that precipitated his transition from "Torah and not Christ" to "Christ and not Torah?" Historical-critical studies remind us that authors reflect on events in specific contexts and shape their rhetoric to achieve intelligible goals in those contexts. Yet I want to stress a somewhat different point, namely, that the event Paul later calls an encounter with the risen Christ would have been at its heart inarticulable in Paul's earlier horizon. In other words, the standard historical-critical warning that temporal distance can distort a report can obscure an equally important insight—namely, that some events become coherent only on subsequent reflection. I do not intend a claim here about Paul's inner life. In the previous sections, I drew on the work of several biblical scholars to suggest a partial reconstruction of how Paul understood Judaism as a public story and set of convictions. Now I want to ask what happens to a person constituted by such public symbols when he affirms (as Paul later did) that Christ has been crucified and resurrected but that Torah-observant Jews like Paul did not enter into the resurrection with him.

Paul's new experience is an anomaly, which is to say that it cannot be adequately articulated in his framework. As Donaldson says, Paul's Damascus experience is "a new, unanticipated and disjunctive experience, one which resists assimilation into the inherited world of understanding, and thus precipitates its disintegration."[18] Yet there is something deeply disturbing about the kind of anomaly Paul faces. If he is a dyadic personality, then the either-or he faces is more than either Christ or Torah as the boundary of Israel. The risk he faces is that if he casts his lot with this anomaly, he can no longer count on the formerly reliable story of his own community. In other words, Paul does not retell the story because he has seen the resurrected Christ; rather, he retells the story to put words to an event his tradition has no words for. He later articulates this event as an encounter with the resurrected Christ, but by then his community's story will have already been called into question. I can agree with Dunn that "the distinctiveness of Paul's conversion experience consisted in . . . a real perception of an encounter with Jesus, albeit in a sphere of existence which cannot be brought within the limitations of visual description."[19] But we must not pass too quickly from "Jesus lives again" to "Jesus was resurrected." To see Jesus alive again would be extraordinary, to be sure; but to see Jesus resurrected would be to see him living already in God's eschatological future, and to make that intelligible, the story has to be told differently.

Those who shared Paul's prior story expected that Israel's punishment would lead to forgiveness while the nations would be judged.[20] But if Jesus alone was raised, then he alone entered God's future without those who, like Paul, were marked among the righteous by Torah observance. Moreover, from Paul's prior perspective, to confess Christ resurrected would be to accept God's vindication of a man whose followers Paul had persecuted, believing he was acting on behalf of the Torah-observant. Consequently, in facing Jesus as the sole human inhabitant of the eschaton, Paul faced a more radical universal judgment than the universalism already entailed in the proselyte model: If Jesus alone was raised, then everyone else was judged (Rom. 3:23). I refer, of course, to the moment of inarticulateness before Paul retells his experience as an encounter with the risen Christ; after this rearticulation he can once again identify the righteous community as those "in Christ." But from his earlier perspective, to articulate "Jesus lives again" as "Jesus is resurrected" would throw Paul's whole world of who is righteous and who is unrighteous into inarticulateness. In short, although "Jesus lives again" might be made coherent within Paul's narrative world, the more eschatologically loaded "Jesus is resurrected" can only be uttered from within a story that is already being retold.

Finally, to confess that this resurrected Jesus is also the Christ involves yet another challenge to Paul's narrative world. Doubtless Paul could have understood Jesus' resurrection as the vindication of a prior claim that Jesus was the Messiah (whether by Jesus or by his followers on his behalf). Yet the problem is not just whether Paul could say "yes" where he had once said "no." Rather, the very meaning of the word *Christ* shifts between its denial and its affirmation. From the perspective of Paul the Pharisee, the Christ represents Israel; yet Paul's expectation was that the Christ and Israel would be raised together. Given Paul's prior story, Jesus would seem to be a Christ without an Israel. Sometime later Paul will redescribe the Jesus communities as "in Christ" through the mediation of the divine Spirit bestowed on Christ. Of course, Paul didn't have to articulate all of this before he could affirm that Jesus was the Christ. Yet one speaks from his later perspective when saying that Paul was confronted by the resurrected *Christ.* Thus it is problematic to regard Paul's reconfiguration of Israel as the simple exchange of one boundary (Torah) for another (Christ); rather, the very meanings of the boundary terms shift in the reconfiguration.[21] Paul the persecutor would have understood the logic of the Jesus communities as entailing some such shift (perhaps unarticulated), but he would have understood their reasoning as error. Before Paul could articulate as truth what he had once perceived as error, he would have to begin to retell his community's story. Though Paul is never without a community, from the moment of his encounter he has to contend for the community's identity if he is to let the risen Christ appear.

It is difficult for us to appreciate the profound difficulty of what Paul attempts. By way of comparison, I am struck by Jean François Lyotard's description of a *differend* (a conflict that cannot be resolved because the disputants do not share the same framework) as "something that asks to be put into phrases":

> In the differend something "asks" to be put into phrases, and suffers from the wrong of not being able to be put into phrases right away. This is when the human beings who thought they could use language as an instrument of communication learn through the feeling of pain which accompanies silence (and of pleasure which accompanies the invention of a new idiom), that they are summoned by language, not to augment to their profit the quantity of information communicable through existing idioms, but to recognize that what remains to be phrased exceeds what they can presently phrase, and that they must be allowed to institute idioms which do not yet exist.[22]

Although Paul in his zeal confidently addresses his world, he finds himself addressed by something that asks to be put into phrases but has no idiom. Yet with respect to what happened to St. Paul, Lyotard's account is inadequate, because the invention of a new idiom hardly captures the tremendous cost Paul bears as a dyadic personality in retelling his own community's story. In choosing to name this unutterable something "the crucified and resurrected Christ" (over the claims of his established narrative), Paul disrupts the comfortable reliability of his own narrated world. Insofar as Torah gives the categories in which Paul's world is articulated, his world is at stake in the retelling; as a dyadic personality, Paul's community and his self-understanding are equally at stake.

2.4 The Detour to Paul's Reconfigured Self:
Paul's Story of Israel

I now turn to the lines of Paul's mature narrative to glimpse, at the end of this account, the sort of self that appears in Paul's reconfigured story of Israel. To sight the communal dimension of Paul's story, I start with Dunn's account of Christ as sacrifice, then turn to Wright and Donaldson to begin to uncover the role of the community in this sacrifice. Yet even in these authors, Christ's role as Israel's representative submerges Israel's particular role at the cross: Israel is judged in Christ, and Israel is at the cross in Christ. But how in particular does God's wrath fall on Israel in Christ? What is the story? Here I offer a reading of Rom. 7, Gal. 3:10–14, and Rom. 3:21–26 to resituate the symbol of sacrifice in Israel's story. Sacrifice symbolizes and anticipates Israel's own experience: Implicated in its own death in Christ, Israel passes through death into resurrection.

2.4.1 Dunn: Christ as Sacrifice for the Sinner

On one hand, Israel's death in its Christ reveals the universal human condition of sin, flesh, and death under the law (Rom. 3:19):

> If Jesus dies, then all are dead. If *the* Christ dies, then no one can
> escape death. When Paul says the "one" (eschatological Adamic figure) died [2 Cor. 5:14], he means that there is no other end possible
> for all human beings. All humankind dies, as he died, as flesh, as
> the end of sinful flesh (Rom. 8:3). Had there been a way for sinful
> flesh to overcome its downward drag, to escape its subjection to the
> power of sin, God's representative man need not and would not
> have died. The one would have demonstrated to the all how the sinful flesh could be overcome. . . . The death of the one signifies that
> there is no way out for the weak and corrupted flesh except through
> death, no answer to the power of sin working in and through the
> flesh except its destruction in death. As Karl Barth put it, "Man
> could not be helped other than through his annihilation."[23]

On the other hand, the human story can go on only if we participate in the story of Christ as the one who died and was raised. How does Israel in Christ participate in the death and resurrection of Christ? First, Dunn appeals to the image of sacrifice, seeming close to the idea that sacrifice is a kind of transaction that absorbs the penalty for sin.[24] Yet that impression has to be balanced against his assertion that the images of sacrifice and representation say the same thing, that is, "Paul's teaching is *not* that Christ dies 'in the place of' others so that they *escape* death (as the logic of substitution implies). It is rather that Christ's sharing *their* death makes it possible for them to share *his* death" (Dunn, *Theology of Paul the Apostle* 223). Dunn adduces Morna Hooker's description of the dynamics of sacrifice: "By the sacrifice the *sinner* was made *pure* and lived *free of that sin*; By the sacrifice the *pure* animal *died*. And we can hardly fail to fill out the rest of the second line by adding: By the sacrifice the *pure* animal was made *impure* and *died for that sin*—by its death destroying the sin" (Dunn, *Theology of Paul the Apostle* 222).

Here is an overarching story in which to situate "due penalty." But it is a story about the individual, not about the community: Sacrifice is a symbol of the individual sinner's death and resurrection. When sin brings death to the sinner, death will make an end of sin. The sacrifice, as symbol, expresses the present reality of the hope that God will raise the sinner into a new life, pure and free from sin. The dynamic that brings an end to sin is just the outcome of sin itself (death), but this outcome is also the wrath of God (Rom. 1:18).[25] "Wrath of God" thus has a double aspect, narrating the consequences of human unrighteousness but also construing these consequences as God's own act of judgment. The consequences of human unrighteousness serve the purposes of God, specifically, to destroy sin where it has lodged itself, in the flesh.

To transfer this storyline to the community, one could say that when Israel participates in Christ as sacrifice it becomes the community that dies (killing sin in the flesh and leaving the old creation) and rises in Christ (entering the new creation). Although Dunn's reading of "participation in Christ" is communal in a certain sense, this participation is not first and foremost the experience of a community.[26] First, Dunn insists that participation in Christ is a mystical experience that takes place in a community (Dunn, *Theology of Paul the Apostle* 395). Second, he still retains a somewhat individualistic reading of Paul's soteriology. Consider, for example, his claim that "up until the end of Romans 8 Paul's exposition of the tension and process [of salvation] *could have been understood in solely individual terms*" (Dunn, *Theology of Paul the Apostle* 508; emphasis added). With Wright and Donaldson, rather, I maintain that the story of salvation in Romans is the community's story from beginning to end.[27] I do not mean to say that Dunn understands salvation solely in individualistic terms. He does not. Still, Dunn's account alone cannot properly set up my own task, namely, a detour to the self through the community. For that reason I now turn to Wright and Donaldson to sight the communal dimension of Paul's story.

2.4.2 Donaldson and Wright: Paul's Story as the Story of His Community

Donaldson argues that in Paul's schema of salvation, both Torah and ethnic Israel retain a soteriological role (Rom. 9–11), but that these roles have shifted. The role of Torah, Paul now sees, was to identify sin and condemn it in Israel: "God has deliberately given the Torah to be the means of concentrating the sin of humankind in one place, namely, in his people Israel—in order that it might then be concentrated yet further, drawn together on to Israel's representative, the Messiah—in order that it might there be dealt with once and for all."[28]

Wright weaves the idea of dealing with sin into Paul's story of Israel by way of the exilic curse (Gal. 3:10–14).[29] On the whole, I have no quarrel with Wright's claim that many first-century Jews would have thought that Israel was still in exile. Yet the exile theme, if pushed too far, can submerge Israel's role in the particular catastrophe that occurred in Paul's own lifetime, namely, the crucifixion of Israel in its Christ.[30] The cross is not only the climax of the exile (the wrath of God) but also the culminating act of sin in the flesh (the outcome of human sin). To the extent that Donaldson and Wright construe dealing with sin as a past transaction that pays for sin and brings an end to the exile, Dunn's more dynamic understanding of Christ as representative is to be preferred. But Dunn, as I have already observed, does not offer a sufficiently communal account of Christ as sacrifice or participation in Christ. Donaldson offers a more communal account of Christ as sacrifice, but doesn't say much about participation. Wright offers a communal account of participation, but he doesn't place dying and rising with Christ at the center of Paul's soteriology. I intend to situate dying and rising with Christ in Israel's story and interpret the theme as communal in its historical provenance (ethnic Israel) and present reality (Israel reconfigured around Christ). To do this, it will be necessary to speak of Christ's bearing the divine Spirit at the cross. So I first address Paul's use of the phrases "Spirit of Christ" and "Spirit of the Son."

2.4.3 The Eschatological Spirit as the Spirit of Christ

Paul's retelling of Israel's story entails a new designation for the eschatological Spirit, namely, the Spirit of Christ (or the Spirit of the Son). What does this new designation imply? First, the genitive denotes that Israel demarcated by Christ receives the Spirit only in Christ rather than as a direct bestowal (Rom. 8:9–11). Consider Rom. 8:1–11: God sent Torah to give life to his people, but the gift of life was blocked by flesh under slavery to sin (Rom. 7:14).[31] Therefore God sent His son to condemn sin in the flesh (Rom. 8:3). Verse 4 ("that the requirement of the law might be fulfilled in us") has the same object as v. 11, that is, that God "will also give life to your mortal bodies through His Spirit who dwells in you." Our death in Christ thus gives us a just share in his resurrection life (which is the gift of the Holy Spirit), and so God righteously renders the covenant judgment on us, "Live!" If Paul formerly accepted the traditional belief that Spirit empowers Torah observance, then his understanding has now been recentered on Christ (2 Cor. 3:1–4:6). Christ alone is obedient (Rom. 5:18); Christ alone is anointed with God's Spirit and has been raised from the dead (Rom. 1:4). The community in Christ receives the Spirit only because it participates in Christ, hence, the community experiences the Spirit of God as the Spirit of Christ (Rom. 8:9).

Second, "the Spirit of Christ/the Son" means that the Spirit brings Christ. Here one has to distinguish carefully between Paul's use of the phrases "Spirit in you/me" and "Christ in you/me." In arguing that Gal. 2:20 ("Christ lives in me") refers to the indwelling of the Spirit, Gordon Fee maintains the distinction between the Spirit and the Son only at the expense of any unique import to Paul's "Christ in me/you" language.[32] But a better interpretation of Gal. 2:20 follows from Malina's model of dyadic personality. A dyadic personality like Paul "needs another continually in order to know who he or she really is."[33] The constitution of the dyadic person in the Torah-centered community already entailed a kind of "Torah in you" language, for example, in Deut. 30:11–14 Torah is "in your heart and in your mouth." When the boundary shifts from Torah to Christ, a similar "Christ in you" language now expresses Christ as the dyadic person's constitutive other. That explanation of Gal. 2:20 better maintains both the distinction between Christ and the Spirit and the unique import of Paul's "Christ in me/you" language. The dyadic personality understands herself in terms of her relation to another (the covenanting God or the neighbor), and that other is now articulated no longer through Torah but through Christ.

A third sense in which the Spirit is the Spirit of Christ is that the Spirit forms the community to the crucified, suffering, resurrected Christ. In a world under wrath, God's glory is manifest in this community by its suffering with Christ for others, "always carrying about in the body the dying of Jesus, so that the life of Jesus also may be manifested in our body. . . . So death works in us, but life in you" (2 Cor. 4:10–12). Keeping in mind the stronger distinction I assert between Christ and the Spirit, I can otherwise agree with Dunn's summary:

> In his life Jesus was a man determined by the Spirit—he lived "according to the Spirit" (Rom. 1:3f); but in the resurrection the relationship was reversed and Jesus became the determiner of the Spirit. In a sense we may say that Jesus was so wholly determined by the Spirit of God that the character of Jesus became the clearest possible visible expression of the Spirit—not merely his actions and words, but Jesus himself became the charisma of God. . . . And so the character of Jesus became as it were the archetype which the eschatological Spirit filled, the "shape" which the Spirit took on as a mould, the shape which the Spirit in turn stamps upon believers.[34]

Such molding and shaping happens in the community of the crucified and resurrected Christ, as witnessed in 2 Cor. 3:17–18.[35] That "the Lord is the Spirit" does not identify Christ with the Spirit but establishes that Lord in the previous phrase ("whenever a person turns to the Lord, the veil is taken away") refers to the Spirit.[36] In other words, the openness of the Corinthians to the Spirit is likened to when Moses turned his unveiled face to Yahweh. Their fellowship, as partaking of the eschatological Spirit, is the living reality of the new covenant (2 Cor. 3:6). What, then, is the mirror in which we behold the glory of the Lord? It is the face of the neighbor who is also being conformed to Christ by the Spirit.[37] The Spirit's transforming work thus becomes visible in everyday face-to-face encounters in a community. The Spirit of Christ forms the community to the crucified, suffering, resurrected Christ. Yet to see how this community dies and rises in Christ, it is first necessary to see how Christ, as the community's representative, goes to the cross anointed with the divine Spirit.

2.4.4 Jesus as the Christ Anointed with God's Spirit at the Cross

In the gospels, of course, it is clear that Jesus goes to the cross anointed by God's Spirit.[38] Yet the relationship between Jesus and the Spirit prior to the cross is difficult to discern in Paul's letters because he focuses on the cross and resurrection to the near exclusion of Jesus' ministry. Dunn observes that the most problematic passage in this regard, Rom. 1:3–4, still does not rule out that Paul "may well have seen Jesus' resurrection appointment *kata pneuma* as in some important sense an outworking of his life on earth lived *kata pneuma* (cf. 2 Cor. 4:16–5:5)."[39] First, the Spirit in Paul's theology is closely tied to Christ's role as Israel's representative.[40] Second, Paul avoided identifying the Spirit as the agent of the resurrection (Rom. 6:4, 8:11).[41] I take Dunn's point to be that if the Spirit can be identified as the Spirit of Christ—and yet the Spirit is not bestowed on Christ simply as the agent of his resurrection—then "Spirit of Christ" can only mean that the Spirit is defined by the relationship of Jesus and the Spirit throughout his life. Consider, finally, that although Rom. 1:3–4 might be taken as a temporal sequence (descendant of David *kata sarka* and Son of God *kata pneuma* through the resurrection), Rom. 8:3 reverses that sequence (if it is a sequence). There it is God's Son who "concerning sin (*peri hamartias*) condemned sin in the flesh." That Jesus is God's Son is thus a precondition of what God accomplishes at the cross, and if the title Son is associated with possessing the Spirit (Rom. 1:4), then Jesus must have gone to the cross anointed with God's Spirit.[42]

But perhaps the strongest reason for understanding Christ as the one who goes to the cross anointed with God's Spirit is that the community that participates in him shares that experience. In other words, if the community represented by Christ possesses the Spirit of Christ, dies to the world under wrath, and is raised in the life of the Spirit (Rom. 8:11, 17), then that must be the experience of its representative, Jesus Christ. That Jesus in his earthly life shares the experience of his community is also attested in Rom. 3:21–26, where God's presence with Jesus is expressed under the figure of mercy seat rather than Spirit.

2.4.4.1 ROMANS 3:21–26. I have argued that a first-century Jew may well have believed that Torah observance was empowered by the Spirit and that God would manifest his righteousness by vindicating Torah-observant Israel. Paul says in Rom. 3:21, however, that God's righteousness is revealed apart from the law, though witnessed by the law. With Sam Williams and Wright, I take *pisteōs Christou* and *pisteōs en tō auto haimati* in v. 22 and 25 to refer to "Christ's faithfulness" and "Christ's blood shed in faithfulness" rather than "faith in Christ."[43] The referent of *pisteōs Iesou Christou* (v. 22) is not likely to be the believer's faith, because *dia pisteōs Iesou Christou* qualifies the same righteousness "manifested (*pethanerōtai*), being witnessed by the Law and the Prophets" in v. 21. In the context, what is witnessed by the law and the prophets is not the righteousness that comes about in the believer's faith but the righteousness God accomplishes in Christ. Christ's faithfulness unto death—as one under the curse and thus outside the covenant (Rom. 8:3, Gal. 3:13)—perfectly manifests the boundary of the covenant community apart from the law. At the cross, God demonstrates the boundary of the covenant community in Jesus' faithfulness, that is, in Christ's ultimate obedience unto death (Rom. 5:18; Phil. 2:

8). When Paul confronted Christ resurrected without the Torah-observant, he recognized that Jesus himself had fulfilled Israel's hope to be the people in whom God tabernacles.

Consequently, *hilasterion* in v. 25 should not be translated as "sin offering" but as "mercy seat," that is, the place where God is present to the world in a people. Dunn contrasts the public death of Christ (*proetheto*) with the hiddenness of the temple cult.[44] Although Dunn concludes from this that he should translate *hilasterion* as sin offering, his argument can point in a different direction. Lyonnet and Sabourin argue, rather, that *hilasterion* should be translated mercy seat because "while the propitiatory was not seen by anyone and could not be seen, Christ is openly and publicly shown by God before the whole human race, as the verb *proetheto* apparently has to be understood."[45] Christ's obedience on the cross reveals the boundary of the community in which God tabernacles, and that is the righteousness of God revealed apart from the law (v. 21).

What does it mean to say that Christ is a mercy seat? At the mercy seat God is present in a voice (Exod. 25:22; Num. 7:89) and a cloud (Lev. 16:2). The cloud fills the tabernacle with the glory of the LORD (Exod. 40:34–35). Exod. 30:6 says simply "in front of the mercy seat . . . I will meet with you." These passages and others like them are at the background of Paul's reference to the mercy seat. Mercy seat and Spirit, each in their own way, testify to God's presence in and with Christ as Israel's representative. Though the two images should not be conflated, the image of Christ as mercy seat is consistent with the insight that Christ goes to the cross anointed with God's Spirit. In Christ, God attains what he had always intended for Israel, namely, that God's Spirit would tabernacle in the world in a faithful people (1 Cor. 3:16).

In this reading I am close to Wright who says of Rom. 3:21–26 that "the Messiah, King Jesus, has been the true, faithful Israelite" and that " 'the faithfulness of Jesus' (which later, in Romans 5, Paul can also refer to as 'the obedience of Jesus') is thus *the means whereby the righteousness of God is revealed.*"[46] With Wright, I agree that the martyrdom motif of Macabees is behind Paul's thought and that behind the martyrdom motif stands Isaiah 40–55.[47] What I now want to add, by exploring Israel's role at the cross, is the storyline that explains how a righteous death "somehow exhausted the divine wrath" (Wright, *Letter to the Romans* 476). The sinner must die to end the deadly tangle of sin in the flesh; but the sinner cannot rise unless he or she acts righteously (Rom. 5:18) and is anointed by God's Spirit. The martyr and the sacrificial cult both anticipate this hope. In Rom. 7 and Gal. 3:10–14, Christ becomes the righteous representative in whom Israel can finally die and rise.

2.4.5 Israel, Torah, and Christ at the Cross

Israel plays a role when God deals with sin, and it does so as a community. Yet that Christ is the representative sacrifice for the community does not of itself explain the community's role. We should ask, rather, what is the particular situation of this community that is answered by Christ's sacrifice? The question leads to Rom. 7 and Gal. 3:10–14.

2.4.5.1 ROMANS 7. With Wright and others, I take the position that the *I* in Rom. 7 refers first and foremost to Israel, whose fall at Sinai recapitulates the fall of Adam.[48] Paul's puzzling marriage metaphor in v. 1–3 becomes clearer when we recall the dyadic structure of the Israelite and, by extension, of Israel itself. From one perspective, Israel is continuous in that she is matched serially with two husbands (Torah and Christ); from another perspective, Israel is discontinuous in that Israel under Torah dies (v. 4). The husband who dies is not Torah per se but the whole dyadic structure of Israel under Torah. In Rom. 6, Paul observes that all those in Christ (both Jew and Gentile) have died with him, will be raised with him, and presently live by the power of his resurrection (6:3–10). In 7:4, Paul further argues that for the Israelite in Christ this death brings a new husband—a new constitutive other. Verse 6 restates the conclusion of the two husbands argument while it anticipates 8:3, namely, that the new life beyond this death is a life in newness of the Spirit. By contrast, although Israel according to the flesh did possess Torah, in that condition Israel could only hope for the promised Spirit. Thus from his post-Damascus perspective, Paul denies the traditional claim that the Spirit already enlivened Torah observance. To anticipate the discussion of v. 9, that does not mean that the Spirit was absent in Israel before Christ. Rather, Spirit was associated not with Torah observance per se but with faith and hope like Abraham's (Rom. 4).

Verse 7 then confronts a possible objection to the argument so far, namely, does the close association between the law and the passions in v. 5 lead to the conclusion that the law itself is sin? We know that Torah identifies sin (v. 7). But what does it mean that "sin, taking opportunity through the commandment, produced in me coveting of every kind" (v. 8)? The majority opinion is that the fleshly human being is tempted by what is forbidden.[49] An analogy with contemporary language philosophy offers another possibility. Charles Taylor observes that an underlying assumption of eighteenth-century linguistics was that "feeling" words expressed a feeling that preexisted the word. Yet contemporary linguistics suggests that "the development of new modes of expression enables us to have new feelings, more powerful or more refined, and certainly more self-aware."[50] Sadly for humankind, it would seem that the same principle applies to sin. To be sure, that the law identifies covetousness as such is a mark of progress. But unfortunately (in a somewhat perverse paraphrase of Taylor) the development of new modes of expression enables us to commit new sins, more powerful or more refined and certainly more self-aware. The narrative of Torah places Israel in a world where sin is identified, but fleshly Israel (Israel *kata sarka*), already vulnerable to sin, now lives in an articulated world where sin can truly flourish. Taking the *I* in v. 8b–11 as Israel, we then obtain the following sequence in v. 8–11:

> Sin is dead apart from the law (v. 8b)
> Israel was once alive apart from the law (v. 9a)
> The commandment came, sin became alive, and Israel died (v. 9b)
> The commandment was supposed to result in Israel's life (v. 10a)
> The commandment in fact resulted in Israel's death (v. 10b)
> Sin took occasion through the commandment, deceived Israel, and
> through the commandment killed Israel. (v. 11)

In the story of Romans, when did Israel have life apart from the law? Specifically, Israel had life apart from the law in the experience of Abraham (4:5–22). There is an elusive connection between Paul's recounting of Abraham's trust in God for the birth of Isaac and a possible allusion to the Aqedah (compare 4:18 and 8:32).[51] If it is true that some first-century Jews believed Isaac had received the Spirit, then Paul might intend by this connection to commend Abraham's very specific hope as the proper shape of Israel's faith. In other words, Israel's proper faith is not to depend on God in the abstract but to trust God to provide the child of promise who will receive the divine Spirit, die, and rise for Israel's salvation (4:17–22; compare 8:32). This conjecture fills out a plausible storyline that can weave together the story of Abraham in Rom. 4 with an otherwise elliptical reference to Isaac in Rom. 8:32.[52]

Taking v. 9b (that Israel died) in the context of v. 4 (that Israel dies in its Christ) would indicate that the process of Israel's dying that began with the giving of Torah came to its climax in the death of its Christ.[53] Verse 10a (that the commandment was to result in life) restates Israel's hope that Torah observance was empowered by God's Spirit. Yet in actual practice Israel's real hope was that its incomplete experiences of the Spirit would be fulfilled in one who, bearing the divine Spirit, would die and rise for Israel's salvation (v. 7, 14; compare 8:4). Until this salvation was fully realized, however, Israel under Torah could only die without rising. Yet Israel did experience the divine Spirit wherever those like Abraham looked forward to the fulfillment of this promise (v. 10b). On the contrary, wherever Israel tried to live solely by Torah apart from this hope, it lacked the faith of Abraham. The proper way to hold Torah, Paul realizes in retrospect, is as the instrument of Israel's death, yet having faith (like Abraham) in the God who gives life to the dead (Rom. 4:17; see 4:24).

How did sin find occasion in the law to deceive and kill Israel (v. 11)? Consider Rom. 10:2–3, where Paul refers twice to Israel's lack of knowledge. First, Israel has "a zeal for God" but "not in accordance with knowledge" (10:2).[54] Second, it is as a result of "not knowing about God's righteousness" that Israel seeks to establish its own righteousness (10:3). This "not knowing" parallels the ignorance expressed in Rom. 7, namely, "what I am doing, I do not understand" (v. 15), and "sin . . . deceived me" (v. 11). Does Paul intend to implicate Israel's zealotry in the death of its own Messiah? Such complicity would be of a piece with Paul's own persecution of the church, and is further supported by Paul's reference in 1 Thess. 2:14b–15a to "the Jews, who both killed the Lord Jesus and the prophets."[55] It may also be that Rom. 11:11 (that the Jews have stumbled, but not so as to fall) has in view "that it was the Jews' rejection of Jesus Himself and their delivering Him to the Gentiles which led to his death."[56] Thus if Rom. 7 has in view the complicity of some Torah-observant Jews in the crucifixion, then "sin, taking an opportunity through the commandment, deceived me, and through it killed me" (v. 11) means that sin used the unwitting zeal of some Jews to prosecute Israel's own death in the Messiah. This interpretation fills out narratively how human sin is concentrated on Israel. In the cross of its Christ, Torah-observant Israel plays a role in its own death, albeit a role that is, as Paul says, "not in accordance with knowledge" (Rom. 10:2).

Sin, not Israel, is the agent in Israel's death in Christ. That sin was dead and became alive (v. 9–10) refers to a former inactivity turned active, a former lack of power become powerful.[57] Israel could participate in Abraham insofar as Abraham's faithfulness was counted as righteousness and his sin was not accounted (4:7–8; compare 14:23b).[58] But when the law was given at Sinai, "sin became alive," means that sin became active (v. 9) and was now accounted (5:13). The irony in v. 9–10 is thus that whereas Israel hoped to be enlivened by God's Spirit when the law was given, sin was enlivened instead. Sin in Rom. 7 is therefore a kind of monstrous counterfeit of God's Spirit, masquerading as Israel's principle of life. In reality, though, sin does not give life but draws life from those it enslaves and kills ("sin became alive and I died"). Consequently, although some Jews zealous for Torah participated unwittingly in the death of Israel's Christ, Torah-observant Israel per se did not kill the Christ (v.

12). Rather, sin was exposed and judged when it abused the Torah to kill the one to whom Torah bore witness, namely, Christ, the righteous one (v. 13; see 3:21).

Does fleshly Israel stand culpable in its own death? In v. 14–20 Paul argues that the *I* in bondage to sin does not understand what it is doing (v. 15) and that sin, not the I, is the ultimate agent of Israel's death (v. 17–20). Without appealing to an exclusively autobiographical I in Rom. 7, it is clear that Paul's own experience parallels that of Israel in Rom. 10:2–3 and (by hypothesis) Rom. 7. In persecuting the Church, Paul had understood himself to be protecting the boundary of the righteous community. Yet in doing so, he had unwittingly participated in destroying the very hope he had sought to defend. To situate Paul's experience in the context of v. 15, we could say that lacking understanding, Paul did not practice what he would like to do (i.e., to protect the boundary of the righteous community) but did the very thing he hated (i.e., persecuted those who constituted the righteous community). Sin deceived an Israel that pursued zeal without knowledge, and in so doing rendered Israel indistinguishable from the whole wrathful situation that had led to the death of Israel's Messiah. Thus the I in v. 7–25 is not simply at the mercy of conflicting desires for good or evil but is deceived about the very content of the good it does pursue. A different principle (sin) operates in the I to bring about an evil even while the I aims at this mistaken good (v. 21).

The I (Israel) is trapped by sin in its flesh and cannot escape (v. 24). Fleshly Israel has to die, for there is no other way to put an end to sin (v. 4, 9, 10, 13). But if Israel is trapped by the sin that dwells in its flesh, sin has likewise been trapped in Israel's flesh to be destroyed (Rom. 8:3). Thus when Israel according to the flesh dies in Christ, the outcome can be narrated both as the consequence of sin and as God's execution of a death sentence on sin (the double sense of wrath of God).[59] Rom. 8:3 is the pivot point between the two understandings of Israel in Rom. 7:4. Rom. 7 depicts Israel who dies joined to its former husband (Torah), and Rom. 8:4–39 depicts Israel who rises with its new husband (Christ). Sin as a power operating in Israel (and in all those in Adam) has been condemned in the very way that Torah had always foreseen, that is, Israel dies and rises in Christ as its representative. The final condemnation of sin (death) will only occur when those in Adam die, but in Christ the outcome of their death is now assuredly a judgment of "life" (Rom. 8:34–39). Christ dies Israel's death with the Spirit on him so that Israel can rise with him at the eschaton, but also so that God's Spirit can now be present in a world presently under wrath (Rom. 8:19–23).

By "works of the law," then, Paul refers to his former expectation that by God's grace, Torah, wisdom, and Spirit would cooperate to bring about a righteous community in the Torah-observant. In retrospect, he comes to see that works of the law was a mistake for Israel in the flesh held prisoner by sin (Rom 7:23). When Paul faces the crucified and resurrected Christ, he is forced to recognize that only one man has fully entered into the righteous community, and even he had to die to be raised. Paul reconfigures Israel's story around this man (rather than the Torah-observant community as he had once conceived it), and that story stands in the background of Rom. 7. Sin is so deeply entwined in human experience (the flesh) that the only way to end its reign is death. Sin dies in Christ's flesh as Israel's representative, and that is the ultimate consequence of sin in the flesh; at the same time sin is judged because this consequence can also be regarded under the aspect of God's wrath. Torah is thus God's saving response to fleshly Israel in bondage to sin, but works of the law is a misreading of that response. Works of the law so understood cannot suffice where sin and flesh are so deeply entwined. A look at Gal. 3:10–14 will underscore why Paul contrasts "works of the law" with "justification by faith."

2.4.5.2 GALATIANS 3:10–14. J. Louis Martyn has suggested that Paul's talk of "two walks" in Gal. 5 has its origin in the doctrine of the two ways, the blessing and curse found, for example, in Deut. 30:19 and Jer. 21:8. Yet Martyn says where the rabbis "find both blessing and curse in God's law, Paul sees that the blessing and the curse do not come from the same source."[60] I cannot finally agree with Martyn in assigning the blessing to God and the curse to a law that is used by God but never given by God (Martyn 366). Nor can I agree that flesh is the "alien, occupying power" in the eschatological conflict (Martyn 530). I do agree, though, that Paul's two walks in Gal. 5 convey the eschatological conflict set up in the community that dies and rises in Christ (Gal. 5:17, 24–25). But the crisis in Gal. 3:10, which narrates the turn of events that inaugurates the walk in Spirit, is not that Israel is under the exilic curse (Wright); nor that Paul's opponents have brought a curse on themselves by trying to bring the Gentiles under Torah (Dunn); nor that Israel is under the curse of a law that is not divine in origin (Martyn). Rather, Torah places the whole walk according to flesh under a curse when sin subjects the flesh to its power, and that is the situation in which Israel *kata sarka* finds itself (Gal. 4:29).

On one hand, Hab. 2:4 (v. 11) asserts that life comes through faith; on the other hand Lev. 18:15 (v. 12) asserts that life comes through observance of the law.[61] The tension is resolved on appeal to Deut. 21:23 (v. 13) interpreted from the perspective of what actually happened to Jesus, namely, that Christ's journey to the cross, passing through the curse, did not end in death but in life (Johnson 311). The conflict resolves itself in favor of Hab. 2:4—Jesus is the one faithful, even outside the covenant and under the curse (Deut. 21:23). Therefore

Hab. 2:4 (and not Lev. 18:15) describes the true boundary of the righteous community—the faithfulness of Christ.

But Israel itself receives the "promise of the Spirit through faith" (v. 14) only when Christ becomes a curse. That does not mean that Israel lacked God's Spirit, but that where the divine Spirit was present in Israel it anticipated Christ. Christ, not Torah observance, is the measure of the Spirit's presence in the world. In Christ, Israel can now embark on the walk according to Spirit, its hope become actual because the divine Spirit is unambiguously present in Christ. Torah, Paul now understands, always anticipated this event (v. 24).

In Paul's retelling of Israel's story, Torah emplots the world dying under sin in the story of the one God with Israel—a people God has chosen to die and rise. Membership in the family of Abraham is thus God's answer to the plight of a humanity that *must die* to be free from sin but *cannot rise* because sin is killing those the Spirit would enliven (Rom. 7:9–10). Sin, that is, has usurped the role of God's Spirit in becoming the subject of humanity's actions (Rom. 7:17). The juridical fittingness of Israel's death under the law refers to Israel's unwitting complicity in the wrathful situation that led to its own death in the cross of its Christ. As Rom. 6:23 says, "the wages of sin is death." Yet this phrase does not intend a kind of tit for tat, which as Jürgen Moltmann rightly worries, can perpetuate a cycle of blaming the victim.[62] First, although Torah articulates the world under wrath as the world of the one God, Israel in Christ no longer lives under Torah and its curse. To revert to life under Torah is to reenter the world in which Christ became a curse (Gal. 3:13; compare 2:24) and sacrifice (Rom. 8:3). Second, even in the world under wrath, "the wages of sin is death" is not strictly transactional. To live in the flesh as described in Rom. 7 is to live toward a future in which we will all die as the outcome of human unrighteousness. That does not mean that each deed meets its matching punishment, but that the whole apparatus is set on self-destruct and that we are all implicated in its perpetuation.

In short, God allows human beings their integrity, even to the point of rejecting the source of their own life (Rom. 7:9). It is just (in the juridical sense) that all should die as the consequence of this radically flawed life (Rom. 1:32, 3:9–23). But God has repaired the situation by allowing that disastrous outcome to take place proleptically in one man whose Spirit now enlivens the community that dies and rises in him, Jesus Christ. By not intervening at the cross, God permitted fallen human history to come to an end in one people—in one representative of that people—to open up the possibility of a life beyond that disaster lest it overtake the whole of creation. That community is called to life as the eschatological community embracing Jew and Gentile in their differences.

By "justification by faith," then, Paul refers to the shape of Abraham's faith fulfilled in Christ. The proper way to hold Torah, Paul now recognizes, is to trust that the God who gives life to the dead will provide a perfect sacrifice and in that sacrifice Israel will die to rise again. Torah was never the means by which God, present in Spirit and wisdom, would graciously bring about the righteous community. Rather, Torah was always God's means to judge sin in the flesh. In Abraham's faith, Paul reaches back to a more original understanding of his community. Paul's understanding has two aspects: that Abraham's hope is the proper way to hold Torah (justification by faith, not works of the law) and that Jesus, as Israel's Christ, fulfills that hope. The first is a public interpretation that Paul may share with other Jews; the second is the revelation Paul proclaims as the good news (Rom. 1:1–17; Gal 1:1–12). Paul's "works of the law" is consistent with covenantal nomism: It depends on God's gracious election, atonement, and empowering presence in Spirit and wisdom. But covenantal nomism is not limited to works of the law because it can also encompass Jews who, like Abraham, await God's perfect sacrifice. Still, Paul asserts, Jesus really does fulfill the Jewish hope (Gal. 3:14) and all will one day confess him as Christ and Lord (Phil. 2:9–11). That does not mean, however, that individual Jews have to convert to Christianity as we know it, for we do yet not fully know who the eschatological Christ is but are only gradually transformed into his image (2 Cor. 3:13–16). Jews of the faith of Abraham (who do not presently confess Jesus as the Christ) can thus join in one eschatological community with those in Christ to await the deliverer out of Zion (Rom. 11:26). The Church, in its worship and practice, is exhorted to make Jesus present in the world as its deliver and Christ (Rom. 12–15).[63]

2.5 Conclusion: The I in an Israel Reconfigured

I turn from Paul's retelling of Israel's story to reflect back on the self disclosed in that story, dividing the reflection into two parts, namely, the self that dies in Christ and the self that rises in Christ. The believer dies in Christ in three senses: First, the believer dies in that her community dies; second, the believer, as a dyadic personality, dies because the constituting other shifts from Torah to Christ; third, the believer's own future death is renarrated in the story of Christ's death. The first two senses can be taken together because of the close connection between community and self in the dyadic personality.

In Israel demarcated by Torah, the Jew relates to God and her neighbor through Torah observance empowered by the Spirit. That dyadic being dies when Israel under Torah dies in Christ (Rom. 7:4). In Israel demarcated by

Christ, the Jew understands herself to relate to God through participation in Christ empowered by the Spirit of Christ. The Jew in Christ thus dies as one kind of dyadic being (I::other-in-Torah) and rises as a different dyadic being (I::other-in-Christ). But this notation might give the mistaken impression that an I migrates from one pair to the other. Rather, as a dyad the I is either I:: other-in-Torah or I::other-in-Christ. There is never a monadic I. Consequently, it is not hyperbole when Paul says, "I have been crucified with Christ" (Gal. 2: 20). As a dyadic personality whose community came to a disastrous end at the cross, Paul the Israelite was really crucified with Christ.

Gentiles in Christ, as full members of the family of Abraham, also experience their death in Christ (Rom. 6:4a). But Gentiles would not in quite the same sense understand their own communities to have died. The true meaning of Torah's story of God with his people (Paul now sees) is that human beings have to die to sin before they can live by the Spirit. The Jew in Christ dies in a world articulated by Torah and rises in a world anticipated by Torah. In retrospect, the Gentile can grasp the *stoichea* (Gal. 4:3) as anticipations of the same reality articulated by Torah.[64] Thus the Gentile experiences the death of her own community only insofar as she, like Paul, discerns the original aim of her community in Christ (Phil. 2:10–11). By virtue of Torah, then, Israel is first among the peoples to articulate "I am guilty" when God's wrath falls (Rom. 5:13, 8:3). Israel in Christ identifies the truth of God and the world (Rom. 3: 26, 8:3–5).

The I thus dies both in its dyadic structure and in the death of its community. In a third sense the "body of this death" (Rom. 7:24), or the flesh enslaved by sin (Rom. 6:6, 7:14), dies proleptically in Christ (Rom. 8:13; 2 Cor. 4:10; Gal. 5:24). Only the sinner's death can finally end the deadly tangle of flesh in slavery to sin.[65] Yet the believer in Christ can identify her own future death with the story of Christ. As a member of the body of Christ, her present suffering belongs to the suffering of Christ (Rom. 8:13; 2 Cor. 4:1–12; Phil. 3: 10; Gal. 5:24; see Col. 1:24). In this way death's liberation from sin becomes a present reality (Rom. 6:7). In sum, "I have been crucified with Christ" conveys the death of the believer's former community, the death of the dyadic I, and the believer's future death renarrated in Christ's story.

But to die in Christ also brings hope because Christ dies, anointed with the Spirit, to rise again. The believer's relation to this Spirit is the clue to the self that rises with Christ. Paul uses two concepts to express this relation, namely, the human spirit (1 Cor. 2:12; see Rom. 8:16) and conscience (Rom. 9:1; 1 Cor. 8:7–13, 10:24–28). These concepts, once they have been situated in the context of Israel's story, can help us glimpse the self disclosed in Paul's story.

Robert Jewett argues that Paul's *pneuma* recapitulates a Hellenistic sense of human spirit as the apportioned divine spirit.[66] The human spirit is thus the believer's share in the Spirit given to the community. 1 Cor. 2:11 deploys a strong form of this differentiation (*pneuma tou anthrōpou*) as a defense against Corinthian presumption. Although Paul never again speaks of the *pneuma tou anthrōpou*, he nevertheless retains the distinction between the human (apportioned) spirit and the divine spirit (as, for example, in Rom. 8:16). "The Spirit," Jewett concludes, "was thought to so enter human possession that it could be referred to as 'mine'" (Jewett 451). Gordon Fee argues, on the contrary, that the stronger autonomy expressed in 1 Cor. 2:11 should be taken as paradigmatic, that is, that spirit "refers to the interior, nonmaterial component of the human personality."[67] Their disagreement centers on whether reading human spirit as the apportioned divine Spirit can adequately express human spirit's autonomy. Jewett is satisfied that although the human spirit is the apportioned Spirit, Paul's "mine" sufficiently expresses its autonomy. Fee's references to the human spirit as a "nonmaterial *component*" of the human being, as a "*place* of intersection of the human and divine," and as the "*place* of the Spirit's habitation" bespeak a more individual understanding of spirit.[68] Fee suggests that only this more individualized notion of spirit adequately grounds the dialogical encounter between "spirit" and "Spirit" in Rom. 8:16, asserting that Jewett's interpretation, on the contrary, "leads to a view that seems nearly indefensible (that the Spirit is merely witness to himself)."[69]

Yet neither Jewett nor Fee situates the dialogue of spirit and Spirit in the community's story. In his life, death, and resurrection, Jesus Christ is identified by his relation to God's Spirit; correlatively, the Spirit bestowed on Israel is identified in Christ's life, death, and resurrection (the Spirit is the Spirit of Christ). The Spirit's story is thus the story of the life, death, and resurrection of Jesus as Israel's Christ. The human spirit is identified in the same story: Paul serves with his spirit in the gospel (Rom. 1:9); our spirit bears witness with the Spirit that we are God's children (Rom. 8:16); Paul's spirit is present in the assembly at Corinth (1 Cor. 5:3–4); and whoever is united with Christ is one spirit with him (1 Cor. 6:17). These story elements testify to the human spirit as the dyadic personality seen under the aspect of an inner dialogue that recapitulates (as "mine") the dialogue in a community. The dialogue in this particular community is guided by the divine Spirit who makes Christ present in face-to-face encounters (2 Cor. 3:17–18).

This intimate relation of the self to the Spirit in the community leads me to modify Malina's account somewhat to say that Paul's personality is best characterized not as a dyadic personality but as a communal personality. "Communal personality" conveys Paul's strong sense that his individual I appears in relation to a community—a sense that is not sufficiently captured in the phrase "dyadic personality."[70] When Paul retells his community's story he appears as one crucified with Christ (Rom. 7); yet the community itself only appears where actual others manifest Christ (paradigmatically in his suffering, 2 Cor. 4:10). Thus for Paul as a communal personality, the self and community are correlates, which is to say that the self and community are each mutually the condition of the other. There are, of course, dangers in construing the self as communal, not the least of which is Christendom's history of scapegoating the Jews. Yet Paul does not scapegoat the Jewish people; rather, he seeks to embrace Jew and Gentile in one community, encompassing those who were misdirected, those who now embrace Israel's hope in Christ, and those who still await that hope (Rom. 11:26).

Like spirit, conscience is another category under which Paul relates the individual to the divine Spirit in the community. Here Malina indicates the interpersonal (though not fully communal) dimension of *syneidesis*:

> The Latin word *conscientia* and the Greek word *syneidesis* stand for "with-knowledge," that is, a knowledge with others, individualized common knowledge, commonly shared meaning, common sense. Conscience then refers to a person's sensitive awareness to one's public ego-image with the purpose of striving to align one's own personal behavior and self-assessment with that publicly perceived ego-image. . . . Conscience is a sort of internalization of what others say, do, and think about one, since these others play the role of witness and judge.[71]

If by extension conscience internalizes the spirit in a community, conscience nonetheless testifies to a distinct other who can bear witness with the spirit in the community (Rom. 9:1; compare Rom. 8:16). Although conscience is therefore in each case "mine" (1 Cor. 8:29), the particular shape conscience assumes reflects the spirit in the community (1 Cor. 11:1). Christ's relation to the Spirit is thus the norm for the individual's conscience, and conscience recapitulates, in the individual, the Spirit's relation to the community.

The categories of conscience and human spirit can now guide the backward glance at the I in Paul's story. In the community in Christ, Christ mediates the believer's relationship to God and neighbor as Torah once did. That Christ is present to the community is the work of the divine Spirit, revealed to the community as the Spirit of Christ. This dynamic in the community is recapitulated in the individual believer, both in face-to-face relations (2 Cor. 3:18) and in forming the individual's conscience (and spirit) by the Spirit in the community (1 Cor. 10:24–11:1, 16:18; Gal. 6:18; Phil. 4:23). Insofar as the Spirit of Christ is the source of this life (and the transcendent subject of the community's life), conscience and human spirit are the believer's "mine" of the Spirit (Rom. 9:1).

Dunn, Wright, and Fee all reconstruct "Christ lives in me" (Gal. 2:20) as the indwelling of the Spirit of Christ.[72] That is because each of them is committed (each in his own way) to a monadic anthropology: The human spirit is the "place," as it were, where the human and the divine Spirit meet, and so the inner relation of Christ to the believer has to be expressed in terms of spirit/Spirit.[73] But if Paul's anthropology is communal rather than monadic, then the individual's relation to a constitutive other (a relation that points outside the self) is nonetheless a dimension of the believer's own inwardness. In other words, "Christ lives in me" does not gesture to the Spirit but to Christ, who relates to the believers as constitutive other. But then is the present reality of Christ reduced to the community? No, as Dunn says,

> The spiritual reality of Christ was not reducible to the faith experience of individuals or to the tangibility of the church. Christ was still a personal reality within the totality of reality, still in direct continuity with Jesus of Nazareth, still the focus of God's saving grace for both present and future. But "personal" in a sense which is no longer the same as the human "person," and yet is more sharply defined than talk of God as "personal."[74]

Even though the believer's experience of Christ as constitutive other is mediated by the Spirit and community, the present reality of Christ is not reduced to the community or to the Spirit. Nor is Spirit just another name for the community's collective experience. Rather, Spirit is the agent who opens the space where the community faces Christ as another.[75] In Paul's account, Christ and the Spirit together constitute the community while each transcends it in a way that is (in some sense) personal.

In facing his neighbor (indeed, in reflecting on his own self) Paul now faces Christ made present by the Spirit. He had formerly understood himself to face his neighbor (and self) under Torah empowered by the Spirit. Paul narrates this shift as the death of his former communal personality and the resurrection of a new communal personality (Rom. 7:4). The Gentile's experience is similar but mediated (from Paul's perspective) by the Jewish experience. The term *stoichea* (Gal. 3:4–5) encompasses both elemental substances and elementary forms of religion (and, it is necessary to add, elementary forms of organized life because these are inextricable from religion in Paul's context).[76] The parallel Paul draws between the law and the *stoichea* in Gal. 4:3 could extend to the function of law in Gal. 3:24, which is to say that the *stoichea* may well function for the Gentile as Torah functions for the Jew, namely, as *paidagōgos* to Christ. Thus the Gentile, like the Jew, would experience a shift in her constitutive other: The constitutive other articulated through the *stoichea* would be revealed in retrospect, like Torah, as having always aimed at Christ (Phil. 2:10–11). That need not mean that all roads outside Christ lead to what we now call Christianity. Rather, if we engage in open dialogue, then we, like Paul, might have to put our own community's story at stake to meet the other as other.

While believers face Christ as their constitutive other, they, like Christ, live at once in two worlds. In the walk according to flesh (that is, in the world under God's wrath) Christ is crucified by the rulers of this age (1 Cor. 2:8) and cursed by Torah (Gal. 3:10–13; Rom. 8:3). Christ cannot be adequately articulated in this present evil age but is, in Lyotard's phrase, a pain that accompanies silence, a something that asks to be put into phrases.[77] Although each individual has to make his or her own decision to forsake the present evil age, such a decision is only possible where the community that lives by the Spirit of Christ opens the way. Like Paul, those who belong to this community are, from their former perspectives, transgressors with Christ (Gal. 2:18).[78] When they suffer, they do so not as the outcome of God's wrath but as suffering with Christ for the salvation of a world under wrath (Gal. 6:17; 2 Cor. 4:11–12; see Col. 1:24). Their suffering is renarrated in the story of Christ, and thus they live in the new creation opened by Christ.

How do believers in this community experience the world under wrath? From Paul's monotheistic perspective, the world under wrath is still God's world, and the consequences of human unrighteousness continue to serve God's purposes. But those in Christ possess a kind of double vision. On the one hand, they agree that the world is under God's just wrath; on the other hand they renarrate the world as aimed at the eschatological community in Christ and its suffering as the suffering of Christ (Rom. 8:17–22). Malachi says to Israel and Judah, "Do we not all have one Father? Has not one God created us? Why do we deal treacherously each against his brother so as to profane the covenant of our fathers?" (Mal. 2:10). Where Malachi saw Israel as one family divided by sin, Paul now sees all the world's peoples as one family in Christ divided by sin (Gal. 3:28).[79]

Although this community renarrates the suffering world under wrath as the suffering Christ, the resurrection life in this community gives every reason for rejoicing (Phil. 3:1). The Spirit in the community is recapitulated in each believer's human spirit and conscience in such a way that each can say "mine" of the Spirit in the community (Rom. 8:16, 9:1; 1 Cor. 2:11). Each is empowered to live a life of faith, dependent on God, which is the true aim of our created humanity in Adam (Rom. 5:18–19). In the community as a whole and in each self, God is present in the world for its salvation (Phil. 2:15). As the community moves toward God's future, each can experience that future now as a foretaste (Phil. 3:12).

"Righteous" is, in a certain sense, a boundary marker that locates the believer in the community God will vindicate. But it also says something more about the self as righteous. When Christ goes to the cross anointed by the Spirit, his one righteous act demonstrates the righteousness of God (Rom. 3: 21–26, 5:18). Christ at the cross is the righteous community acting righteously. Righteousness, therefore, is not just a boundary term but also describes God's judgment on what this community does—what it does, that is, as the body of Christ empowered by the Spirit. Each believer's "mine" of this Spirit joins the believer to Christ, who lives in the fullness of God's righteous community. Thus the traditional interpretation of "Christ is our righteousness" (1 Cor 1:30) is not wrong when the individual's righteousness is understood as mediated by the Spirit who joins the individual to Christ. God judges Christ righteous at the cross, and Christ merits that judgment in his righteous act; the believer's continuing walk in spirit participates in the righteousness of Christ; God's judgment "Righteous!" arrives at the believer in Christ, that is, as belonging to the body of Christ (2 Cor. 5:21). For a communal personality like Paul, there is no conflict between the righteousness of the community and the righteousness of the individual.

Yet before the final judgment, practical life in this community remains ambivalent, stretched as it is between two walks, the walk according to the flesh and the walk according to the Spirit (Gal. 5). Notwithstanding, this very ambivalence (that this community *can* walk according to Spirit) is God's gift to a world whose single-minded descent had ended disastrously in the cross of Israel's Christ. Wherever believers say "mine" of the Spirit in this community and walk accordingly, Christ's righteousness is active in the world (Gal. 5:16–26; Rom. 6:17). That is not to say that the world outside of the community in Christ is unambiguously headed for its own destruction. Rather, although God's salvific power is aimed toward the world opened by the resurrection of Christ (Phil. 2:10), the source of this power is wider than the Spirit of Christ (1 Cor. 15:24–28). God's Spirit is among all peoples moving the world toward Christ's future; the event Paul narrates (the life, death, and resurrection of Jesus Christ) opens that future; and Israel's retold story makes that future present in a community that bears the Spirit of Christ to a world presently under wrath.

Paul's realism is compromised when traditional Pauline anthropologies do not take into account the relation of self and other that constitutes a communal personality. Paul is really under a curse because in the world under wrath, his constitutive other (the neighbor, community, and spirit disclosed through Torah) condemns the sort of being he is in the flesh (Rom. 7:14). Christ really becomes a curse because as Israel's representative he bears the climactic outcome of human unrighteousness in his own body (as a Jew under Torah who comes under its curse). Paul really dies in Christ, that is, his former communal personality dies in the shift from Torah to Christ, and his future physical death is renarrated in the story of Christ's death. Paul is really raised into a new life, which is to say that he has a new communal structure, facing his neighbor in Christ. Finally, the walk in Spirit in this community is a real foretaste of Israel's final justification and the transformation of the cosmos.

The burden of the remaining chapters is to ascertain to what degree the realism of Paul's "I have been crucified with Christ . . . Christ lives in me" can be reawakened in our context. But before I embark on that task, I respond in the next chapter to a possible criticism, namely, that Paul's communal personality may be an artifact of an ancient thought-world that must be demythologized.

3

Rudolf Bultmann's Story of Paul: The Detour Not Taken

The pronoun *I* in St. Paul's letters can carry a profoundly communal sense, and the background of this usage is Paul's retelling of Israel's story. As someone who retells Israel's story, Paul is a locus of his community, and yet he transcends it: His spirit and conscience assert "mine" of the Spirit in his community. That Spirit, Paul now recognizes, is the Spirit of Christ, and Israel's boundary has always been faith, not Torah. The Spirit of Christ fulfills the original promise given to Abraham (Rom. 4) that by dying and rising, Israel would fully correspond to the God who gives life to the dead. The I in this community lives simultaneously in two worlds—dying to the world under wrath but alive by the power of the resurrection to God's eschatological future. The community appears in Paul's retelling of Israel's story and Paul recognizes himself only in relation to that community. So I have proposed a highly communal interpretation of Paul's use of I. Is it true? There are a number of difficulties.

It is one question whether the description is true to the communal self evident in Paul's letters. That is a question about the accuracy of my exegesis and my use of biblical scholarship, and here I submit to the criteria of biblical studies. But the question cuts deeper if it asks whether Paul's use of *I* should remain, in any sense, normative for us. Is Paul's I, rather, an outmoded understanding of selfhood—a husk we should shell to get at the kernel? To answer that question, I propose that we should interpret Paul's horizon, interpret our horizon, and narrate the continuity between the two as the historical life of one community. A genealogy of selfhood from Paul's time to ours, though, would be a massive undertaking on the order of Charles Taylor's *Sources of the Self.*[1] What I offer here is strong evidence that such a genealogy is possible. I interpret the self in Paul's horizon (chapter 2), in our horizon (chapters 4 and 5), and correlate the two (chapter 6). This correlation constitutes strong evidence of a historical kinship between Paul's sense of self and ours.

It is a difficult path. There can be no absolute justification for taking it, so I first try what seems an easier road—to appeal to a transcendental structure of human existence that we share with Paul. That insurmountable difficulties lie along this road leads the inquiry back to the original path that although difficult, is at least navigable. The road I have chosen to travel for a while is Rudolf Bultmann's interpretation of Paul. In the first section of this chapter, in a critical engagement with Gareth Jones's *Bultmann: Towards a Critical Theology*, I isolate the presuppositions in Bultmann's work that allow him to circumvent the long detour that I maintain is necessary.[2] In the second section I interpret Bultmann's mature account of Paul's theology in his *Theology of the New Testament.*[3] I then raise three intertwined criticisms that indicate why his attempt to avoid the detour cannot be sustained. First, Bultmann identifies eschatology and transcendental analysis to such an extent that he fails to show adequate concern for actual social conditions. Second, in his decontextualized eschatology, the encounter between the hearer and the proclaimer loses the character of a genuine encounter between self and other: The other is no longer different from the self, and genuine alterity is lost. Third, this loss of alterity corresponds to a related loss of community in the kerygma. Following this critique, I retrieve two crucial aspects of Bultmann's work. First, I continue to assert with Bultmann that a phenomenological account can articulate transcendence in the encounter with the risen Lord. Second, I employ a variant of demythologizing to bridge the gap between Paul's time and ours—albeit demythologizing in a mode that invites greater suspicion of our own framework while affirming attestations to the work of the Spirit in our community.

3.1 Bultmann and Heidegger: The Relation of Phenomenology and Theology

Gareth Jones proposes to study the "philosophical deep structure" of Bultmann's thought through his relationship to Heidegger—the true nature of this relationship having been obscured through overattention to Bultmann's use of

Being and Time (Jones 4–11).[4] It is precisely this "deep structure" that lets Bult-mann avoid the detour to the self. His project takes off in the wake of Albert Schweitzer's claim that the eschatological Jesus "passes by our time and returns to his own" (Jones 33–34).[5] If Jesus is such an utterly alien figure, then how are we to respond to him today? Regarding eschatology, a good deal of water has flowed over the dam since Schweitzer.[6] Yet a variant of Bultmann's ques-tion still stands at the heart of my own project: How should we approach St. Paul as someone who is other than us but who nevertheless remains in gen-uine communion with us? Bultmann's response to a similar question leans so hard on what we allegedly share with Paul that it fails to engage Paul as gen-uinely other. In the end, though, what I offer is not a rejection of Bultmann but a critical retrieval.

Bultmann's teacher, Wilhelm Hermann, drove a wedge between exegesis and dogmatics in his distinction between *Geschichte* and *Natur*, that is, that the "historical Christ" exceeds the "natural Jesus" as "a lived, experiential encoun-ter with God in the present moment" (Jones 26). Bultmann sought to heal this division in an alternative distinction between *Historie* (a causal account of the connection of events) and *Geschichte* (a personal story of encounters with the risen Lord). In so doing he restored a theological purpose to exegesis, albeit a negative one, namely, "to lead the individual away from culturally relative im-ages of Jesus Christ, and towards the encounter with the risen Lord" (Jones 27). To a degree, then, Bultmann could agree with Schweitzer that the historical Jesus passes by our time and returns to his own. Yet the historical Jesus points to a figure who does remain, namely, the risen Lord. Rather than the two figures of Jesus posited by liberal theology ("Jesus" and "the Christ") Bultmann posits three:

1. the *historical Jesus* who lived and died on Earth;
2. the *kerygmatic Christ*, that is, the Jesus who lives and dies in stories; and
3. the *risen Lord*, that is, the Christ of faith, the mystery of salvation. (Jones 34)

The point of christology is to distinguish between one and two and thus to lead the believer to three, the risen Lord. The unity of the historical Jesus, the kerygmatic Christ, and the risen Lord is their mutual inherence in the single eschatological event in which the believer encounters the risen Lord. Yet by "eschatology" Bultmann intends something different than Schweitzer, namely, "the non-objectifying expression of God's will to save the individual" (Jones 41). Eschatology, that is, opens onto the transcendental conditions of human existence. Eschatology in this sense, Bultmann argues, is implicit in the message and mission of Jesus but only becomes explicit in the kerygma of the early church, especially in Paul and John.

Who is addressed by the kerygma? Bultmann pursues "the human question" by first reducing the horizon of early Christianity to its transcendental conditions of being (as being-toward-God) and time (as the moment of decision) (Jones 63–85). Human existence is always realized in act; yet presupposed in every act is a prior fundamental decision to accept or reject one's existence as being-toward-God. Bultmann says he discerns this transcendental structure in Paul's letters. For example, by *soma* (usually translated "body"), Paul intends the subject's ability to relate to herself reflexively. So as *soma* the individual understands herself as God does, namely, as open to encounter. The transcendental condition of this openness is human "being" as "being-toward-God." If in the eschatological encounter I receive my authentic self, then I must already be (transcendentally) being-toward-God ready to be accepted or rejected. Similarly the "moment" of my decision has to transcend temporal causality or else I remain the same being simply choosing Christ as a new ideal or exemplar.

Given these two conditions of being and time, how does the one who hears the gospel encounter, as Jones says, "the kerygmatic Christ as the story of the historical Jesus, told as the eschatological event" (Jones 85)? The risen Lord encounters the believer in her actual existence through the kerygma as the story of the historical Jesus. What confronts her is her own authentic existence as a modification of her actual existence. So in the eschatological moment, the kerygma becomes the hearer's story (*Geschichte*), uniting the proclaimer, the hearer, St. Paul, and the historical Jesus all in the same eschatological purpose.

Two presuppositions underlie this account. First, in telling the story of Jesus as the Christ of Israel, Paul intends to tell the story of the human person in general. On Bultmann's reading, then, Paul's story is not first and foremost the story that identifies God and his people. Second, what unites the historical Jesus, the risen Lord, and the hearer is their shared eschatological purpose to exist authentically—a purpose acted out by Jesus, proclaimed by Paul in the kerygma, and recapitulated in the hearer. Eschatology is thus collapsed without remainder onto a shared encounter based on these conditions of human existence. One question that occupies the critical remarks below is whether this sense of "encounter" is adequate to what it means to encounter an other, like Paul, in his actual difference from us.

How does this encounter with the risen Lord reveal God? To understand Bultmann's answer to "the God question," Jones urges, we have to understand him as an "event theorist" in the tradition of Heidegger:

Bultmann, therefore, never remains simply the exegete of primitive
Christianity and its texts; the phenomenologist of being and time;
the theologian of the kerygma. Rather, he is all of these things, at
different stages. But it is only as the thinker of the eschatological
event that each of those other tasks finds its rightful place in the
scheme of Bultmann's thought. Without the eschatological event,
there is Non-Being rather than theology. In his recognition of this as
the meaning of human being as being-towards-God, Bultmann reas-
serted the primary role of Christology with a degree of philosophical
rigour and theological insight unparalleled in the story of twentieth-
century theology. (Jones 123–24)

Jones characterizes Heidegger's method in *Being and Time* as a "hermeneutic phenomenology," which is to say that it is a phenomenological reduction
on a historical horizon that aims, not at a transcendental ego, but at the transcendental conditions of the horizon (Jones 93–99).[7] The later Heidegger abandons hermeneutic phenomenology for a new line of inquiry that Jones calls
"event theory," referring to Heidegger's turn to interrogate language as the
event that discloses the truth of beings that emerge out of concealment.[8] Here
Heidegger turns away from a particular historical horizon (the Dasein of *Being
and Time*) to interrogate the relationship between the horizon (Being) and the
being in whom Being appears (the ontological difference, or the difference
between Being-as-such and beings).

Bultmann, however, never becomes concerned with the general question
of Being. Rather, he continues to perform his phenomenological reduction on
a particular horizon, namely, Christian faith as a way of being-in-the-world.
When Heidegger turns to the ontological difference, he abandons any transcendental claims because of the generality of the interrogation; Bultmann, by
contrast, believes that if the event of revelation to which this way of being bears
witness is the unique event of revelation—the event that reveals the meaning
of (human) being for all of us—then there is no need to abandon the claim
that its conditions are transcendental. Event theory then functions for Bultmann not as an alternative to hermeneutic phenomenology but as its comple-
tion in a description of how language becomes the revelation of God (Jones
117).

Bultmann finds his way from phenomenology back to faith, Jones suggests, in Heidegger's distinction between faith as a mode of existence *coram
deo* (believing) and faith as a form of historical existence (understanding).[9] As
believing, faith is only open to the revelation—the event—of God in Christ; as

understanding, however, faith is open in principle to phenomenological analysis (Jones 105). How to move, then, from the phenomenology of faith as an understanding mode of existence to the theology of faith as belief? Both points of view are joined in the event of the ontological difference. For Heidegger, the event of revelation brings beings into unconcealment ("truth" as *a-lētheia*) against a background of concealment. In the presocratics, to encounter a being authentically is to be open not only to the particular being but also to the horizon in which it has its meaning and the process by which the former emerges from the latter. In Plato and Aristotle, however, Heidegger locates a different understanding of truth that covers over this more original understanding: Truth is the correspondence of description and appearance (Jones 112). Thus after Plato, the coming-out-of-concealment is itself concealed, and this concealment can only be thrown off by what transcends it, namely, Being-as-such.

Bultmann, Jones observes, holds that "in the earthly life of Jesus, the eschatological significance of the Christ event is concealed until Easter Sunday" (Jones 118). What the resurrection reveals is *alētheia* as "the divine Being, the essential Being, which is also my essential being, and which is closed to me and remains closed to me, unless through the divine revelation the border is opened and I become raised up" (Jones 117). Here Bultmann transforms Heidegger's philosophical distinction into a theological understanding of the event of revelation—that God revealed in Christ is the light that brings me before my authentic existence and empowers me to choose. Bultmann singularizes Heidegger's understanding of the event and refers it exclusively to the revelation of the authentic structure of human existence. For Heidegger, on the contrary, the event of revelation takes place wherever beings are recognized as emerging out of concealment.[10] Thus Bultmann, unlike Heidegger, continues the Western tradition in taking the individual self as the locus par excellence of the God question (Jones 75).

The kerygma thus initiates the hearer into a process whereby she sees her own authentic existence emerge out of God as the horizon. So theology has two tasks: first, to retrieve from the mythical language of the New Testament whatever can elucidate the actual situation of the addressee. What the New Testament offers, however, is not a description of some actual mode of existence but an analysis of the formal structure of human existence (Jones 106–7). Second, the theologian "must hear the Word of God" and proclaim it anew in nonobjectifying language (Jones 120). Practically, that means that the theologian, to be effective, has to live in the process of perceiving her own authentic existence emerge out of the Christ event. In our context, this process has to be described in relational (not mythological) terms.[11] Yet the description will be empty unless it facilitates an encounter with God in Christ and God wills to meet the hearer. Without articulation, the encounter is unintelligible; without encounter, the articulation is empty. Theological language thus speaks of God by the only avenue open to the sort of being who stands before God as the light that reveals her own authentic self. Christology articulates that event.

How, then, does Bultmann avoid the detours to the self? First, he understands Paul's story as the one true story of the human person in general (or "everyman"). I have argued, rather, that first and foremost Paul's story identifies a community and only secondarily the self within that community. Second, the method of demythologizing identifies Paul's eschatology with a reduction to the transcendental conditions of human existence and so prescinds from any consideration of shared background. I propose that these two presuppositions empty the encounter with the risen Lord of genuine otherness, so Bultmann's attempt to avoid the detour founders. On the way to that proposal, I first turn to Bultmann's account of St. Paul's theology in his *Theology of the New Testament*.

3.2 Bultmann's Story of Paul

Starting out from Bultmann's account of Paul's formal structure of human existence in *Theology of the New Testament* (1951), I enlarge on the elements comprised in the claim that human "being" is being-toward-God. I next take up Bultmann's description of the "human plight" or flesh under the domination of sin—a crucial topic in Paul that is not closely addressed in Jones's analysis.[12] Finally, within Bultmann's account of Paul's story, I trace the role community plays in the human plight and its solution, that is, "man under faith."

3.2.1 Bultmann's Account of Paul's Formal Structure of Human Existence

Bultmann's claim that Paul presupposes a formal structure of human existence is tied to a crucial insight that I continue to assert: that in telling the story of Christ, Paul intends to transcend his own context and, moreover, that he succeeds in doing so. My disagreement with Bultmann, as I make clear in the concluding section of this chapter, is over the way he understands Paul's eschatology and anthropology. For now I simply want to examine the key elements that Bultmann assigns to Paul's formal structure of human existence and ask how they fare, as an interpretation of Paul, in light of the interpretation of Paul's kerygma as the story of Israel.

The key concept in Bultmann's account of Paul's formal structure of human existence is *soma*. For Bultmann, *soma* is the self considered as the object of one's own conduct as subject (Bultmann, *Theology* 1:196). Because I have such a relationship to myself, I can also subject myself to the will of another: My relationship to myself as *soma* is the transcendental condition of being responsible for my own *soma* or for surrendering it to another. *Soma* serves a double function in this interpretation. First, it is a transcendental condition of human existence expressed mythically, namely, that human existence is openness to the other because it is primordially openness to oneself as another. We understand Paul's use of *soma* because we share this transcendental condition. Second, this condition grounds the continuity between Paul's "I have been crucified with Christ" (I encounter the decision for my authentic existence in the kerygma) and "nevertheless I live" (I persist as a being who can submit himself to another). Despite this relational aspect, Bultmann's *soma* differs from Paul's more communal sense of I in that for Bultmann the otherness of other people recedes behind two other sorts of alterity: self as other to itself, and self as other to God. Bultmann is right to worry, of course, that the role of other people in the constitution of selfhood should not reduce the self to its relations. In chapter 6 I propose that Ricoeur's dialectic of self and other responds to Bultmann's concern while giving other people their due in the constitution of selfhood. As it stands, though, Bultmann's *soma* cannot adequately express Paul's communal personality.

Bultmann understands Paul's use of *pneuma* to denote "the self that lives in man's attitude, in the orientation of his will" (Bultmann, *Theology* 1:206). The divine Spirit is itself guided by a will and so it is also a kind of subject. To be led by the Spirit is to have one's will oriented to the will of this divine subject so that "the divine *pneuma* . . . has become the subject-self, so to say, of the Christian" (Bultmann, *Theology* 1:208). In *soma* the human person submits herself to herself or another; in *pneuma* she lives toward the actual end that she wills in doing so. In chapter 2 I followed Robert Jewett, who says that the human spirit is the person's "mine" of the Spirit in the community. Perhaps, then, we should understand Bultmann's *pneuma* as the transcendental condition of this ability to say "mine" of the Spirit. Yet by relating human spirit and divine Spirit solely through the category of will, Bultmann severely truncates his notion of spirit. The spirit in a community is expressed not only in willing the same end but in shared language, praxis, stories, and patterns of interpersonal relationship, and Bultmann's reconstruction of *pneuma* cannot articulate those dimensions of spirit.

Syneidesis, Bultmann says, had by Paul's time shifted in meaning from "joint knowledge with another" to "knowledge shared with one's self" (Bultmann, *Theology* 1:216). Here it might seem that Bultmann's reconstruction is altogether incompatible with the dialogical and communal account of conscience I proposed in conversation with Bruce Malina. Yet that account has as its focus some actual conscience, whereas Bultmann seeks its transcendental conditions. Bultmann fully grants that in conscience the self relates to the transcendent in some actual context—for Jews, Torah, and for Gentiles, the political state and human conventions (Bultmann, *Theology* 1:261). In its demand of absolute obedience, the conscience attests to a transcendent authority; its particular commands are always the inward recapitulation of a public discourse. It is in conscience that the self is called to decide for her own self (Bultmann, *Theology* 1:219).

Nevertheless, if we accept Malina's reconstruction of Paul's background, then Paul's notion of conscience would have retained a significant dimension of joint knowledge with another that is lost in Bultmann's account. Bultmann might well respond that it should be lost, that is, demythologized. After all, his reduction proceeds from the insight that Paul can say "mine" of his conscience. Yet as an alternative interpretation of Paul's conscience, Paul Ricoeur's account has much to recommend it: Ricoeur's dialectic of selfhood and otherness can account for the "mine" yet preserve the place of the other in the constitution of conscience.[13] My point here is not to defend one account against the other (I leave that for chapter 6) but to suggest that what "conscience" means (even phenomenologically reduced) does not escape interpretation. In *soma*, *pneuma*, and *syneidesis* Bultmann believes that his analyses have receded beneath the level of interpretation (Jones 167–78). Yet my somewhat different account suggests that even the articulation of a transcendental condition is subject to a dialectic of suspicion and attestation. Bultmann's purpose is clear enough: to honor Paul's intention to let his claims about *soma*, *pneuma*, and *syneidesis* transcend his particular context. But on the way to capturing its transcending intention, Bultmann sacrifices too much of the claim's context. In the critical comments, I suggest that Bultmann's problem is that he attempts to hold together the past and present by collapsing eschatology onto the phenomenological reduction; the solution is a different understanding of eschatology and anthropology.

3.2.2 *The Ontic Situation of the Human:* *Sin, World, Law, and Death*

For Bultmann, human life is lived *coram deo*. Each person's ontological possibility to be good or evil is realized ontically as the decision for or against a relationship with God, which is the true human life. As being-toward-God, the human person experiences the drive toward true life as a *telos*, and that drive is also a command. In Paul's Jewish context, that command is expressed in Torah. Sin is a misdirected pursuit of this life that brings about its opposite, death. The primordial sin is thus "the false assumption of receiving life not as the gift of the Creator but procuring it by one's own power, of living from one's self rather than from God" (Bultmann, *Theology* 1:232). By depending on something other than God, the human being becomes enslaved to the very thing she had sought to control. Thus Rom. 7 is not about Paul or Israel but the human in general who as inwardly split "loses his self, and 'sin' becomes the active subject within him" (Bultmann, *Theology* 1:245). So the problem identified by Rom. 7:7–25 is not that human beings fail to do the good but that they bring about an evil (their own death) under the form of pursuing the good, that is, true life (Bultmann, *Theology* 1:247). Bultmann is correct, of course, to finger humanity as the source of its own destruction. Yet he proceeds as if Paul is speaking about the general situation of humankind rather than the particular disaster that befell Israel in the death of its Messiah. Interpretation has to travel in the reverse direction, from the reconstruction of the story to the self presupposed in the story.

Rom. 5:12–21, in Bultmann's account, does not refer to inherited sin but to the fact that Adam's disobedience brings about a new possibility for human existence, namely, sin unto death. Each human being has always already appropriated this possibility through an individual act, and we now share a world that promotes our continued apostasy:

> Since human life is a life with others, mutual trust is destroyed by a *single* lie, and mistrust—and thereby sin—is established; by a *single* deed of violence defensive violence is called forth and law as organized violence is made to serve the interests of individuals. . . . So everyone exists in a world in which each looks out for himself, each insists upon his rights, each fights for his existence, and life becomes a struggle of all against all even when the battle is involuntarily fought. (Bultmann, *Theology* 1:253)

Although the origin of such a world remains a mystery (expressed mythologically in the story of Adam), we are each responsible for its perpetuation— the human world only exists through us. The human world (*kosmos*) grows up out of human selves until it "comes to constitute an independent super-self over all individual selves," namely, the "spirit of the world" (Bultmann, *Theology* 1:256–57). Mythologically expressed, the *kosmos* is the domain of demonic spirits who exist only insofar as they take their power to exist from humans who surrender their own power to exist to them (Bultmann, *Theology* 1:258). These powers exist *for us* in the sense that we exist in dependence on them in a way that properly belongs to God alone. The divine Spirit grants us life and demands our dependence; we give over this life to spirits who live through us and kill us while we grow to depend on them. Such spirits are thus counterfeits of the divine Spirit. For Bultmann, of course, these are all existential realities in mythological dress (Bultmann, *Theology* 1:257).

The law brings this situation of bondage to its logical conclusion—the death of the sinner. However, it is God's mercy that the law leads us into death because we must die to be delivered from our desperate situation. What is this "death?" In the encounter with the risen Lord, the individual faces the objective truth about humankind and, correlatively, the truth about herself—a truth that confronts her as a sinner. Faith presents the sinner with the possibility of a continuous life restored to its proper dependence on God. She understands her prior life as under sin and death; yet in dependence on the creator, she no longer cedes her life over to the powers of "sin" and "world." She is crucified with Christ, yet Christ lives in her (Bultmann, *Theology* 1:257). Sin and world are defeated because they receive their power to exist from the human who has now left that cycle. So Christ's victory over sin and death occurs in the moment of faith.

I agree with Bultmann that Christ's victory over sin takes place in the individual's decision of faith.[14] Yet that the decision of faith is a shared experience presupposes language and community. Bultmann, however, construes community solely as a temptation away from authenticity (echoing, perhaps, Heidegger's attitude to "the They"—*das Man*—in *Being and Time*).[15] Consequently the solution Bultmann discerns in Paul does not involve a challenge to the hearer's community per se but to her stance toward that community. Thus for Bultmann the influence of the community asserts itself in the perpetuation of the problem, while the solution cuts the individual loose from her community. It remains to be seen whether Bultmann's discussion of the kerygma as an actual encounter between persons entails a more positive role for the community in salvation.

3.2.3 The Human Person under Faith

As I trace what Bultmann means by the individual's righteousness *coram deo*, I ask the reader to keep in mind that I intend a similar claim by a different path—the kerygma as the story of Israel (chapter 2) and an ontology of the self in community (chapter 5). If the self and its community are correlates, then to admit that the kerygma is the story of a community does no harm to the claim that in the encounter with the risen Lord the individual believer is righteous *coram deo.*

Righteousness for Bultmann is the condition for which receiving life (salvation) is the result. Righteousness does not denote the condition of being innocent but of having been acknowledged innocent in a courtroom setting; "one's own righteousness," by way of contrast, is self-empowered striving (Bultmann, *Theology* 1:273). *Righteousness* thus refers first and foremost to the relationship between the individual and God. For all that, righteousness is objective because it is revealed (it becomes a real possibility for humankind) in the Christ event (Bultmann, *Theology* 1:275). "This saving occurrence . . . is the eschatological event by which God ended the old course of the world and introduced the new aeon" (Bultmann, *Theology* 1:278). It is not simply that a new idea arose in Christ but that an old eon passed and a new one opened. Note, however, that the "new eon" is not a communal category per se. Rather, the new eon is present in every Now in the decision of faith of every believer. But then are faith and the eschatological event relative to the individual believer's subjectivity? Bultmann claims, rather, that faith belongs to the eschatological event itself, and to understand what he means by that we have to look more closely at his account of the kerygma.

The cross becomes the eschatological event in the kerygma, which is to say that the cross of Christ becomes the eschatological event in the believer. All the images Paul uses to describe the death of Christ articulate one reality with two objective dimensions (Bultmann, *Theology* 1:292–300).[16] First, Christ's death outside of us was needed for our salvation. Second, in the kerygma the hearer encounters another (the risen Lord) who offers the hearer her own self as gift. If the subject of this event is the historical Jesus, what gives it its eschatological significance? Each of Paul's images presupposes some conviction on the part of the hearer, for example, that Jesus is the preexistent Son of God or that he was raised. Bultmann distinguishes between two "acts" of faith:

> The first is belief (in the narrower popular use of the English word): willingness to consider true (= believe) the facts reported of the preexistent Son of God—incarnation, crucifixion, resurrection from the dead—and to see in them a demonstration of the grace of God. The second is a faith which is a self-surrender to the grace of God and which signifies the utter reversal of a man's previous understanding of himself—specifically, the radical surrender of his human "boasting." (Bultmann, *Theology* 1:300)

If these are two discrete acts, then a belief that presupposes some particular historical framework (faith₁) conditions surrender (faith₂). Bultmann claims, however, that there is only one act: "The decision-question whether a man is willing to give up his old understanding of himself and henceforth understand himself only from the grace of God" turns out to be the same as "the question whether he will acknowledge Jesus Christ as the Son and God as Lord" (Bultmann, *Theology* 1:301). The implication is that if I come to the same decision for authentic existence as Paul (faith₂), then I need not share much of the background presupposed in Paul's faith₁. Why? Because leaving my old self-understanding for the new one counts as the acknowledgment that Jesus Christ is the Son of God. The minimum we have to share with Paul is to proclaim the eschatological purpose of Jesus and thus confront the hearer with the decision for her authentic existence.

One encounter of this sort is Paul's own encounter with the risen Lord. In this encounter, Bultmann says, Paul "risked himself as a Jew" against a formerly "unimaginable new possibility of understanding himself."[17] In so doing, Paul, when he confesses that Israel's hope was fulfilled in Jesus, proclaims that Jesus brought the ultimate decision for human existence into the world. Here Paul "has simply taken the Jewish concept of Messiah radically" (Bultmann, *Theology* 1:242). If Paul affirms that *this* man is the hoped-for Messiah, then the new age has already begun, and the Messiah can no longer be anticipated as the fulfillment of Jewish striving after righteousness. As a historical event, the Messiah is God's own eschatological salvation. Yet as a crucified Messiah, this historical event entails a paradoxical judgment on Jewish (and ultimately on all human) striving for righteousness: The one who represents the highest hope of works righteousness was crucified, and to confess this man as the Christ is to resolve that works righteousness is a perverse pursuit of death under the figure of life. In that resolve, in the wake of this contingent historical event, Paul confronts the possibility of his own authentic existence. Bultmann is mistaken that all of first-century Judaism was a striving after righteousness. Yet it is true enough that for Paul to confess "Jesus is the Christ" he first has to retell Israel's story. In doing so he is indeed taking the Jewish concept of Messiah radically, and it is the historical fact of the crucified Messiah that makes the retelling of Israel's story necessary.

But then how is the new age opened by this historical Messiah anything more than Paul's own subjective experience? First, although the evidence is only visible to faith, the new reality is manifest in a world-event, namely, "the new age is real in that Christ is being preached" (Bultmann, "Significance" 243). The power to preach is the risen Lord himself in the preaching—a power visible only to faith and yet really present in the world. That Paul exists authentically is the presence of the risen Lord in his preaching. Preaching proclaims an act of God in history, namely, the transformation of the proclaimer by the historical event of the cross and the offer of that transformation to the hearer. But preaching also belongs to that historical act itself because it is the condition of the event being repeated again and again in people who hear it and respond. The new age becomes a world-event not only as *historische* but in its transforming work on those who hear (*Geschichte*). But then does the reality of this world-event depend on an act of the hearer (faith)? Not if faith belongs to the eschatological event. That faith is a "walk in Spirit" means that the genuineness of the walk is hidden with God: the I does not have disposal over its own faith. That people now walk according to Spirit is itself part of the eschatological event and faith belongs to that eschatological event.

Finally, the new eon is a reality in Paul's context not only in the preaching but through the historical Jesus. That does not mean that the world develops out of Jesus' personality (whether as the effect of his human character or as an ideal) for if that were so then "the new age would simply be an epoch of spiritual development" (Bultmann, "Significance" 245). That such a man lived in history is taken up into the kerygma; the kerygma comes to us in history; and yet as *Geschichte*, the kerygma confronts us with the same eschatological purpose of Jesus, namely, to exist, as he did, for God. Thus the historical Jesus, the kerygma, and faith all belong to the same eschatological event. The claim that Jesus is the Christ, the risen Lord, is of a piece with the claim that eschatological existence is present in the world. All of this might seem to indicate that for Bultmann the Church partly constitutes the salvific power of the kerygma, but in the critical remarks that follow I argue that for Bultmann the Church is actually a second-order effect of the kerygma's transformation of individuals.

3.3 A Critical Engagement with Bultmann

I propose the following organization for my critical remarks. On one hand, I raise three criticisms. First, I offer a different eschatology following Jürgen Moltmann's critique of Bultmann's eschatology. Second, I argue that genuine alterity cannot appear in the encounter with the risen Lord as Bultmann describes it. Third, I argue that Bultmann fails to adequately account for the role of community in the kerygma. On the other hand, I retrieve two important insights from Bultmann. First, that some form of phenomenological analysis must continue to assert itself against totalizing discourses that would reduce the self and other to language, praxis, narrative, interpersonal relations, or community. Second, that some chastened version of Bultmann's demythologizing remains necessary because we no longer share Paul's world.

3.3.1 Time and Eschatology

There are three ways, Moltmann suggests, to relate eschatology to time. First, one could take the temporal category for the Last Things to be the "already" of the present and the "not yet" of the future, creating a futurist eschatology in which history and eschatology "lie along one and the same temporal line."[18] Here the "Last" is empty in "Last Things" because all futures recede into the past. Second, one could take the temporal category for the Last Things to be eternity. But then how does one relate Last Things to the present and future "since eternity is simultaneous to all times, and is equally indifferent towards them" (Moltmann, Coming of God 6)? Bultmann pushes such an eternalizing eschatology. Moltmann offers a third way to escape the oscillation of futurist and eternalizing eschatologies, namely, "the Advent as eschatological category, and the category Novum as its historical reverse side" (Moltmann, Coming of God 6).

The transposition of eschatology into eternity does begins not with Bultmann but with Barth. Barth's eschatology disrupts the optimism of the Protestant concept of time while inadvertently affirming it because an eternalized eschatology still creates no real crisis in history (Moltmann, Coming of God 18). Bultmann's eschatology, like Barth's, depends on the eternal moment, although Bultmann understands the moment in terms of a phenomenological reduction of human existence—the Last Things are present in the moment of decision. In consequence, Bultmann's eschatology does not concern the future of this world but rather "depriv[es] the world of its worldhood" (Moltmann, Coming of God 19). Moltmann counters that to "replace world history by the historicity of existence does not make world history disappear":

> Christian eschatology teaches hope not only for the soul . . . but also for the body; not only for the individual but also for the community; not only for the church but also for Israel; not only for human beings but also for the cosmos. This supra-individual horizon of hope can then only be called mythological if one has no concern for the conditions over which this horizon spans its bow. . . . To say this does not rule out the fact that "my decision" plays a decisive part even if the whole world is against me: on the contrary. But the Christian rebellion of conscience, which leads to personal conse-

quences in the form of resistance, persecution and suffering is a
public rebellion against public demons, injustice and acts of violence. (Moltmann, *Coming of God* 20–21)

In short, each person's moment of decision draws on and advances real
historical struggles. From the Church's perspective, "community" does not
denote the simple ingathering of authentic selves but the historical engagement of the church with Israel's hope that God will indwell His creation in a
people. Our embeddedness in time should motivate us to force Bultmann's
individualized eschatology out of timelessness and into God's future, recognizing the actual (not simply transcendental) conditions of human existence.
No doubt, theology must find a way to speak of the believer's decision as her
own, and phenomenological analysis is one such option. Yet eschatology concerns first and foremost God's future in which God indwells the creation—a
future that encompasses the future of the individual, community and nature.
Thus although reflection on human existence remains one locus of theological
reflection, eschatological reflection as such should not be reduced to this one
locus.

For Bultmann, talk about God is always analogical because God is only
known indirectly as the one who brings us to the moment of decision. Just as
Paul demythologized Jewish apocalyptic, the corresponding demythologizing
move on our part is to express the kerygma in the language of relationality,
that is, analogical speech about God:

God's love and care, etc., are not images or symbols; these concep-
tions mean real experiences of God as acting here and now. Especially in the conception of God as Father the mythological sense van-
ished long ago. . . . As applied to God the physical import of the
term father has disappeared completely; it expresses a purely personal relationship. It is in this analogical sense that we speak of God
as Father.[19]

Yet Bultmann's appeal to the analogy of relationship raises as many questions
as it is intended to answer.[20] Is this analogy really free from objectivizing myth?
Is it true, for example, that in speech about God, the physical import of the
term father has disappeared? Can we speak of a personal relationship without
speaking of the person and being of God? If the encounter with the risen Lord
is to transcend each particular encounter, then Bultmann's analogy of relationship must be joined to some more adequate analogical understanding of God's
being. Moltmann offers as the analogy for God's mode of being the future in

which God indwells his creation—the coming God (Moltmann, *Coming of God* 24).

Moltmann narrates God's Being through acts in history rather than a timeless simultaneity (eternalized eschatology) or becoming (futurist eschatology). These acts are paradigmatically, though not exclusively, the great stories of Exodus, the return from exile, and Christ's resurrection. Experiences of the partial fulfillment of God's promise in history do not simply bring about a transcending of the world (as Bultmann maintains) but open new possibilities of existence that can transform the person, the community, and nature. Here the eschaton is not the transcendental condition of time but the advent of the coming God as the source of such conditions (Moltmann, *Coming of God* 26). Theology doesn't speak of God, as Bultmann does, exclusively on appeal to phenomenological analysis, but in the actual "What happened?" narrated as the advent of the coming God.

In sum, Moltmann rejects Bultmann's timeless eschatology because the eschaton has to embrace not only the transcendence of eternity to every moment but the actual future of the world. The resurrection is a novum—a demand placed against the conditions of human existence—not the irruption of eternity into time. Paul responds to just such a demand when he retells Israel's story to let what cannot be said—the crucified and resurrected oChrist—come into phrases. For Paul the crucified and resurrected Christ is not simply an irruption of eternity into time but an event that demands a new understanding of Paul's world, community, and self. Consequently Paul's claims about *soma*, *pneuma*, and *syneidesis* transcend his context not because they are timeless or eternal but because they belong to the eschaton as the future of the world.

3.3.2 Kerygma and Alterity

Bultmann develops his eternalized eschatology not only to establish the transcendence of Paul's claims but also to defend his own understanding of justification by faith. If justification is *sola fide*, then assent to the framework that makes faith$_1$ intelligible to Paul cannot be a prerequisite for our encounter with the risen Lord (faith$_2$). The minimum we have to share with Paul, Bultmann argues, is the intent to proclaim the eschatological purpose of Jesus, namely, to bring the hearer to a decision for her authentic existence. My second criticism of Bultmann, then, is that such a shared eschatological purpose is not enough to connect our proclamation with Paul's.

I can understand Robert Jenson's frustration when he finds bizarre Bultmann's position that for a past event that poses an eschatological possibility "the temporal course of that event must be irrelevant to its meaning."[21] Bultmann's point, though, is that the historical event of the cross can become the eschatological event only when the hearer meets the risen Lord in the kerygma; otherwise its effect is reduced to mere historical causality. Yet David Fergusson rightly observes that Bultmann's either/or (either historical causality or encounter) fails to account for the many ways responsible agents breach the natural continuum of cause and effect every day—ways in which the intentions of these agents are bound up with a public, observable world (Fergusson 122). Under a different account of causality, it might be possible to join description and encounter such that we could speak of the eschatological event transmitted and preserved in a community of believers. For now it is enough to observe that Bultmann's dichotomy of history and encounter responds to the distance between a historical event whose intelligibility recedes (Paul's faith₁) and the need for the kerygma to address each hearer anew (our faith₂).

Bultmann resolves this tension in two moves. First, he limits the eschatological in Jesus' purpose to that which transcends every context (Bultmann's eternalized eschatology). Second, he makes the historical claim that his demythologizing recapitulates Paul's project now. In this double move, the temporal distance between the present hearer and the first-century hearer is overcome in the eschatological moment. Consequently, distance in time no longer matters because the eschatological event of Christ is the unique, world-disclosing event of revelation. Bultmann thus tears asunder the immediacy of the event of revelation (the risen Lord) and the interpreted historical event that initiates it (Paul's relation to the historical Jesus). In so doing, Bultmann preserves an immediate grasp of immanence that is not immediate self-knowledge but rather the copresence of all human beings in the eschatological event. What matters is not the language in which the encounter is articulated (the background presupposed in faith₁) but the reality of the encounter itself as an encounter with another, the risen Lord (faith₂).

Yet Bultmann admits that an encounter with another always requires some background against which faith₁ is intelligible, because the kerygma does not encounter the hearer as text but as preaching. That means that the hearer encounters the proclaimer's authentic existence, in the presence of the risen Lord, put to her own inauthentic existence as a challenge. This encounter happens in a shared world where two contemporaries meet in their differences. But then precisely what makes the kerygma effective in the present is utterly lacking in the demythologized encounter with Paul—genuine alterity. Bultmann's demythologizing cannot deliver Paul's alterity because it "tends to isolate the individual from the personal and social relationships that shape human identity" (Fergusson 142).

For Paul in his first-century context, the objectivity of the experience is in the confession that Jesus is the Christ. Demythologizing, however, abstracts from any actual social implications of that confession to go straight to its meaning for Paul's existence. Here Bultmann claims he is simply recapitulating Paul's project. Against this claim I raised a first objection: that Paul intends to narrate the identity of the eschatological community, not the story of the human in general. So Bultmann first occludes Paul's alterity in misconstruing his intent. Recall that for Bultmann, one speaks of the eschatological, which is the transcendent, by reducing phenomenologically from all particular contexts. Yet transcendence so understood, Ricoeur observes, is invincible only at the cost of being empty.[22] Here a second objection arises, specifically, that Bultmann gives no account of the shared background against which we can understand the equivalence of our decision and Paul's. Bultmann could answer that we share the same eschatological purpose, but now the circle appears vicious: The eschatological purpose prescinds from context, and context is precisely what is at stake. Without access to genuine alterity, it is difficult to see how, despite Bultmann's best intentions, the encounter with the risen Lord does not collapse into an encounter with an ideal or exemplar. The logic of Bultmann's own position demands more. I maintain that the way to preserve the appearing of the eschatological event through time is to situate it in a historical community, and that leads to my final criticism of Bultmann.

3.3.3 Kerygma and Community

How can the kerygma's challenge to the individual facilitate the messy business of creating community, given that its eschatological content abstracts from context? Here I follow Bultmann's logic of transformation as it bears on community, arguing that his demythologizing leaves behind the communal dimension of the kerygma.

For Bultmann, there is a kind of sociality that precedes the gospel and is represented paradigmatically in Torah. The basic principle of this sociality includes love of neighbor, but it also contains a curse that commands obedience through fear of retribution. There is a significant sense, then, in which this framework is not yet real community. Nonetheless, the law is beneficial insofar as it expresses the human *telos* to pursue "life." This *telos* appears to Gentiles in the political state (which is originally ordered by God) and in human conventions (insofar as they are genuinely good) (Bultmann, *Theology* 1:261). There is thus a God-given framework for human community, but in the hands of sinners it has been abused by organized violence until there is no real community (Bultmann, *Theology* 1:253). Faith fulfills the law, not out of fear of retribution but because it brings about the love of neighbor (Bultmann, *Theology* 1:315). The new self, living out of love of neighbor, has "the right . . . to find for one's self" what is properly Torah (Bultmann, *Theology* 1:342). So love of neighbor resolves all of the problems associated with forming community, and in love those of faith properly discern the signs of God's guidance. The gospel does not transform social structures per se, but transforms individuals who, in love of neighbor, discern what truly belongs to the law.

Yet how are we to apply the love of neighbor criterion to a claim that the law does or does not apply in some particular case? Bultmann's focus on the agent's authenticity loses sight of the actual procedures we use to evaluate such claims. The love of neighbor criterion might well be turned about, asking instead how one is to decide which action best comports with love of neighbor. Jones puts the problem succinctly when he observes Bultmann can say, "I have faith only when I have it ever anew in my duties and exigencies" but cannot give an account of "what those duties and exigencies actually are" (Jones 206). That the believer is free is an aspect of her own inwardness, to be sure, but to articulate that freedom, even to herself, she has to appeal to public symbols that do not escape interpretation.

In construing the kerygma as the story of the human in general, the only community that Bultmann implicitly recognizes is the human race. Yet the kerygma so understood cannot deliver the resources needed to realize the goal that the human race should be one community; that the human race should be one community remains a task even if it is already given to faith in an actual historical community (Gal. 3:28). This community must be able to embrace others in their alterity lest it suffer the consequences of becoming either a community in name only (ignoring alterity) or a totalitarian community (destroying alterity). What can create such community? When Paul faced the silently suffering other, he did not simply stake a claim about what was genuine in the law. Rather, he staked a claim about the identity of his community. In so doing, he did not apply the law from a perspective above it but risked a radical reinterpretation of the original call of his own people to embrace the suffering other as other. He reestablished the story of his own life only at the expense of retelling his community's story.

3.3.4 Demythologizing and Community: An Appreciation of Bultmann

Bultmann's demythologizing has two laudable concerns. First, it allows a message in an unfamiliar framework to continue to address us in the present. Second, it asserts the transcendence of the individual hearer, the proclaimer, and the risen Lord within the encounter. Although Bultmann is right that not everything brought forward in reconstruction should bind the interpreter's practice, no method can infallibly assign in every instance what is background and what is message. If we follow the clue that the gospel is a story that identifies a community, we have to recognize that Paul is genuinely different from us while he participates with us in one community. To put Paul's words into present practice, then, is of a piece with our debate as a community about how we should embrace Paul in his difference from us. So the criterion of what can be demythologized is not a fundamental structure of existence but an ongoing conversation about the identity of our community with Paul.

Here the family resemblance between my approach and Bultmann's becomes evident. Like Bultmann, I also claim that this project carries on Paul's project in the present. Where Bultmann sees Paul's project as a precursor to phenomenological reduction, I see it as the project of narrating the continuity of the self and other in one community through time. What recommends the latter project is that it does not reduce all differences between the present interpreter and the author but narrates the shift from the one to the other as the historical life of a community.

But why not simply grant that Bultmann's reduction and my communal account are just two different analogies for appropriating Paul's words in our context—analogies that fall within an allowable range of reasonable interpretations of the text? Why not simply acknowledge a diversity of interpretations, within the limits of what Ricoeur calls the ideal meaning and eschew the pursuit of (as the title of a recent book suggests) "what St. Paul really said?"[23] To suggest why I think it remains crucial to assert that our interpretations aim at what Paul really meant, I want to contrast my retrieval of Bultmann with that of Jones, who proposes the following four stage process of interpretation (Jones 174–75).

The first stage "involves, straightforwardly, the *religionsgeschictliche* analyses, in so far as it is possible, of the motifs, symbols, events and utterances described within it" (Jones 168). In the second stage, the reconstructed text is allowed to speak analogically in its own context, albeit a context reconstructed by the interpreter. The analogy operative at stage two is the analogy the author uses to express the community's relationship to God. In the third stage, the interpreter interprets her own horizon, an exercise in suspicion. In the final stage, the interpreter places her interpretation in an analogical framework that lets the author's voice speak again to the interpreter's community.

So in the case of Pauline interpretation there will be two analogies—Paul's (as reconstructed by the interpreter) and the interpreter's own analogy. Bultmann joins the two by fiat: Paul and the present-day interpreter share the same eschatological purpose. I claim, rather, that the two analogies should be joined by a narrative that identifies a community. Gadamer, somewhat famously, joins the two by what he calls a "fusion of horizons."[24] Jones offers a different metaphor, namely, that hermeneutics is like the construction of frames for windows (Jones 172). I take him to mean that one window looks out on the present and another window looks out on the past through the present. Historical-critical exegesis opens a window onto texts that tell stories about Jesus. Sociopolitical and historical-economic analyses open windows onto "the *context* in which *we wish to see Jesus of Nazareth* in his soteriological significance (given that we are Christians)" (Jones 172). At each stage there is a possible plurality of interpretations. Notwithstanding, the ideal meaning serves as a criterion against which certain interpretations should be called wrong (Jones 144).

So far I agree with Jones, but I worry that he too readily dismisses the claim that what is reconstructed at stage two (Paul's context) is the author's original publicly articulated intention. Jones suggests that although various analogies may be probative within their own discourses, all analogies are necessarily partial and may complement rather than supersede one another. Even at stage two (the search for "the text's own voice") the interpreter "must move towards recognizing that voice as itself an interpretation, one representation among several" (Jones 169). Here I am concerned that Jones may restore Paul's alterity only at the cost of our community with him: We confess that Paul is other than us only by positing that who he is finally escapes our grasp. Paul's otherness is restored only as a mystery that forever escapes us, and he can no longer assert his otherness in conversation with us.

I certainly do not mean to claim in response that interpretations can be transparent; but I do want to stress that if what eludes us about Paul's alterity is something we can talk about, then it has to show up in some interpretation. Such interpretations can themselves be subjected to suspicion—perhaps Paul is *not* such a mystery after all! I am somewhat mollified by Jones's assertion that some interpretations can be judged wrong with respect to the text's ideal meaning, but my discomfort returns when he identifies ideal meaning with "context-bound" meaning and contrasts it with "objective truth" and "what really happened" (Jones 166, 145). Unless we intend to banish such phrases from our language, we at least have to admit them as regulative ideals that guide interpretation. No interpretation is judged against the real except in some other interpretation. If that is understood, I see no problem with the claim that an interpretation aims at "objective truth" or "what really happened" as long as these phrases are not tied to a metaphysical realism that purports to judge interpretation against an uninterpreted event.

As compared to Bultmann's understanding of the gospel as a kind of story of everyman, the recommendation to understand the gospel as the story that identifies a community is indeed another analogy among a plurality of analogies. For Jones, the ideal meaning of a text does not impose an order among these analogies but just sorts the wheat from the chaff. I want to amend this a bit by suggesting that these analogies can be ordered within a narrative that identifies the community. To make that case I need a present-day analogy for a narrative that identifies a community, which I locate in the sort of narratives interpreters give when challenged to justify their reconstructions of an author's intention.[25]

Terence Donaldson's *Paul and the Gentiles* is a recent attempt to reconstruct Paul's intention. Donaldson reconstructs a "convictional world" behind Paul's rhetoric as a backdrop to his mission to the Gentiles.[26] Convictions, Donaldson claims, structure a social world: They are the background against which our lives make sense. The most important aspect of convictions is that they are public, not subjective or idiosyncratic beliefs of individuals. What I want to draw from Donaldson's study is the general shape of such an argument: that in general, interpretation seeks to reconstruct a discursive background for the publicly articulated intention of a real author. Jones refers to this interpretive act as the imposition of a window on the past, but there is an ambiguity in his metaphor. Is it an empirical claim about what usually happens in interpretation, that is, that in practice interpreters never get the ancient interlocutor's intention right? Or is it a phenomenological claim about the experience of the interpreter? Although I agree with the former, I have to reject the latter. Does the interpreter really intend, at the end of the day, to say "Perhaps, after all, what I have achieved is only a best guess at my ancient interlocutor's publicly articulated intention, framed by my own window onto the text?" Or does the interpreter intend, rather, to aim at what the historical writer really meant— no matter how often in practice that mark may be missed?

The interpreter always acts within a community, and the implications of that can become apparent if we reflect on the act of interpretation. Jürgen Habermas offers four criteria to evaluate communicative acts.[27] First, my act has to be *intelligible*, that is, I have to speak in a way that invites another to grasp a publicly available meaning. Second, my act has to be *true* in the sense that its success as a speech act is possible in practice. Third, my act has to be *truthful* in the sense it represents my explicit intention and is not aimed at some peripheral effect. Finally, my act has to be *right* in the sense that it adheres to the norms of the situation. When I say "I am in pain" to express a psychosomatic state, if I do not use a public predicate like *pain*, then my statement will be unintelligible. If the statement does not represent my psychosomatic state, then I do not speak the truth. If I intend just to manipulate someone, then I do not speak truthfully. If I draw attention to my own minor injury when a doctor is trying to save someone else's life, then I do not speak rightly. Of course, I would not answer explicitly to each of these criteria in every speech act, but I could be challenged retrospectively on any one of them. Habermas asserts that these criteria apply to any communicative act whatsoever, but I only need the weaker claim that they apply to Paul's context and ours.[28] So two related claims meet in an act of interpretation—the author's claim to express an intention in a public idiom and the interpreter's claim to recover that publicly articulated intention against a reconstructed background.

To assert (as Jones does) that the interpreter's claim presupposes a window of interpretation could be expressed by qualifying it as limited to a community whose norms establish its rightness, for example, "This interpretation is intelligible, true and truthful *within the community of contemporary biblical scholars.*" Although such a qualification would make the interpreter less broadly accountable, the claim loses some force because in practice communicative actions are submitted to norms from various discourses. For example, David Tracy's three publics of the theologian (society, academy, and church) mark three broad discursive domains in which the theologian participates.[29] In the qualified claim, the interpreter's audience may well wonder why the interpretation might *not* be intelligible, true, truthful, and right in the theologian's other two publics—and whether that failure is culpable within a larger community where the theologian traverses all three publics. Without such a qualification, however, the interpreter is liable, at least in principle, to give an account of how her interpretation is right in each of these discursive domains.

Such an account would be a sort of story of interpretation that should accomplish three things: first, to situate the interpreter's claim within the context of a public practice of interpretation; second, to locate the claim within the historical sweep of a community of interpreters; and third, to locate the claim within the rules of the various discourses for which it is claimed to be right. Now a story of interpretation that concerns itself only with intelligibility, truth, and truthfulness might well aim no further than a community like contemporary biblical scholars. But when someone challenges the rightness of a claim, the interpreter could be called on to respond from any discursive domain in which she participates and to all those persons her larger community recognizes as genuine others, past and present.

Consider, as an example, Jones's claim that although Bultmann pursues biblical interpretation for the sake of a theological and pedagogical intent, E. P. Sanders "and other scholars who share his general methodology, have no such theological intent. They simply aim to discover more about Jesus of Nazareth" (Jones 195). To use the biblical texts as historical documents is already an analogy at the last of Jones's four stages, and Jones interprets Sanders as implicitly qualifying this use as right for a community of historical-critical interpreters. Yet to admit something more about Jesus (or St. Paul) into discourse has deeper implications for a community that seeks to embrace the historical other in his genuine difference from us in one community. However much Sanders may qualify it, his claims have inescapable implications for the larger community that appears in his acts of interpretation—a community that traverses Tracy's three publics and joins past and future interpreters in one community.

In the conversation that ensues on a challenge to a claim's rightness, the interpreter's story of interpretation articulates a community that may be at stake in the act of interpretation, and this kind of story better approximates the genre of Paul's gospel than the story of everyman. The requirement to narrate our community with the author is not just one more analogy but orders other analogies with respect to the good of a community. Plurality is still possible, though, because the community aims to embrace others in their actual differences. Jones's path to plurality misses the connection between the act of interpretation and the good of a community by focusing on the interpreter's choice of analogy. The plurality modeled on what Paul accomplishes is more costly: In articulating the other in her concrete difference from us, the interpreter, like Paul, may have to risk the identity of her own community.

The claims of Scripture are claims from within our community across time: Someone in our community once made such a claim. To hear these claims anew, I agree with Jones that we have to interpret the author's horizon and interpret our own horizon; I want to add that we must also narrate the continuity between the two as the life of one historical community through time. Then when we let the claims of ancient authors affect us, we will not witness the fusion of two horizons but the event of our own community coming to embrace others in their alterity. Retrospectively we can recognize the same imperative in Paul's gospel.

I want to emphasize that the publicly articulated intention of an author can only come into conversation in a reconstruction that is itself susceptible to suspicion. Moreover, the author's intention does not trump all other considerations but asserts within a larger conversation, "Here is how Paul would have understood the matter according to the best arguments available to us." That Paul understood something in a certain way need not decide the issue for us. We may be led to say, "Paul responded this way, but in our context and our situation we must respond in a different way."

How can this correction to demythologizing help us think about transcendence in a way that bridges our distance from Paul yet doesn't reduce eschatology to timelessness? Paul's kerygma is the story of a community where all human beings meet in their actual differences while each tells the story of his or her own life in its scope. This community is given to faith (Christ's presence in the Word and Sacrament), but in practice it remains a hope. In Moltmann's terms, to encounter this hope is to encounter the novum of the resurrected Christ. The response to temporal distance is to narrate the continuity between different ways of expressing this novum in one community of the living and dead in Christ (Moltmann, *Coming of God* 108). "If God's Being is in his coming," Moltmann says, "then the future that comes to meet us must become the theological paradigm of transcendence" (Moltmann, *Coming of God* 24). What would it mean to let "future" be the paradigm of transcendence? What Paul accomplished in retelling Israel's story can serve as a model for us.

In reconfiguring his community's narrative around the crucified and resurrected Christ, Paul does not simply strip the Christ event to its transcendental presuppositions. Rather, he lets the Christ event transform the historical horizon in which his world, community, and self are disclosed. Specifically, the community that represents the eschatological community is not demarcated by Torah but by faith manifested publicly as the Spirit of Christ in a people. When Paul makes a claim about "the human" from within this representative community, then that claim can exert a norm for others to the extent that this community preserves its aim to embrace others in their genuine alterity.

Clearly there are varying degrees to which claims about the self depend on context. For example, though the potential for conscience might be posited as a capability of the human organism, an actual conscience presupposes a person in community with others. It is not difficult to see that the latter sort of claim about "the human" does not escape interpretation.[30] But what about so-called potentialities of the human organism? There are two indications that even such potentialities do not escape interpretation. First, the self who responds is only actual in a particular dialectic of self and other, self and community. Consequently, we only ever glimpse the responding self in a particular context, and we can never hope to answer every skeptical charge that our certainty about who responds is context-dependent. Second, the self who responds is always already enabled to act and reflect by immersion in a public world and can only reflexively articulate and reflect on her experience using public symbols that do not escape interpretation.

The way to establish transcendence, though, is not to escape from the fact that claims about selfhood betray commitments to actual communities but to make good use of it. Challenges to the normativeness of the self revealed in the kerygma can take three forms. First, the speaker could appeal to a more original understanding of her community, as Paul does when he refers the boundary of his community to the faith of Abraham (Rom. 4; Gal. 3). Second, the speaker could claim to opt out of the community altogether. Yet that sort of a view from nowhere is unintelligible without a commitment to some community. Hence a third, more intelligible possibility is that the speaker could claim to speak from the horizon of some other community.

For its part, the Church aims to represent the eschatological community that embraces all peoples in their genuine alterity. In preserving this aim, the Church is bound to the first possibility, that is, to appeal to a more original understanding of the community. So the normativeness of the self revealed in the Church's proclamation is ultimately tied to its claim to embrace others in their alterity. The claim itself entails a praxis: As representing the eschatological community (proleptically, partially, and under the sign of the cross) the Church risks its own identity in embracing the other as other. Objections from other horizons are overcome only if the Church's praxis demonstrates that it can effectively embrace the neighbor in her genuine otherness.

This praxis applies not only to the Church's mission to the world but to its connection with its own past. Bultmann is right that if Paul's message can still speak to the present then we must share the same eschatological horizon. But if eschatology is understood in Moltmann's sense rather than Bultmann's, then to show that we share the same eschatological horizon becomes a task, namely, to demonstrate that we are one historical community with Paul. Yet if Paul is not to disappear as a concrete other, then we must interpret Paul's horizon, interpret our own horizon, and narrate the continuity between the two as one historical community through time. In Moltmann's terms, the historical perspective on that continuity (its novum) is the living stream of genuine encounters between self and other in the community; the transcendent perspective on that continuity (its advent) is the work of the Spirit of Christ, active in practice as each I says "mine" of the Spirit in the community.

The crucial function of demythologizing is thus served by a more complex communal process—to interpret the past, interpret the present, and narrate the continuity between the two. The community can hope that the Spirit of Christ guides this process.[31] Yet because the Spirit is the Spirit of the *crucified* Christ, the community's decisions—themselves born out of a conflict of flesh and spirit—remain subject to all modes of suspicion. Suspicion, though, can only be met by greater attestation. So despite the real ambivalence of the Church's practice, it remains the case that "we all, with unveiled face beholding as in a mirror the glory of the Lord, are being transformed into the same image from glory to glory, just as from the Lord, the Spirit" (2 Cor. 3:18).

Here an objection may arise, namely, that in letting the message address the present through the work of the Spirit in the community, I may compromise the second concern of Bultmann's demythologizing, specifically, that the individual should transcend her community. Briefly (and the claim is not fully developed until chapter 6) I argue that the transcendence of the self to community continues to be asserted in the self's "mine" of the Spirit in a community. This transcendence can be articulated using phenomenological analysis, yet it never escapes the dialectic of suspicion and attestation. Such a response will say too much for some and not enough for others. Such is the fragmentary nature of attestation of the self, "credence without any guarantee . . . trust greater than any suspicion."[32]

By way of conclusion and as a transition to *Oneself as Another* in the next chapter, I want to briefly touch on Ricoeur's interpretation of Bultmann. Ricoeur observes that when Bultmann reduces notions such as "act of God" to the surrender of the will he "makes hardly any demands on this language of faith, whereas he was so suspicious about the language of myth."[33] Yet if this language of faith is truly nonobjective, as Bultmann claims, then faith language "is no longer of the order of signification at all" and "with faith, there is no longer anything to think, anything to say" (Ricoeur, "Preface to Bultmann" 66). Here Ricoeur makes a similar point to one I raised earlier: If the claim that we share the same encounter with Paul (faith₂) doesn't also involve a shared background, then the claim is empty of meaning. Yet more is presupposed in the encounter than meaning, namely, "that the word itself belongs to the being who addresses himself to my existence" (Ricoeur, "Preface to Bultmann" 70). If the encounter is to have objective significance, then language has to articulate being: the being of the proclaimer, of the hearer, and of God present in the risen Lord. Bultmann, Ricoeur says, has taken a short cut through Heidegger's work "without having made the long detour to the question of being" (Ricoeur, "Preface to Bultmann" 70). It is only the detour through the actual (in Heidegger's phrase, the *existenziell*) that prevents the collapse of the conditions of existence into "abstractions of lived experience, of a formalized *existenziell*" (Ricoeur, "Preface to Bultmann" 71).

So the distance between Ricoeur's ontology of the self and Bultmann's formal structure of existence arises in part because Bultmann and Ricoeur stand in somewhat different horizons. Bultmann has already taken Heidegger's turn to the event of revelation, but he remains firmly committed to the I as the unique locus of reflection on the ontological difference. For Ricoeur, on the contrary, "Authentic Dasein is born from the response to Being and, in responding, preserves the strength of Being by the strength of the word."[34] The self that names beings in the world is called forth in responding to Being. This self is not nothing, but neither is it immediate in the sense of Bultmann's copresence of every I in the eschatological moment. Rather, the self only ever comes into conversation in a word that is subject to interpretation. The self must be encountered in looking over one's own shoulder in an itinerary of detours through language, praxis, narrative, and ethics. So Ricoeur's project in *Oneself as Another* can help correct the loss of alterity consequent on Bultmann's decision to collapse eschatology into a certain type of phenomenological reduction. At the same time, however, Ricoeur's critique of Bultmann labors under the same construal of the kerygma as the story of the human in general. Thus although Ricoeur can help correct Bultmann's inordinate rush to let Paul's story of everyman map onto the hearer's story, his itinerary needs one more detour—a detour through stories that identify communities. I turn, then, to explore the community presupposed in Ricoeur's *Oneself as Another*.

4

The Deferred Self: Paul Ricoeur's *Oneself as Another*

In the next two chapters I leave off Bultmann's more direct method of joining the past to the present (by the fiat of the eschatological moment) and embark on a more arduous path through detours suggested by Paul Ricoeur's *Oneself as Another*.[1] To appropriate Paul's "I have been crucified with Christ" (Gal. 2:20) in our context without hyperbole requires an understanding of the self as the correlate of a community. I find the beginnings of such a project in Ricoeur's book. Yet in his ontological sketch of the self, Ricoeur focuses on the relation of self and other rather than the relation of self and community. That is not to say that the role of community in the constitution of the self is absent from Ricoeur's account; rather, it never becomes an explicit theme. I propose to take it as a theme here, that is, to take a last detour to the self through community. Armed with these findings, I reconfigure Ricoeur's ontology of the self in the next chapter, but now from the perspective of the self in community.

4.1 The Detour through a Philosophy of Language

Ricoeur begins his itinerary with what he calls a "semantics of identifying reference" that brackets the speaker and situation. At this level the person is not yet a self (i.e., is not self-designating) but is something referred to in sentences. To identify a given particular we

classify it as either a *body* or a *person*.[2] Three constraints characterize this grammar: First, a person is at the same time a body; second, the physical and mental
properties of a person are attributed to one and the same entity; third, the
mental predicates maintain the same meaning as they circulate among the
personal pronouns (I hurt, you hurt, she hurts, etc.). There is thus double
attribution (physical and mental predicates to a person) without double reference (as in the Cartesian body and soul). This kind of identity is *sameness*, that
is, identity characterized by language's ability to identify the same thing over
and over again (Ricoeur, *Oneself as Another* 32). How the self belongs to the
framework is not set up as a problem for a semantics of identifying reference.

The semantic level, of course, cannot cover all of what can be said about
the human. By *aporia* Ricoeur indicates any phenomenon that cannot be adequately accounted for in the framework under consideration (here, the semantics of identifying reference). A first aporia appears when semantics is
called on to account for the strange property of a body that is at once mine and
yet a body among bodies. A second appears in accounting for ascription as the
way two sets of predicates (physical and mental) can be attributed to one and
the same entity. A third aporia appears in accounting for the way I feel my
own pain but can only observe yours.

On a new level, speech act theory promises to address these aporias by
putting the speaker back into play. Yet anchoring the I to an utterance is not
as easy as it may appear. Speech act theory does not attribute reflexivity to a
subject but to the utterance as an event in the world. This ontology of events
is limited, however, in what it can say, because a single subject speaks many
utterances. Therefore the I cannot be linked to the utterance, so it escapes the
ontology of events. Here is the "aporia of anchoring," namely, "the lack of
coincidence between the 'I' as the world-limit and the proper name that designates a real person" (Ricoeur, *Oneself as Another* 51).

In response, Ricoeur undertakes a synthesis between the semantics of
identifying reference and the theory of speech acts. In identifying reference
the third person is person by a transfer from the first to the third person, which
is to say that when I speak of a third person as another self, I affirm that she,
like me, affirms responsibility for her own speech acts. On one path, then, I
transfer self-designation from myself to the third person; on the opposite path
I am anchored in discourse myself only because I am in turn a person for
others. How does this happen? The social institution of naming inscribes the
I within a social map of persons in the world. Yet an aporia remains—what
kind of being is both a basic particular and a reflecting subject? This question
moves the inquiry to the philosophy of action.

4.2 The Detour through a Philosophy of Action

Ricoeur now aims at a more comprehensive description of ascription, no longer considered purely with respect to sentences but in the relation of action to agent. The semantics of action pursues the what of action through the question "why?" in the sense of the *intention* that characterizes the action. There are three canonical forms of intention corresponding to the verb tenses of past, present, and future. The first two, past and present, are adverbial, namely, the intention with which something is done. When the adverbial form of intention takes first place (as it does in the analytic theory of action), it is easy to regard reasons as falling within a Humean causal framework.[3] This is not wrong, but if it is taken reductionistically the agent can disappear again into an ontology of events. Ricoeur argues that what is called for, rather, is a framework of teleological (not Humean) causality that can situate the analysis of action within a phenomenological interpretation of the lifeworld (Ricoeur, *Oneself as Another* 78–79). Here the future tense of "to intend" comes to the fore, and the phenomenon of intentionality becomes the capacity to project oneself across one's own projects through time. Ricoeur dubs this alliance of analytic philosophy and phenomenology a "pragmatics of action."

Yet aporias persist and propel the next detour to narrative identity. The first aporia is the gap between ascription to self and other. To become public, mental predicates have to be suspended from particular ascriptions (they cannot be merely idiosyncratic), and that can only occur in agreements between self and other. Thus a purely descriptive discourse cannot fully account for ascription because it cannot adequately articulate the lived experience of self and other. But then might ascription just be a weak form of moral imputation? Ricoeur objects that imputation itself presupposes something that amounts to a second aporia, namely, the *power to act* attested in "the assurance that the agent has the power to do things" (Ricoeur, *Oneself as Another* 112). Any attempt to give conceptual clarity to this power runs into Kant's third antinomy: first, that agents have to be able to initiate their own actions to be held responsible and, second, that for the agent to remain free the search for causes has to remain open.[4] Such a power to act is thus a primitive datum—something attested.[5]

What is the relationship between this power to act and other forms of causality? Once an ontology of events is set aside, it becomes apparent that the responses to "who?" and "why?" match the two sides of Kant's antinomy. That is, the search for who (the agent) ends, and the search for why (motive) goes on. Kant's antinomy sends the theory of action back to interrogate the sort of agent who can stand at the intersection of two kinds of causality, teleological and systematic-Humean. If we are to articulate this agent, then the aporias of ascription have to be resolved in another discourse, specifically, narrative identity.

4.3 Narrative Identity: From Description to Prescription

Ricoeur stipulates by *ipse* (selfhood) the temporal projection of self-constancy and by *idem* (sameness) the permanence through time of a core of the self. Is there a form of permanence in time that responds to the question "who am I?" (selfhood) rather than "what am I?" (sameness)? In everyday language we have two models for permanence in time, namely, *to keep one's word* and *character* (Ricoeur, *Oneself as Another* 118). On the one hand, when someone "acts in character," selfhood and sameness reach their closest approach. There is no conflict between this "who" and its "what," that is, its previously constituted character. On the other hand, when someone "keeps her word," selfhood and sameness may reach their furthest point of separation: In promising, I pledge to keep my word in spite of the leanings of my character. The lesson of promising is that an account of selfhood should not replace an account of sameness but rather should pass through it as a detour. Selfhood and sameness are dialectically related.

Because selfhood can only appear in its dialectical relation to sameness, Ricoeur begins with a recent account of personal identity as sameness, Derek Parfit's *Reasons and Persons*.[6] Parfit takes as his point of departure Locke's limit cases concerning mental and bodily identity.[7] To put the question baldly, in a tie between mental and bodily continuity (for example, a mind or soul transplanted into another body), which wins? Locke never doubts that mental continuity wins. But for Hume, the more thoroughgoing empiricist, these puzzling cases become genuine paradoxes, and the idea of the self becomes an illusion. Still, Hume does not utterly reject the idea of selfhood but says that it rests on imagination supported by a set of (reasonable) beliefs. Parfit, following Nietzsche, concludes that selfhood should no longer be supported by such beliefs. Ricoeur replies that the beliefs on which the self is founded actually belong to the order of attestation—that we have such beliefs attests to the being of the self (Ricoeur, *Oneself as Another* 128).

The three ordinary beliefs under consideration are first that the self has a core of permanence; second, that a determined response can always be given to puzzling cases threatening this core; and third, that this core must exist for the sake of moral responsibility. To these ordinary beliefs Parfit opposes his "reductionist thesis," namely, that a "person's existence just consists in the existence of a brain and body, and the occurrence of interrelated physical and mental events (Ricoeur, *Onself as Another* 131)."[8] To superimpose a core of identity onto this scheme is to appeal to "a separate further fact."

Ricoeur answers that what Parfit first discounts is not the self per se but the phenomenon that actions, mental states or the body are for each person "mine." Parfit thus jettisons the ordinary belief in a core identity only at the expense of being able to adequately account for certain phenomena. He jettisons the second belief by substituting for a question about selfhood ("Am I going to survive?") a nonequivalent question about sameness ("Will there be a person who will be the same person as I?") (Ricoeur, *Oneself as Another* 135). Finally, Parfit argues that if "who?" is undecidable in these puzzling cases, then the question is empty; moreover, what matters for ethics is not "the self" but shared experience as such. Ricoeur counters, "How can we ask ourselves about *what* matters if we could not ask *to whom* the thing mattered or not" (Ricoeur, *Oneself as Another* 137)? In other words, the question "who?"—even if it is undecidable in certain cases—is entailed in the very grammar of the ethical. So the question "who?" reasserts itself on the detour where identity is sameness (*idem*) without selfhood (*ipse*). *Narrative identity* can better articulate the self as the sort of being who appears in a dialectic of selfhood and sameness.

When we describe action, narrative emplotment configures discordant events into a "discordant concordance."[9] As plotted, contingent physical events attain, albeit in retrospect, a narrative necessity. Ricoeur applies this well-known operation of emplotting to characters: "characters, we will say, are themselves plots" (Ricoeur, *Oneself as Another* 143). The conjunction of these two uses of emplotment is "the true response to the aporias of ascription" (Ricoeur, *Oneself as Another* 146). First, narrative identity responds to the aporia of self-designation on the level of semantics, the aporia of ownership of actions on the level of pragmatics, and the aporia of how each can say "mine" of his or her own body on the level of Parfit's reductionist thesis. The one side of each aporia is joined to the other because action and plot are just two perspectives on one phenomenon, the self in its world. An emplotted character is thus the kind of being in whom the questions who? what? and why? finally meet up. Second, although the mental predicates do circulate among the first, second, and third persons, stories reestablish the attribution of predicates to particular characters. Third, because plot and character develop together, Kant's third antinomy receives a "poetic reply": The person can effect a relative beginning

in time while "the narrative as such [has] the power of determining the beginning, the middle, and the end of an action" (Ricoeur, *Oneself as Another* 147).
The dialectic of character and selfhood are inscribed in discourse in a narrative.

Narrative identity not only responds to aporias but moves the itinerary to
the final detour because it finally relates ascription to imputation and description to prescription—first by extending the field of action theory and second
by revealing another aporia that moves the itinerary to ethics (Ricoeur, *Oneself
as Another* 152). Narrative extends the field of action theory by stretching the
structure of action beyond the simple action chains studied by an analytic
theory of action. The self owns its actions under the rubric of *practices*, that is,
public constitutive rules that nest actions within a hierarchy of ends. Such
practices are interactive: A patient and an agent together constitute the action,
and, as a living tradition, the constitutive rules precede the individual agent
and patient. Practices as such need not contain narrative scenarios for narrative
identity to connect up with them. Rather, the link is that the sort of organization
characteristic of practices can be articulated in a narrative. In other words, the
organization of practices has a prenarrative quality—a quality that Ricoeur calls
elsewhere mimesis$_1$ or "narrative prefiguration."[10] Mimesis$_1$ refers to the susceptibility of the lifeworld to be articulated in narratives (mimesis$_2$) that can
then transform the world of a reader (mimesis$_3$). Mimesis$_1$ reminds us that
even though the lifeworld can only come into discourse in narratives, the lifeworld as such is not a narrative.

The narrated self embeds itself in practices by projecting permanent or
provisional *life plans* (to be a student, a doctor, a husband, etc.). In projecting
life plans the self situates itself within fragmentary practices that have their
own unity, all within a more or less dimly sighted unity of a life. Finally, the
unity of a life is itself articulated in a narrative, the well-known "narrative unity
of a life" proposed by Alasdair MacIntyre.[11]

Yet the question of which story I ought to tell about my life leads out of
narrative theory toward ethics. For Ricoeur, this "ought" is most evident in the
act of promising. Promising reinscribes, through the metaphor of an account,
a commitment on the level of mimesis$_1$ between an agent and a patient: I am
accountable to you who can count on me. Promises thus articulate traces of
the interactions between self and other on the level of mimesis$_1$—traces that
prevent the narrative unity of a life from devolving into an arbitrary "Who shall
I be today?" These traces mark commitments that transgress the bounds of
narrative theory toward ethics.

4.4 The Detour through Ethics

Two inquiries led the itinerary so far—who speaks? and who acts? Both led to aporias indicating that the self stands at a crossroads: The person is at once object of discourse and self-designator; the agent is at once systemic cause and teleological cause. Narrative identity finally gives an adequate account of the kind of being who stands at the crossroads. Yet reflection does not stop here, as if the self were simply reduced to its narrative, because the question "who tells her story?" cannot stand apart from the question "who is responsible?"

Ricoeur stipulates (not for etymological reasons, but as a convention) the term *ethics* for the teleological perspective (commonly associated with Aristotle) and *morality* for the deontological perspective (commonly associated with Kant). Though necessarily fragmented, his reflection on the self in ethics and morality attains a certain unity in a tripartite thesis: First, ethics has primacy over morality; second, in spite of this primacy, the ethical aim has to be subjected to the test of the moral norm; third, when the moral norm leads to conflicts, as it inevitably does, these conflicts can be resolved only by returning to the ethical aim—to aim at "the 'good life' with and for others, in just institutions" (Ricoeur, *Oneself as Another* 172).

4.4.1 First Thesis: The Primacy of Ethics over Morality

Reflection on the self in ethics moves from actions called good back to the self who esteems itself as responsible for these actions. *Self-esteem* accompanies the reflexive self-regard toward actions called *good*; *self-respect* accompanies the reflexive self-regard toward actions called *duty* (Ricoeur, *Oneself as Another* 171). In the detour through teleological ethics Ricoeur takes each component of the ethical aim in turn ("the good life," "with and for others," "in just institutions") to mark off a corresponding tripartite structure of esteem: self-esteem, solicitude, and equality.

To aim at the good life the self faces practices (the *is*) on the one hand and the ethical aim (the *ought*) on the other. Standards of excellence in a practice constitute the meaning of its *internal goods*, and these goods in turn aim at the telos of the practice. But how can goods in a practice, aimed at its internal telos, also aim at the *good life*? Ricoeur takes his cue from Aristotle, who recognizes that in wise deliberation (*phronēsis*) the one who deliberates (the *phronimos*) can also be at stake. If a chosen life plan stresses the voluntary side of self-formation, then the narrative unity of a life stresses the larger story not at the self's disposal. The good life stands at the apex of this hierarchy but not as something other than life stories. Rather, the content of the good life is "for each of us, the nebula of ideals and dreams of achievements with regard to which a life is held to be more or less fulfilled or unfulfilled" (Ricoeur, *Oneself as Another* 179).

In self-esteem, I esteem myself as directed toward the good life. Yet self-esteem so understood harbors a danger of solipsism. In what sense is the good life a life "with and for others?" If interpersonal relationships are not to be guided entirely by moral norms, then a prior desire to live well together has to precede morality. Here arises the second component of the ethical aim, solicitude, which is the desire to live well with and for others. The solicitude that characterizes friendship permits us to hope that a mutuality of self and other persists even at the moral limit situations where the initiative of self or other seems to be annihilated. In solicitude the self perceives itself among other selves. If from a solipsistic point of view my esteem of the other seems problematic, my esteem of myself is no less puzzling because I can only esteem myself in my relations to others. Paradox is averted if the dialectic of self and other renders equivalent "the esteem of the *other as a oneself* and the esteem of *oneself as another*" (Ricoeur, *Oneself as Another* 194). The example of friendship suggests therefore that it is at least thinkable that self-esteem does not close in on itself in solipsism but unfolds—even prior to the moral law—into a desire to live well with and for others (Ricoeur, *Oneself as Another* 180).

If self-esteem unsupported by solicitude threatens to descend into solipsism, solicitude unsupported by a desire for equality threatens to confine relationships to dyads lacking esteem for third parties. Hence the third component of the ethical aim: to live well with and for others *in just institutions*. Is there, prior to political institutions, a desire to live and act together in just institutions—a desire, that is, for equality (Ricoeur, *Oneself as Another* 194–95)?[12] Human action is social, and one can discern in actions, albeit retrospectively, a prior commitment to esteem third parties. Yet "publicness taken in this sense is, as we well know, more a task to be accomplished than something already given" (Ricoeur, *Oneself as Another* 196). For this reason "it is perhaps reasonable to give to this common initiative, this desire to live together, the status of something *forgotten*" (Ricoeur, *Oneself as Another* 197). This forgotten desire for equality is nonetheless real for all that and can be glimpsed reflexively in an analysis of the concrete structures of our life together, namely, institutions that are just.

In self-esteem, I esteem myself as directed toward the good life; in solicitude, I esteem myself as another, the other as another self; in the desire for equality, I esteem myself as one among equals, each equally worthy of esteem. If the scope of solicitude is the other I encounter face to face, then the scope of equality is all of humanity (Ricoeur, *Oneself as Another* 202). (As will become apparent shortly, I characterize the scope of equality rather as in practice a community, though its aim is all of humanity.) The desire for equality—predicated on a sense of justice prior to the recognition of authority—stands at the foundation of the self's orientation toward just institutions. Yet this sense of justice can never be glimpsed apart from life in institutions; it is always broken and remains a task rather than an accomplishment; and it is, for the most part, forgotten as the basis of authority. For all that, deontology presupposes a self oriented to justice, and it is the burden of Ricoeur's eighth study to show how deontology emerges when the ethical aim is submitted to the test of universality.

4.4.2 Second Thesis: The Ethical Aim Submitted to the Moral Norm

Ricoeur turns in the eighth study to the second part of his threefold thesis, namely, that deontological morality arises when the ethical aim is subjected to the moral norm. An imperative is dialogical ("*I* command *you*") and places a constraint on the hearer, recognized or not, that gives meaning to the judgment obeyed or disobeyed. Kant places this dialogue inside the autonomous self, recasting inclination as the power to obey or disobey imperatives (Ricoeur, *Oneself as Another* 275). In autonomy, obedience loses its relationship to another who commands, and "the good will" becomes the only good without qualification.

Yet Ricoeur observes three aporias in Kant's account of autonomy that betray its forgotten origin in teleological ethics. First, Kant's deduction of autonomy descends to an attestation, namely, the well-known fact of reason. This fact of reason is none other than "the specific form taken by the attestation of 'who?' in the moral dimension" (Ricoeur, *Oneself as Another* 212). The fact of reason attests to a commanding self who lays down the moral law and to a receptive self who is affected by its commands. This receptivity approaches the character of being affected by another in the feeling of respect for the law, which constitutes a second aporia.[13] The third aporia appears when Kant posits, at the origin of evil, a distorted yet fundamental maxim that orders inclination before law—a maxim that "*affects* the use of freedom" (Ricoeur, *Oneself as Another* 216).[14] Here autonomy is radically affected at the very level where respect beckons the subject—an "original wound" in human choice (Ricoeur, *Oneself as Another* 218). In these aporias, the autonomous self appears by turns as receptive, passive, and finally even powerless (Ricoeur, *Oneself as Another* 275).

If the first two aporias point to a forgotten telos at the origin of deontology, the third indicates the need to submit teleology to the test of universalization. Ricoeur suggests that Kantian respect for the moral law is esteem of myself as directed toward the good but having subjected that good to the rule of universalization. I thus esteem myself as one who belongs to a tradition and who operates within its canons of practical wisdom; I respect myself as one who puts the intuitions of that tradition to the test of universality in the hope of more certain shared convictions. In interpersonal relations, respect for others is not added on to self-respect from the outside but is solicitude submitted to the test of universalization.

To glimpse the moral self on the level of institutions we have to explore the connection between the deontological rule of justice and the teleological desire to live well with and for others in just institutions. Although in principle "the just" faces both the ethical aim and the moral norm, violence appears to have utterly eroded the original connection between the just and the good. Procedural justice seeks to expose this violence by a third appeal to universalization at the level of institutions—the fiction of the social contract. Unlike the moral "ought," though, the social contract is not attested as a fact of reason. But what makes this fictional contract seem plausible is its "formalization of a sense of justice that it never ceases to presuppose" (Ricoeur, *Oneself as Another* 236). In other words, the appeal to a social contract trades on a forgotten desire to live well with and for others in just institutions that it subjects to the rule of universalization. That desire is attested in our willingness to believe such a fiction.

4.4.3 Third Thesis: Morality Returns to Ethics to Resolve Conflicts in Situation

The third component of Ricoeur's thesis is that deontological morality has to return to its roots in teleological ethics to resolve certain conflicts. Only at the end of this final detour does the responsible self appear in its fullness: a self that is constituted in the horizon of an ethical aim, submits that aim to the test of the moral norm, and returns to that aim where no norm guides unambiguously. The question "who is responsible?" thus moves the itinerary beyond the false choice between a transcendental ego (the self of deontology) and a self that is a work of art (the self of teleology). Rather, the self is glimpsed as it navigates a dialectical course between these two extremes. We can best follow this course through conflicts that require the self to return to the ethical aim where no moral norm guides certainly.

Ricoeur's evocation of Hegel is unmistakable. Yet he explicitly denies any closed resolution of conflict in a moment that sublates ethics and morality.[15] For Hegel, deontological morality (*Moralität*) sets rational limits on individual action but cannot give it content. Action receives its content from a historical dialectic of natural society and *Moralität* (Ricoeur's dialectic of ethics and morality finds its inspiration here). The outcome of this dialectic is not arbitrary because it is oriented toward the rational Idea, which finally bodies forth in *Sittlichkeit* (objective moral obligation embodied in the state). Hegel allows that there are historical moments in which *Moralität* exerts a higher claim when social structures are as yet inadequate. But there is a movement in history to transcend these inadequacies toward a synthesis in which it is finally appropriate for obligations to the community to take precedence over the obligations of *Moralität*. Ricoeur (aware, as Hegel could not be, of the state-sanctioned terrors of the twentieth century) denies any such synthesis. Rather, he proposes tragedy as a model for the sort of conflict in which morality takes recourse to ethics. Tragedy instructs the state not only in its infancy but even "at the advanced stage of morality" (Ricoeur, *Oneself as Another* 294). In this final leg of his itinerary, Ricoeur reverses the order of the previous studies. He moves from institutions to individuals, starting from the native ground of *Sittlichkeit* to redescribe *Sittlichkeit* as a moment in the exercise of practical wisdom (Ricoeur, *Oneself as Another* 250).

On the level of institutions, the horizon of political discourse Ricoeur interrogates is Western democracy. Conflicts that arise in democratic institutions concern disputes about the various estimations of "good" assigned to shared goods. The challenge is to chart a middle way between the naive assurance that some norm always guides these estimations unambiguously, and the playful proliferation of discourses. Still, the democratic thinker must acknowledge a fundamental indeterminacy as to the basis of political power and interpersonal relations (Ricoeur, *Oneself as Another* 260). To resolve conflicts that concern the very basis of political power, interlocutors must have recourse to something beneath the fiction of the social contract. What is brought to mind in this search beneath the social contract is "the memory and the intersection in the public space of the appearance of the traditions that make room for tolerance and pluralism, not out of concessions to external pressures, but out of inner conviction, even if this is late in coming" (Ricoeur, *Oneself as Another* 261). What commands our attention in these diverse traditions is that we discover there a prior conviction to live well together that is also *ours*, even if those who bore these traditions were, like us, not guiltless of violence in imposing them. To the extent that true *phronēsis* operates in these traditions (i.e., insofar as they compel without violence), *Sittlichkeit* and *phronēsis* can be said to be equivalent in the social structures they generate, albeit a modest *Sittlichkeit* subject to suspicion in a way Hegel could never allow.

Descending from institutions to interpersonal relations, is there a role for *phronēsis* in articulating genuine exceptions to rules for the sake of others—maxims that although not universal, are also not arbitrary? For example, the maxim to lie to a dying person under certain circumstances may be justifiable without its attaining the status of a "duty to lie to the dying" (Ricoeur, *Oneself as Another* 269). Or again, a deft hand is required in assigning moral estimations to stages of fetal development where "the dichotomy between persons and things is akimbo" (Ricoeur, *Oneself as Another* 272). These situations at the beginning and end of life place in stark relief a challenge that faces moral respect every day, namely, to balance the universal and the particular. In these situations, respect has to return to solicitude—but not in a way that abandons what has been gained through the universal.

Finally, on the level of the self, conflict can be carried back to the very heart of autonomy, making it necessary to resituate the autonomous self in its history and community (the postmodern deconstruction of the self). The self loses its transcendental status, but do all claims to universality fall with the transcendental ego? Ricoeur proposes a three-stage reconstruction of Kantian formalism to throw into sharp relief the conflict between universality and con-textualism already hidden in Kant's autonomous self. He then uses this recon-struction to show that claims about the self can be asserted with the certainty of attestation even under contextualist pressure.

At the first stage, Ricoeur places autonomy at the end rather than at the beginning of moral discourse because the autonomous self has to be glimpsed reflexively as one who responds. At the second stage, Ricoeur criticizes Kant's exclusive use of internal contradiction to test maxims. Rather, morals can be described on analogy with a legal system where "specificatory premises" are the analogs of legal precedents (e.g., "Thou shalt not kill *except in defense of another*"). As a contingent fact, though, the public treasury of specificatory premises is characterized by both benevolence and violence. So the self has to exercise *phronēsis* to apply tragic wisdom (the recourse to the ethical aim) to unmask abuses.

At the third and final stage, Ricoeur enters into dialogue with Jürgen Ha-bermas's project to reconstruct Kantian formalism on a morality of commu-nication (Ricoeur, *Oneself as Another* 280). Habermas admits that formal ar-gumentation only gains content when we argue about actual practices, and in this admission Ricoeur sights a course between universalism and contextualism. For example, in the debate on human rights, we should continue to assert the moral norm but leave open a possible recourse beneath it to the ethical aim (Ricoeur, *Oneself as Another* 289). On one hand, all parties should continue to argue from their accepted principles; on the other hand, each should be prepared to recognize potential or inchoate universals in the discourse of the other—universals that might reawaken a more original understanding of one's own ethical aim. Such recognition can take place only if we imaginatively try on the possible truths of others, albeit not at the level of argumentation.

From this point of view argumentation is not simply "the antagonist of tradition and convention, but . . . the critical agency operating at the heart of convictions . . . carrying them to the level of 'considered convictions' " (Ricoeur, *Oneself as Another* 288). A conviction "expresses the positions from which re-sult the meanings, interpretations, and evaluations relating to the multiple goods that occupy the scale of praxis" from practices, to life plans, to the unity of a life, to the good life (Ricoeur, *Oneself as Another* 288). Considered convic-tions shape our common life in a way that can be justly styled a more modest *Sittlichkeit* "stripped of its pretension to mark the victory of Spirit over the contradictions that it itself provokes" (Ricoeur, *Oneself as Another* 290). Our argued positions attain solidity only in considered convictions that are disclosed in open conversations with others who are different from us. By reflecting on what goes on in such conversations, we can hope to catch a glimpse of the self who responds to the question "who is responsible?"

"Who is responsible?" means "who is responsible at the end of each of the detours?"[16] The detour through linguistics and pragmatics culminates in a self whose actions can be imputed under the ethical and moral predicates *good* and *obligatory*. *Imputability* thus articulates a self who seeks to own her actions under ethical and moral predicates in accord with the wise in the tradition. The detour through narrative identity culminates in a self who, with respect to the future, can admit responsibility for consequences where there was no orig-inal intention to harm. With respect to the past the self can accept responsibility for a tradition, in all its ambivalence, as "mine." With respect to the present the self agrees to be held accountable as the same one yesterday, today and tomorrow. *Responsibility* thus articulates a self who owns her past and future actions in the present, even where she may not have originally intended. The detour through ethics and morality culminates in a self who recognizes itself as another (and the other as another self) throughout the crisscross of auton-omy, interpersonal relations, and plurality. *Recognition* thus articulates a self who esteems herself and others as transcending and yet inseparable from the interpersonal and plural relations in which each always already finds herself.

4.5 A Critical Reflection on the Self and Community as Correlates

As a general observation, I want to affirm that there is no inherent problem in Ricoeur's bracketing community at any of the levels below the dialectic of self and other. Now, however, I reflect back from the end of his itinerary on the role of community throughout. Community is most evident at the level of narrative and ethics, so studies five through nine are the main focus of this critical section. In seeking a path between the transcendental ego and its de-struction, Ricoeur emphasizes the encounter of self and other rather than the location of the self in community. He fully acknowledges, though, that the encounter of self and other requires, first, the presence of third persons and, second, institutions in which "the human" is constituted (Ricoeur, *Oneself as Another* 254). By "institution," Ricoeur says, "we are to understand here the structure of *living together* as this belongs to a historical community" (Ricoeur, *Oneself as Another* 194). Yet because Ricoeur does not take a further detour to the self through community, he does not note that the self and its community may be at stake together in conflictual situations. In such conflicts the self and community stand out most clearly as correlates, which is to say that each is mutually the condition of the other.

4.5.1 Community from the Perspective of Language and Pragmatics

For action predicates to become public, it must be possible to suspend the relationship between an action and its agent. This back-and-forth of suspension and appropriation presupposes a space where self and other meet; such a space appears, however, only where self and other meet. In the earlier studies Ricoeur speaks of this space in terms of third parties and not yet community. But from the perspective of the later studies, we can reflect back on the role of com-munity in the earlier studies. At the level of linguistics the treasury of predi-cates (I hurt, you hurt, he or she hurts) circulates in a community, and social institutions like naming are ordered within a community; at the level of prag-matics, the community opens the space where self and other meet as each suspends and appropriates predicates.

The self participates in the life of a community whenever it speaks or acts. Any mundane, unreflective involvement at the level of the lifeworld (I eat with a fork) can in principle be challenged (why do you insist on eating with a fork in a Chinese restaurant?). In facing such a challenge, the self, in responding, narrates the action. Narrated in retrospect, utterances and other actions are disclosed as having committed the self anew to a community and as having expressed the prior commitments of a self always already engaged in a community.[17] On one hand, that the self expresses prior commitments means that when the self employs public resources in speaking and acting, those resources can in principle be traced back to a particular community. (Such a search is a public affair, and conclusions about which community the speaker is committed to remain subject to conversation.) From this perspective the self and other meet in the space opened by the community. On the other hand, that the self commits anew to the community means that when the self uses public resources, it may initiate new involvements in the community. Narrated in retrospect, after some sort of challenge, some involvements may constitute implicit claims that could in turn be cited by others. From this perspective the community lives in the self and other. Thus self, other, and community are correlates in the sense that each is mutually a condition of the others, and none is properly the a priori of the others. The question of the kind of being who depends on a community's resources yet in whose acts the community appears leads to the theory of narrative identity.

4.5.2 Narrative Identity and the Community's Narrative

Narrative identity articulates what cannot be said in a purely descriptive discourse, namely, the dialectical relationship between *ipse* and *idem*, selfhood and sameness. To guard against reducing the self to its narrative, though, the question "why should I tell *this* story and not some other story about my life?" propels the itinerary into ethics. In promising I commit to a relationship that transcends the vagaries of my character. Such commitments become points of articulation for narrative identity. (Why *this* narrative? Because it better articulates the commitments posited in my promises.)

Ricoeur uses the problem of how a life story is anchored to send his itinerary into ethics, but I want to stress that promising is not the only anchor for the self's story. Myriad other communal involvements anchor the self's story—involvements expressed in actions, practices, life plans, and possible life stories. Such involvements do, in retrospect, attest to selfhood, though perhaps not in such a contrastive way as promising. So although these mundane involvements do not provide as much payoff in terms of an ontology of the self, they are crucial in two ways to my inquiry into the self as the correlate of a community.

First, the community supplies resources for telling stories that constitute the self as a meaning. Whatever one might claim about the universality of given literary images, themes, stock characters, or genres, it is clear that these narrative elements circulate in actual stories that belong to the life of particular communities. Second, the self owns its actions only within publicly shared practices with constitutive rules, and these rules are given only through the mediation of a tradition carried by other people. Here Ricoeur speaks of others and tradition without yet speaking of a community of practitioners (which first appears in his seventh study) (Ricoeur, *Oneself as Another* 176). Yet from that later perspective, it is clear that the self acts in concert with others by internalizing practices that circulate in the life of a community. Provisional life plans (to be a student, a politician, a doctor, etc.) also circulate within a community (for example, I cannot take Samurai warrior as a provisional life plan in my time and place). And actual communities have paradigmatic understandings of what it means to be an author (or coauthor) of a narrative, of what constitutes a valid beginning or end of a narrative, and how narratives can be joined together (because we are always already "entangled in stories").[18] In short, all the elements of a narrated unity of a life—though unique in their combination and application—circulate within a community.

Thus in actions as diverse as attending a university, watching television, using the Internet, taking prescription drugs, or undergoing a medical procedure, people express prior involvements and involve themselves anew in the life of a community. Moreover, these actions are intertwined in public ways that make it difficult for agents to pick and choose among aspects of the community they may wish (or not) to acknowledge as "mine." A narrative that articulates more of these involvements is better attested than one that articulates less. Involvements in a community therefore are intimately tied to the response to the question "why should I tell *this* story and not some other story about my life?"

This reflection on community brings into focus two related problems that Ricoeur does not consider in *Oneself as Another*. First, in the phenomenon of conversion—a limit case of narrative identity—the reservoir of practices, life plans, and life stories in the community might be at stake alongside an individual's life story. Second, the story that identifies the community might be at stake in some of the most fundamental conflicts in the dialectic of ethics and morality.

4.5.3 Community in the Dialectic of Ethics and Morality

In the dialectic of ethics and morality, the self is glimpsed reflexively as the correlate of a community when conflicts put the self and community at stake together. In such conflicts, the need to identify the community in a narrative attains the status of something attested, and constitutes a first aporia in Ricoeur's account. A second aporia appears when imputation, responsibility, and recognition are affirmed of the self who is the correlate of a community. This aporia is overcome by letting the community appear as person through the metaphor of the spirit in the community.

4.5.3.1 COMMUNITY AND THE ETHICAL AIM. Ricoeur observes that "with respect to its content, the 'good life' is, for each of us, the nebula of ideals and dreams of achievements with regard to which a life is held to be more or less fulfilled or unfulfilled" (Ricoeur, *Oneself as Another* 179). Is this "for each of us" simply an individual matter? I do not claim that Ricoeur would contend that. Indeed, much of his ninth study centers on the shared hopes of people in democratic societies. It is not that Ricoeur fails to understand the good life in terms of community but that he never takes as an explicit theme the stories that identify communities.

The story of a community would exhibit some features of what Jean-François Lyotard calls a metanarrative.[19] Lyotard prefers, rather than a metanarrative that orders other language games, a local consensus where the temporary contract supplants permanent institutions. Ricoeur's engagement with Habermas and the contextualists is a modest recovery of the solidity of institutions without appeal to metanarratives. Ricoeur thus follows Lyotard in rejecting metanarratives. But should that put out of consideration, from a philosophical perspective, all stories that identify communities? Here a first aporia appears in Ricoeur's account: The phenomenon that cannot be articulated when the community's story is not taken into account is the real cost borne by the community when its language games are reordered.[20] To be sure, Lyotard's new idiom or Ricoeur's emplotment can each articulate a formerly inarticulable suffering.[21] But at what cost to a community? I see no better means to express this cost than by referring it to the identity of the community, an identity that (as in the case of individuals) is best expressed in a narrative.

Stories of communities are of course subject to the same dialectic of attestation and suspicion as stories of selves—suspicion, for example, that the community's story may hide the suffering of another. Yet the probity of such a claim depends on identifying an actual other who suffers or who might suffer. There is no need, then, to accept at face value the skeptical claim that any story that identifies the community might in principle conceal the suffering of others. An appeal to such stories can thus satisfy the substance of Lyotard's objection to metanarratives without succumbing to the outright rejection of all nonlocal narratives.

What sort of conflicts put the community's story at stake? In the particular community presupposed in Ricoeur's itinerary, the paradigmatic conflict would involve the community's aim to let equality extend to all of humanity (Ricoeur, *Oneself as Another* 202). To reach this conflict it is necessary to follow the path by which this desire for equality reaches all of humanity. But I first have to address a preliminary question—where is the desire for equality located? Does it belong to the human organism? Does it belong to conditions of discourse in general? Does it belong to those communal institutions that are conditions under which, as Ricoeur says, the self becomes human (Ricoeur, *Oneself as Another* 254)?[22] Ricoeur simply shows that deontology presupposes such a desire; he never tries to establish its locus.

I want to be clear as to what Ricoeur does and does not say about the desire for equality as a condition of experience. He does not intend the strong claim that it is a transcendental condition of all experience; rather, he claims that this desire is everywhere presupposed in analyses of our own horizon and should not be abandoned in dialogue with others. The desire for equality operates between a self and another, but Ricoeur rejects the opposing tendencies to regard either the self as a condition of the other or the other as a condition of the self. Rather, self and other are correlates, that is, each is mutually a condition of the other. I extend Ricoeur's reflections to say that self, other, and *community* are all constituted reciprocally: Each is mutually the condition of the others. Whatever we might say about the locus of the desire for equality, then, the object of reflection (i.e., the self) where that desire appears is always already involved in a community. Consequently there is no contradiction in saying that the locus of the desire for equality is both the self and its community. But could the self be held responsible if its very desire toward others is constituted at least in part by its community? Ricoeur argues, and I concur, that each self is responsible precisely in taking on the heritage of its own community as "mine" (Ricoeur, *Oneself as Another* 295). There is only a conflict between responsibility and communal involvement if responsibility is tied to a solipsistic understanding of autonomy that is neither tenable nor necessary.

What happens, then, when the community's ethical aim toward equality is misdirected, and as the outcome of some challenge (paradigmatically, in response to the inarticulable suffering of another), a member of the community addresses that misdirection? If the one who responds does not intend to abandon the community, then she has to reinterpret the community's aim more originally than those in whom it is misdirected. If her reinterpretation succeeds, then the self and the silently suffering other can appear in one community, but as a consequence the self, other, and community may all have to be reinterpreted.

Given these considerations, I can affirm with Ricoeur that the scope of equality is all of humanity (Ricoeur, *Oneself as Another* 202). But what has been said here? One must never lose sight of the horizon of Ricoeur's questioning. He claims that the horizon in which we live and act has as its condition the desire for equality of all humanity. The self is the locus of this desire insofar as institutions are only instantiated where self and other meet; yet it is also true that the self and other only ever meet in community. In this particular community, the self is ordered by a desire for equality toward all of humanity. In short, a desire that all of humanity should be equal while the alterity of each is respected appears as the aim of an actual community. What is ultimately at stake, then, in a conflict where a suffering other cannot come into conversation is the story that identifies this community, not just the stories of the individuals affected.

4.5.3.2 COMMUNITY AND THE MORAL NORM. My remarks about community in Ricoeur's eighth study ("The Self and the Moral Norm") can be relatively brief because the priority of teleological ethics over deontological morality is prefigured in the seventh study and recapitulated in the ninth. What the eighth study adds to this account is the necessity to submit the ethical aim to the moral norm. I briefly explore the implications of this necessity for community.

The ethical aim is the original soil of morality, but the need for morality arises because the self is always already wounded at the fundamental level where it is affected by respect for the law (Kant's radical evil). When the autonomous self is resituated in community, then that original wound also places a question mark over the community. If the community and self are correlates, then orientation to the good is simultaneously at stake for both the community and the self. Morality recognizes this danger and puts even the ethical aim to the test of universalization. What is this drive toward universalization when it is expressed in terms of community? It is just what I proposed in accounting for the desire for equality, namely, that the other should be embraced by the community in his or her alterity, perhaps even at the cost of the identity of the community and its members.

4.5.3.3 COMMUNITY IN THE RECOURSE FROM THE MORAL NORM TO THE ETH-ICAL AIM. I turn finally to Ricoeur's ninth study, which traces the appeal from morality back to ethics, where no norm guides certainly. Ricoeur can agree with Hegel that "the individual . . . becomes human only under the condition of certain institutions" and that out of this commitment arises the duty to serve these institutions (Ricoeur, *Oneself as Another* 254). After all, the community provides the social structures in which the self and other meet. Ricoeur objects, though, when Hegel contends that the obligation to serve the community is different from and higher than morality and ethics. Hegel's account is insufficiently attentive to those times when the spirit of a people has been misdirected into a deadly *Sittlichkeit*. In such times "the spirit takes refuge" in "the moral consciousness of a small number of individuals" or in the "beautiful soul" (Ricoeur, *Oneself as Another* 256). Ricoeur does not reject the idea that a spirit animates a people; instead he rejects the concretization of spirit in a set of institutions cut loose from the intentions of actual citizens. Spirit has to transcend the community, yet for transcendence to be actual one has to be able to point and say "in *this* beautiful soul (or in *this* moral enclave) lives the authentic spirit of this people."

Spirit, as Ricoeur appropriates it from Hegel, is not an ontological term but a metaphor for the collective life of a community in its ethical aim. To say that "spirit lives *here*" is to reinterpret the ethical aim of the community from out of the past, take responsibility for that aim in the present, and assert that one's actions embody the way spirit should journey into the future. As traversing the life of a community in its ethical aim, spirit stands to community as selfhood stands to person. As I understand the argument, then, Ricoeur does not specifically reject positing spirit as person, but (acknowledging the lessons of twentieth-century political terror) he stipulates that spirit should never be posited as a person that is self-sufficient and cut loose from actual individuals. In the conversation about what institutions are just, the claim "spirit lives *here*" puts the identity of self and community at stake together. Thus at the level of institutions, the self and community are correlates.

Moving from the level of institutions to the level of interpersonal relationships, Ricoeur aims his reflexive glance at the self in its search for exceptions to moral rules on behalf of others. I extend that glance to encompass the self and community as correlates. The community has a store of specificatory premises that can serve as precedents in applying moral rules to particular cases (e.g., "Thou shalt not kill except in defense of another"). But sorting through the benevolence and violence that characterize this store requires wisdom. The wise self is not radically individual because to apply specificatory premises wisely involves a prior estimation of who are the wise in the tradition (Ricoeur, *Oneself as Another* 273). Moreover, such an application is not arbitrary because *phronēsis* balances three related sources, namely, the moral norm, the self's feeling for the other as another self (solicitude), and the accumulated wisdom of a tradition. Here the community opens the space in which the self and other meet in their alterity.

Yet the reciprocal condition should also be asserted, that is, that the community appears in such decisions. This reciprocal condition is evident when we ask what constitutes such decisions as intelligible and the right action in the given circumstances. If I say that an action was intelligible and right, I claim retrospectively that others could in principle repeat my *phronēsis* to find it intelligible and right. But bear in mind that *phronēsis* has two sources besides the moral law. So even if my action is intelligible and right, others might not recognize it as such: They may not have had the sort of encounters that affected my solicitude, or they may not share my estimation of who are the wise. In defending my action I assert that encountering others in this way is right and that it is consistent with the best wisdom in the tradition. In so doing, I make explicit a claim that was already implicit in my action, namely, that the community is manifest more originally in performing the action than in opposing it.

Here the community emerges in the resolution of conflicts: Sedimented traditions are redeployed as considered convictions that can be cited by others. As on the level of the search for just institutions, so on the level of interpersonal relationships the community and self appear as correlates. Success in establishing genuine exceptions for others attests to a community that can encompass others in their alterity without violence. The identity of the community may be at stake in the claim that such actions are intelligible and right, but insofar as I assert that the action is a genuine exception, the adjustment within the community is potentially less devastating than in the last sort of conflict Ricoeur examines, specifically, conflicts at the very heart of autonomy. Finally, then, I turn to the aspects of community and self disclosed in Ricoeur's dialogical understanding of autonomy. I first explore the role of community in Ricoeur's dialectical mediation between universalism and contextualism; I then reconfigure Ricoeur's notions of imputability, responsibility, and recognition to encompass the self and community as correlates.

In encounters with others the self may come to recognize that "other potential universals are contained in so-called exotic cultures" (Ricoeur, *Oneself as Another* 289). What does this mean? Note that although the assertion has in view something new from other communities, the overall drift of the argument is to clarify the sort of truth (attestation) that belongs to universals already held by the community. Each interlocutor thus approaches the other by drawing on what is already attested in her own community yet remains open to potential universals that emerge in the encounter.

There is, of course, no general answer to the question "is such a convergence always possible?" At the same time, there is no a priori reason to cede the outcome to incommensurability. Is such a convergence, to use Gadamer's phrase, always a fusion of horizons?[23] There are two other possible ways for the community to narrate its identity at the outcome of such a conflict. On the one hand, one or the other horizon may "win" the exchange in such a way that the other community is swallowed up as other. The winning community would then tell the story of the other as a community that either lacked original independence or has now ceased to exist. On the other hand, both interlocutors may discover that in some sense they have always already shared one community. This shared community may only become articulable, however, once debate about the present conflict is allowed to reorder their respective understandings of their traditions. Here both communities persist in their distinction from one another *in one community* while each in its own way tells the story of this encompassing community as the telos of its own story. Only an ongoing conversation can decide which sort of story should be told at the end of any particular conflict: There is no a priori reason to eliminate any one of these potential stories.

But at what cost to the community is its story retold? Clearly there is no general answer to the question. Where the issue at stake is the silent suffering of others, some beautiful soul or moral enclave must have new encounters and search the tradition anew. At the end of this search, these individuals may challenge the community to recognize others in a way that has not formerly been understood as intelligible or right. A similar challenge faces the community in assessing an exception to a moral norm. But this new challenge is more profound: Now the community is asked to embrace others in their differences where such differences have formerly been understood to exclude. If this extraordinary claim is intelligible and right (within a better telling of the community's story), then individuals may turn out to be culpable in retrospect for harm where no intention to harm could formerly have been articulated. The claimant says, "We are such a community as should have always embraced these others, once excluded, in their difference from us." The speaker asserts that the community now appears more originally in her embrace of the suffering other than in those who reject that embrace; yet in drawing on the tradition she stands in the space opened by her community.[24] Here the self and community appear as correlates, even at the furthest distance between self and the community. I can agree with Ricoeur that where there are "concealed forms of suffering . . . the incapacity to tell a story . . . can always be made meaningful through the strategy of emplotment" (Ricoeur, *Oneself as Another* 320). Yet the potential for devastation that can follow the resolution of this sort of conflict attests in the strongest way to the need to tell the community's story. A reconfigured personal narrative is not enough to make such a speaker or group of speakers intelligible to others. Rather, it is only in a reconfigured story of her community that the speaker can hope to make herself intelligible again.

So at each stage of Ricoeur's itinerary, the self and its community are revealed as correlates—in the conversation about just institutions, interpersonal relations, and a chastened autonomy sighted in the conflict between universalism and contextualism. In concluding this detour to the self in community I extend Ricoeur's notions of imputability, responsibility, and recognition to encompass the self and community as correlates.

In imputation the self owns the actions it intends in accord with the wise in its tradition; in responsibility the self owns the past and future of the traditions that constitute it in the present; in recognition the self recognizes self and other as constituted with and for each other and yet genuinely different (Ricoeur, *Oneself as Another* 291–96). When imputation, responsibility, and recognition are predicated jointly of the self and community as correlates, a second aporia appears in Ricoeur's account: One has to speak, at least in an analogical sense, of the community as person. The notion of spirit will serve this function, subject to the qualification that any claim about spirit should also gesture to some actual individual or individuals in whom spirit is manifest.

First, I esteem myself as capable of letting my community and its identity be at stake both in my actions and in my bids to enclose those actions in practices, life plans, and the narrative unity of a life. I accept that one and the same action can be jointly imputed to the self and community where profound collective misdirection appears retrospectively as an intention to harm. *Imputability* thus articulates a self who, in seeking to own her actions in accord with her intentions, also owns these actions on behalf of a community when there has been profound collective misdirection.

Second, in solicitude I understand that where genuine exceptions on behalf of others are justified, to seek out the appropriate specificatory premises to embrace those others in their genuine difference is a mark of the ethical aim of my community. This search is not individualistic but aligns the self with the wisest in the community. I accept as mine the community that is my correlate, bearing responsibility for its wise direction in the present and future. In the struggle to distinguish what constitutes genuine alterity and what should be excluded, I accept that at the furthest point of disagreement with the community as collective I remain rooted in the community and accept responsibility for telling its story. *Responsibility* thus articulates a self who owns the consequences of her actions—even, perhaps, where there was no original intent to harm—and in so doing seeks to live out the community's ethical aim in accord with the wise in the community.

Finally, in being led by the desire for equality I recognize others as selves who in their genuine difference from me belong to my community in its original aim. At the same time I recognize that the other, like me, is the correlate of a community and bears responsibility for telling the story of his or her own community. *Recognition* thus articulates a self who, in embracing the other in one community, honors the responsibility of the other to tell her own community's story.

Does this account reduce the self to its community, as Bultmann worried? No, because although self and other appear in the space opened by a community, the community itself only appears where self and other meet in their genuine difference. We are thus permitted to ask, on this last detour to the self, "*who* is authorized to speak more originally on behalf of the community?" or "*who* embodies the spirit in the community?" What is attested in this itinerary of detours is neither the self, nor the other, nor a community alone but a living confluence of all of these correlated dimensions of the lifeworld. This confluence has to be told in a story. The appropriate vehicle for the telling is not a metanarrative but a story that identifies the community and is at stake in a conversation in the community.

No doubt, the self that Ricoeur uncovers is referenced to the horizon of Western democracies. This reference merits at least a weak accusation that it is relative to that particular horizon; but for all that, the self can only ever be glimpsed in some horizon. I am permitted to point to this itinerary of detours and say, "*There* is the structure of the self glimpsed as the correlate of *this* community." The response "I belong to some other community with a different story and a different understanding of the self" is equally subject to attestation and suspicion. Do radically incommensurable understandings of self and community exist? Perhaps. Yet the possibility has no a priori force to end the conversation. Perhaps, instead, the parties may discover that one story better narrates a community that embraces them both in their differences; yet how each party would encompass his or her own community's ethical aim in that one story has to be decided in conversation. The self is not a foundation, and the gesture to the self does not settle all arguments about truth. The self is only ever glimpsed in reflection on the actual discourse of some existing community; the structure of the self and the shape of its community are at stake together.

Somewhat paradoxically, in recognition both the self and other may be called on to recognize their own respective communities as embracing the other in one community. It is possible, though by no means guaranteed, that each interlocutor may be able to assert "mine" of the spirit in his or her own community in such a way that both self and other appear together in one community. If that is the outcome, then both sides affirm that in their actual differences one spirit animates the two communities. Is this an attempt to get something for nothing? There can be no general method to account for what is gained or lost in such transitions. If the transition is nontrivial, then clearly

THE DEFERRED SELF 99

one or the other community—or perhaps even both communities—surrenders some aspect of its own self-identity insofar as that identity was formerly established on the basis of exclusions now surrendered. Only a continuing conversation will determine which of the three sorts of story each community will tell: a fusion of horizons, an assimilation, or a more original understanding of the community's ethical aim.

I am now prepared to discuss Ricoeur's ontological sketch of the self, retrospectively applying the insights gleaned in this detour to the self in community. On the basis of this ontology I can finally appropriate Paul's "I have been crucified with Christ" and "Christ lives in me" in our context.

5

Narrative Expresses Being: An Ontology of the Self in Community

5.1 Toward an Ontology of the Self

The first nine studies of *Oneself as Another* are a hermeneutics of the self pursued through aporias in various ways of describing the self in its world. The question that occupies the tenth study is whether there can be an ontology of the self. Narrative articulates the self, yet the self is not its narrative. Is there a discourse that is not just another narrative but that can articulate the being of the self? Paul Ricoeur proposes to reawaken the possibilities of Aristotle's meanings of being.[1] In the first meaning (being as truth), attestation achieves ontological status as testimony to a self who resists being reduced to any one dimension (e.g., language, speech acts, praxis, story, community, or law). Yet that the self is attested need not mean that there is one entity, "the self," who inhabits all of these dimensions. So a second reappropriation of Aristotle's meanings of being (*dunamis-energeia*) aims at a more modest ontology of the self as a unity: not self as substance but an analogical unity of selfhood on a ground of potential and act. A third dimension of the ontology of the self is a double ontology of the Same and the Other: The dialectic of *ipse* and *idem*, expressed ontologically, enters a dialectic with otherness expressed ontologically.

After certain extraordinary encounters (like Paul's encounter with the crucified and resurrected Christ), the community's story has to be retold to let the suffering other come into phrases. How does an ontology of the self fare in such encounters? The answer to that question is essential to assessing how we should appropriate Paul's "I have been crucified with Christ" and "Christ lives in me" in our context. To anticipate a conclusion not yet won, an ontology of the self is the correlate of a conversation in a community. The real that resists being interpreted otherwise can only be articulated properly when one considers simultaneously the self, the other, and the community in which they meet—a community that correlatively only appears where self and other meet. Such an ontology could be superseded, but only at the expense of a profound challenge to the community's self-understanding.

5.2 The Detour by Way of Analysis: Being as Attestation

After the detours through analysis, the self ceases to be the vacuous ego-pole of the phenomenalist tradition and gains credence as a response to the question "who?" posed to analysis. Yet these detours are as diverse as the objects of the question (Who speaks? Who acts? Who tells his or her story? Who is responsible?). Why even try to unify these accounts under the rubric of selfhood? Even if such a rubric were justified, would the unification refer to anything but the accidental agreement of modes of reflection? Are we justified in speaking, then, of a self that exists as a unity beneath these diverse reflections?

Recall that attestation is the assurance that aporias along the itinerary testify to the self. What is the self's ontological bearing? Ricoeur expands Aristotle's being-true and being-false (in linguistic reference) to encompass attestation and suspicion (in a hermeneutics that interprets the background of reference). For Aristotle the relation of being-true to being-false is disjunctive, but the relation of attestation to suspicion is dialectical. Because a hermeneutical phenomenology articulates the background against which statements are intelligible as true or false, one could never claim that a hermeneutics of the self as a whole is true in the referential sense, or the whole project would descend into a vicious circularity. Nevertheless, we should not say that what is attested is deficient in truth just because attestation is dialectically related to suspicion. Rather, any contrary assertion would be of the same order, that is, attested as being true. Attestation is not inferior to referential truth but belongs to a different order. The comparison between the two orders brings to mind what is similar (referential truth and attestation both supply warrants) and what is different (attestation and suspicion are not related in the same way as referential truth and falsity). Attestation warrants that an existing self resists being reduced to language, discourse, or community.

5.3 The Dialectic of Selfhood and Sameness: Being as Potentiality and Actuality

The self exists, or so the aporias attest. But should we posit one self that underlies the diverse responses to the question "who?" The next challenge is to articulate the self under some ontological heading of the Same where this Same is stretched between *ipse* and *idem*—selfhood and sameness. Narrative identity articulates the dialectic of selfhood and sameness for hermeneutics, but can this dialectic be expressed in an ontology? Ricoeur attempts to reinscribe the dialectic of *ipse* and *idem* within Aristotle's *dunamis-energeia* pair (potentiality and actuality).[2] Two aspects of Aristotle's account are especially appealing. First, although human action is central to *dunamis-energeia*, the pair is not limited to human action and so does not simply repeat the analysis of action in an ontological key. Second, all of Aristotle's examples are designed to decenter reflection toward a "ground of being, at once potentiality and actuality," a ground in which *dunamis* and *energeia* are related dialectically (Ricoeur, *Oneself as Another* 308). Aristotle's meaning of being as *dunamis-energeia* thus maps nicely onto the limitation that *ipse* (selfhood) only ever appears in a dialectic of *ipse* and *idem* (sameness). This correspondence might justify the move from an analogical unity of the meanings of action (speech acts, praxis, narration, and acting responsibly with and for others) to an ontology of potentiality and actuality reconstructed on Aristotle's *dunamis-energeia*.

Ricoeur offers Spinoza's *conatus* to connect his hermeneutics of the self with a ground of potentiality and actuality against which selfhood stands out (Ricoeur, *Oneself as Another* 315). *Conatus* designates the striving of each entity to persevere in its own being.[3] Though *conatus* is discerned first and foremost in human beings, it pertains to all entities—human and nonhuman—because all things strive to persevere in being. Thus the first characteristic to recommend *conatus* as a reappropriation of *dunamis-energeia* is that it exhibits the same fruitful dispersion as Aristotle's *energeia* across human and nonhuman motions. The second characteristic to recommend *conatus* is that although *conatus* is a kind of potentiality, this potentiality is only ever disclosed in actual being. It is in reflecting on actions of real beings that we glimpse in retrospect a striving to persevere in being (a *conatus*) as the ground of selfhood. Potential and actual are thus related dialectically in *conatus*, which is necessary if it is to express the dialectic of *ipse* and *idem* in an ontology. Ricoeur never completed his appropriation of Aristotle by way of Spinoza.[4] Nevertheless, *conatus* exemplifies what Ricoeur means by a ground at once potential and actual. *Conatus* articulates a self that is narrated yet not reduced to its narrative.

5.4 The Dialectic of Selfhood and Otherness: Being as a Dialectic of the Same and the Other

Self is constituted in its *sense* (that is, in its *meaning* or *intention*) only with others. Yet on reflection, the self is disclosed against a background that a speculative, ontological discourse is permitted to articulate as a ground at once potential and actual, paradigmatically, Spinoza's *conatus*. When self is constituted *as meant*, others contribute; yet in retrospect, in virtue of this meaning, we glimpse a self who responds. In the earlier studies, every advance in interpreting the self had to be met by a corresponding advance in interpreting others. Ricoeur now proposes a second-order ontological discourse to articulate the dialectic of self and other in our first-order discourses. The objective is to let whole ontologies face one another dialectically—an ontology of the Same (itself tied to a dialectic of *ipse* and *idem*) faces an ontology of the Other (yet to be determined).

Here phenomenology, an interpretation of the lifeworld, is taken up into an ontological, speculative discourse. This speculative discourse employs the self's experiences of passivity (a theme of phenomenology) as attestations of otherness (a theme of ontology). Three headings cover these experiences of passivity: the experience of one's own *flesh* as another mediating between self and world; *intersubjectivity* or the experience of other people; and *conscience* as "the relation of the self to itself" (Ricoeur, *Oneself as Another* 318). Each of these experiences (on the phenomenological level) becomes a locus for a new investigation (on the speculative level) into the dialectic of Same and Other.

5.4.1 The Passivity of the Self with Respect to the Body: Selfhood in a Dialectic with the Flesh as Other

In the first nine studies, the body is where various analytic discourses meet up with phenomenology. In sentences persons are bodies (linguistics) and yet the body is in each case "mine"; the body is central to actions as events in the world (pragmatics) and yet actions are authored or owned by an agent; the body is where mental and corporeal criteria of identity meet (philosophies of personal identity) and yet it is the irreplaceable anchor of self-constancy. For all that, Ricoeur suggests that his earlier studies never sufficiently took into account the phenomenon of suffering—the limit case of how self and other intertwine in the meaning of action. Suffering is concealed where the decrease of my capacity to tell my story spirals into a corresponding loss of power to exist (*conatus*). The category flesh (a translation of Husserl's *Leib*—sometimes translated as "living body") expresses ontologically the self's experience of its own body as its most intimate other. This experience is attested most profoundly in a phenomenology of suffering.[5]

The body is other to the self in the sense that the self is affected by the body in several ways: in the body's resistance to self-initiated effort; in the body's susceptibility to moods; and finally, in the body's resistance to external bodies. The body thus occupies a middle position between self-presence and the external world. Husserl's enduring insight is that my capacity to regard my body both as "mine" (*Leib* or flesh) and as a body among bodies (*Körper* or body) is integral to the constitution of the ego (Ricoeur, *Oneself as Another* 324). Moreover, we can disentangle this useful distinction from Husserl's larger (and in Ricoeur's estimation, ill-advised) project to ground the constitution of the intersubjective world in the transcendental ego. What, then, is an ontology of the flesh freed from its role in Husserl's transcendental project?

The flesh is characterized by its being for each person "mine" and in its capacity to feel (paradigmatically, the sense of touch). In reflection the mediating role of flesh comes to my attention. But I can recognize in retrospect that the otherness of the flesh is everywhere presupposed in my unreflected actions. Public ways of speaking reinscribe the otherness of the flesh in discourse, yet discourse does not create its otherness. "Flesh" thus articulates a prelinguistic otherness of the body to the self (Ricoeur, *Oneself as Another* 326). Flesh as the center of the world-as-meant replaces the nullity at the center of selfhood in Heidegger's *Being and Time* (Ricoeur, *Oneself as Another* 352). Yet flesh is not *self-presence* in a metaphysical sense because flesh is also *other* to the self. Thus even attestation of the self's relation to its own body does not escape suspicion: Though attestation as the assurance of being oneself acting and suffering is "the ultimate recourse against all suspicion," such attestation "is always in some sense received from another" (Ricoeur, *Oneself as Another* 23).

Consequently the body as flesh can be alienated, and this is the condition of the more concealed varieties of suffering. Under this heading, first is "the incapacity to tell a story, the refusal to recount, the persistence of the untellable" (Ricoeur, *Oneself as Another* 320). Responding to Jean-François Lyotard and others, Ricoeur is optimistic that such episodes can in principle "always be made meaningful through the strategy of emplotment" (Ricoeur, *Oneself as*

Another 320).[6] Yet to deprive the self of the discursive resources to articulate its own suffering imposes even greater suffering. That the flesh is ontologically prior to narrative corresponds to the intuition that suffering is real even where it cannot be articulated. The second concealed form of suffering is "the decrease of the power of *acting*, experienced as a decrease of the effort of *existing*" (Ricoeur, *Oneself as Another* 320). Here actions directed against the body (on a scale from restraint to torture to murder) are not only felt as physical pain but as the self's alienation from its own body, an ownness that is always prior to the act of violence. These concealed forms of suffering are wrong, yet the wrong may not be articulable as such where discursive resources are denied or the other is not regarded as another self. Yet the wrong can be disclosed as such once these discourses are placed against the backdrop of an ontology of the flesh.

That I exist presupposes that I relate to my body as another (flesh). I am supported in this relationship by public ways of speaking that enable me first to talk about my relation to my body in my life story and second to relate to my body without fear of alienation. Yet the otherness of the body is not an epiphenomenon of these discursive strategies; rather, in reflecting on suffering, these strategies are seen to articulate a more primordial otherness of the body.

5.4.2 The Passivity of the Self with Respect to Other People: Selfhood in a Dialectic with Other People

The self's passivity is manifest, second, in relation to other people. Can we specify the role of other people in co-constituting selfhood without sacrificing selfhood to otherness—as if another, or language, or community spoke "in" the ego? If the self were a mere locus, then properly speaking, there would be no self at all. There would be no distinction between the self we glimpse reflexively and the I that accompanies every action. In such a philosophy, the self would be just one pole of an inquiry—a place where discourse happens.

Ricoeur offers the ingenious suggestion that the failure of philosophies that take self or other as a unilateral starting point attests to a dialectic of Same and Other in the constitution of the ego. Two such unilateral attempts (at opposite extremes) are Husserl's transcendental ego and Levinas's responsible ego.[7] Neither unilateral starting point, Ricoeur argues, yields an adequate account of the actual encounters between self and other. That one cannot construct an ontology from one pole or the other suggests that an adequate ontology must be dialectical. The clue to an adequate dialectic is the distance between the two notions of the Same, namely, *ipse* and *idem* (Ricoeur, *Oneself as Another* 331). Because the ontology of the Same expresses a dialectic of *ipse* and *idem*, an ontology of the Other has to do likewise. Self and other each have to recognize a genuine dialectic of *ipse* and *idem* in the other—that the other is another ego like me (*ipse*) and yet irreducibly other than me (*idem*).

The dialectic of Same and Other derives its force from what is attested in genuine encounters. The locus of these encounters is the intersection of two domains—the domain of meaning (where the *ego* in alter ego attains sense) and the ethical domain (where the *alter* in alter ego receives content). But then does the ontology of selfhood fracture along the border of phenomenology and ethics? Not if a dialectic of Same and Other can articulate the kind of being (the self) who stands in a conversation across both domains. The ineluctable requirement to employ ethics and phenomenology together attests to the self as the kind of being in whom Same and Other are related dialectically.

What does this mean? First, the constitution in me of the sense of the other ego presupposes that genuine alterity confronts me prior to this constitution. Second, the constitution in me of the sense of my own ego as a responsible self presupposes that genuine others confront me prior to this constitution. So I am permitted to posit a predialogical self (or other) as long as I acknowledge that I always do so from within an already existing world-with-others. That is, the predialogical self and other are always already intertwined in discourse. Thus any ontological account of self and other remains subject to suspicion, but escapes the hyperbolic doubt that characterizes the philosophy of Levinas.

5.4.3 *The Passivity of the Self with Respect to Conscience: Selfhood in a Dialectic with the Other of Conscience*

Third, the self's passivity is manifest in relation to itself in conscience. Does the metaphor of a voice or call in conscience contribute anything new to the dialectic of Same and Other? Three cautions are in order. First, eagerness to employ the metaphor of voice or call in an ontology has to be checked against Nietzsche's suspicion that conscience is an epiphenomenon of social conditioning (Ricoeur, *Oneself as Another* 345).[8] That is, conscience might not testify to a unique dialectical relation of selfhood and otherness but to an other who speaks in the self. Second, even if a kind of premoral conscience can be posited, the inquiry will have to find its way back (as Heidegger never did) from premoral conscience to moral conscience, connecting the ontological call to the moral injunction and debt. Short of this return, the call of conscience would only attest to the bare "I can." Finally, does the sort of injunction or debt characteristic of conscience testify to a unique mode of otherness, or does it just repeat the otherness of other people? In the latter case, there would be a genuine attestation of selfhood in conscience (contra Nietzsche), but it would simply repeat the dialectic of selfhood and other people. But then a phenomenology of conscience would contribute nothing new on the ontological level to a dialectic of the Same and the Other.

By what right, first, do we descend beneath the phenomenon of conscience to a premoral conscience? What if, rather, Nietzsche's is the better account, and conscience is just the internalized demand of another echoing in an otherwise empty space? In following Hegel, we can submit historical realizations of conscience to suspicion but still glimpse an attestation of selfhood in conscience. In Hegel's account, I recognize the voice of the other that invokes me in conscience as my own voice. Yet I also recognize that my community and I have arrived at this conviction in a dialectic that is, to say the least, not altogether benign. Notwithstanding, I recognize in retrospect that the dialectic in all its ambivalence has been guided by Spirit. Traveling with Hegel, then, the self can suspect moral conscience along its halting progress, but still hear in conscience a voice that is for each person "mine." Whereas Hegel locates the sense of conscience in its teleology, Nietzsche locates it in its genealogy. For Nietzsche, "to state the origin is to abolish the aim and its alleged rationality" (Ricoeur, *Oneself as Another* 346). Thus in Nietzsche's account, the terror of the historical dialectic that leads to conscience is never superseded. Under the tutelage of terror, the I has become the responsible animal, and this "progress" never leads to a self that is free in any real sense. Ricoeur suggests, rather, that the attestation of selfhood marks a middle way between the hyperbolic doubt of Nietzsche and the hyperbolic certainty of Hegel's absolute Spirit. Yet Nietzsche's radical doubt stands as a sober warning that attestation must remain forever in tension with suspicion. The question posed to a dialectic of attestation and suspicion is whether there are other, stronger testimonies to the voice of self in conscience that can counter Nietzsche's suspicion.

This question leads to the second challenge—does the phenomenon of conscience testify to anything other than an inward recapitulation of the common precepts of morality? These common moral concepts do belong to an objective domain that can be described without reference to conscience. Conscience, however, "reinscribes these concepts within the dialectic of the Same and the Other, under the guise of a specific modality of passivity" (Ricoeur, *Oneself as Another* 342). So the phenomenon of conscience attests to a unique relation of the self to itself as one who recognizes these concepts as other. Ricoeur takes Heidegger's account of the call of conscience in *Being and Time* as the clue to a premoral understanding of conscience (Ricoeur, *Oneself as Another* 348–52).[9] What differentiates this call from the modes of otherness previously considered is that although it is immanent, it also has a vertical dimension. The call of conscience is not just an internal conversation but also places a demand on the self—a demand that might testify to a unique mode of otherness addressed to the self in conscience.[10]

But does this analysis add anything to the mere assurance that in every act I recognize the "I can," that is, the assurance that I am a potentiality-for-being? In Heidegger's *Being and Time*, what is disclosed in the call of conscience is the passivity of fallen Dasein, thrown to existence and regarding itself as part of that existence.[11] In the call of conscience, fallen Dasein is thrust against the possibility of its own nonbeing. Here Heidegger locates a more original guilt or debt that is not owed to someone else: a mode of being (being-guilty) that precedes ethical indebtedness. In this bold stroke, Heidegger claims to have freed conscience from ethics. But is this nonmoral conscience recognizably *conscience* any more? Ricoeur concludes that all Heidegger can provide in terms of a return from ontological to ethical conscience is a kind of moral situationism—conscience as a silent summons attests only to the brute fact of Dasein's thrownness. Conscience cannot orient action; instead, it calls the self out of the domination of the They to assume responsibility for its own thrownness. But what difference does it make that I know I am thrown? To put the same point somewhat differently, what concrete action could ever attest to my own authenticity—even that I would recognize myself? (The problem is symmetrical with the one raised in chapter 3 with respect to Bultmann's account of the eschatological encounter, namely, that nothing could ever count as evidence of the encounter—even in my own inwardness.) Heidegger offers no help; the path from ontological back to moral conscience appears blocked, and Heidegger's nonmoral conscience attests to no more than the bare "I can."[12]

Ricoeur suggests a middle path between the deeply suspect moral conscience and the radically nonmoral ontological conscience of Heidegger's *Being and Time*. He proposes that the phenomenon of conscience attests to a unique dialectic of Same and Other, namely, "being-enjoined" and "call" (Ricoeur, *Oneself as Another* 354). As being-enjoined, the idea of debt regains its dialogical structure but only at the expense of a reawakened suspicion: My being-enjoined might be the empty echo in me of the threat of domination. Yet the greater testimony posed to Nietzsche's radical doubt is precisely the engagement of ethics and morality that occupied Ricoeur's prior three studies (his "little ethics"). That account attests to a self on a journey from the ethical aim, to the moral norm, and back to the ethical aim where no norm guides certainly. Conscience reinscribes this journey, through the metaphor of a call, in a dialectic of Same and Other (Ricoeur, *Oneself as Another* 352). First I am enjoined to live well with and for others in just institutions. Yet because of the real threat of violence (even, perhaps, a radical evil that affects the self's orientation to the ethical aim) this desire to live with others has to be given the form of a law. So I am enjoined, second, before the court of conscience. It is this metaphor of conscience as a courtroom that occasions Nietzsche's radical doubt. Yet there is a third dimension of conscience (unacknowledged by Nietzsche) beyond the courtroom. That is, I am enjoined finally to return to the ethical aim where no norm guides certainly. The passivity of the self with respect to this triple call corresponds on the ontological plane to the mode of selfhood designated as being-enjoined (Ricoeur, *Oneself as Another* 354).

Finally, then, what mode of otherness belongs to the Other who enjoins the self in conscience? Bear in mind that Ricoeur means that the self is other to itself in the call of conscience (elsewhere he calls conscience "the dialogue of the self with itself").[13] Thus the call of conscience can be identified with another's voice only as mediated by some interpretation.[14] Consequently, when Ricoeur asks about the otherness of the Other of conscience, he refers to a conscience always already recapitulating in the self an injunction from another. The phenomenon of conscience thus *attests* to the self as other to itself while it *testifies* to an Other who invokes the self. What can be said in general (within the purview of philosophy) about the otherness of the Other to whom conscience testifies? Though Ricoeur shares Levinas's conviction that the call reaches the self from actual others, he wants to "maintain a certain equivocalness of the status of the Other on the strictly philosophical plane" to head off any reductionism:

> To be sure, Levinas does not fail to say that the face is the trace of the Other. The category of the trace seems in this way to correct as well as to complete that of the epiphany. Perhaps the philosopher as philosopher has to admit that one does not know and cannot say whether this Other, the source of the injunction, is another person whom I can look in the face or who can stare at me, or my ancestors for whom there is no representation, to so great an extent does my debt to them constitute my very self, or God—living God, absent God—or an empty place. With this aporia of the Other, philosophical discourse comes to an end. (Ricoeur, *Oneself as Another* 355)

The notion of the trace memorializes both the attestation of the self (the trace is *in me* who responds) and the other (it is a trace *of the other* who invokes me). Yet to say more about the mode of otherness in the trace would overstep the boundaries of a philosophy that recognizes itself as subject to Kant's critique of the limits of reason.[15] Still, philosophy should at least not elide the equivocalness of the Other recapitulated in conscience. A philosophical account should end in equivocalness: The Other manifest in the call of conscience cannot be reduced to the other person, or to the ancestor, or to God, or to an empty place—the Other of conscience exhibits characteristics of each of these figures.

5.5 Critique: The Self in Community, a Community of Selves

The remaining task is to clarify how things stand with Ricoeur's ontology once the self and community appear as correlates. The self is disclosed as potentiality-for-response only within a community that calls the self before its ethical aim; at the same time, the community only lives in and through the selves it comprises.

5.5.1 Attestation in Community

In placing attestation and suspicion within Aristotle's being-true and being-false, Ricoeur asserts that a hermeneutics of the self attests to the real, which is the first basis of his ontology of the self. Ricoeur offers his ontology in hope that it will finally ground the movement from empirical analysis to universal claims, albeit always subject to a dialectic of attestation and suspicion (Ricoeur, *Oneself as Another* 301). The clue to follow here is that attestation only appears in actual conversations—whether among persons in one community or among persons in different communities. So the background against which the distinction between the empirical and the universal stands out is neither the self nor the community per se but the self in community, a community of selves. Thus with respect to the ontological status of attestation, Ricoeur's ontology of the self already appears against the backdrop of the self and community.

Does placing the ontology in this context invite a relativistic conclusion? No, because the distinction between the universal and the empirical is not relative to a community in any strong sense if the boundary of the community is at stake in the conversation. If I am wrong about the universality of some claim, I may also be wrong about the boundary of my own community. So the real attested in a hermeneutics of the self (the real that is reinscribed in an ontology) is not just a self but a self in community, a community of selves. Could this real be otherwise than what is articulated based on what is attested? There is no response to suspicion but better and stronger attestation.

5.5.2 *Potentiality and Actuality in Community*

Ricoeur identifies Spinoza's *conatus* as the closest metaphor to what he means by a ground at once potential and actual.[16] The problems confronting a contemporary appropriation of Spinoza's *Ethics* are profound, as Ricoeur himself admits. I make no claim to have worked out all the issues here, but I direct my inquiry to uncovering the communal aspects of Ricoeur's chosen metaphor.[17]

Ricoeur distances himself from Spinoza's theology, suggesting that what appeals to him in Spinoza's notion of God as *essentia actuosa* is that God is "acting energy" (Ricoeur, *Oneself as Another* 315). *Essentia actuosa* is thus the sort of ground against which selfhood might appear in a dialectic of selfhood and sameness. It would be helpful to relate what is at stake in Ricoeur's reservations about Spinoza to his reservations about Hegel's ontologizing of *Geist*. Unlike Hegel, of course, Spinoza never speaks of God as person or *Geist*. Yet there is a similar tendency in both thinkers to regard the ground of the individual entity as secondary to that which grounds all entities. We have seen that Hegel's ontologizing of *Geist* articulates the transcendence of institutions to persons but prematurely closes the dialectic of attestation and suspicion. By contrast, Ricoeur finds a kindred spirit in Spinoza, for whom *conatus* is always read indirectly off of actually existing entities. Yet for Spinoza, the *conatus* of the individual is not only deferred empirically insofar as it must be read through detours; it is also deferred ontologically insofar as the *conatus* of each individual expresses a ground in which the individual is joined to all other entities (God as *essentia actuosa*).[18] Unlike Hegel, Spinoza does not attribute an aim to this ground—he posits no personal God or *Geist*.[19] Nevertheless, Spinoza still executes the sort of unification from above that Ricoeur eschews in his own more modest ontology.

I can then restate this difference between Hegel and Spinoza in terms of community: Hegel attributes a power and actuality to the institutions that make community possible (*Geist*), but forecloses the argument about which individuals and institutions best instantiate the ethical aim of the community; Spinoza recognizes the detour through the power and actuality of concrete individuals (*conatus*) but too quickly unites these individuals under the *essentia actuosa* (God, or nature). Spinoza thus asserts by fiat a prior community of all beings. The argument about who speaks for the community can continue, but the community is not called by an Other who transcends it. So in Spinoza's account the conversation may be infinite, but it is not open—not open, that is, to an Other who transcends the community. Reconstructing the problem this way opens a way to preserve the first person perspective in an ontology that articulates the self and its community as correlates yet allows for transcendence.

One community of all human beings is deferred in two senses. First, the community, as the correlate of the self, is adequately attested only at the end of an itinerary of detours. An ontology of the self only articulates the analogical unity of this itinerary; to refer to the self as that which unifies the itinerary from above would send the whole project into a vicious circularity. Ricoeur averts this circularity by placing the dialectic of Same and Other inside his ontology, but he never takes as a theme the location of this dialectic in a community. Second, the community of all beings remains a task for actual communities whose ethical aim includes the imperative to embrace others in their differences in one community. The individual's *conatus* may express a communal hope, and yet that hope might still attest to an Other who calls the community. I must add, though, that I mean something different than Spinoza does when I say that the *conatus* expresses an Other. Spinoza posits an ontological identity between the self and its ground (*essentia actuosa*) which, Philip Clayton points out, is finally untenable: Spinoza never makes it clear how the infinite could ever be expressed in the finite.[20] In my account (following Ricoeur) *conatus* expresses the ground it depends on not through identity with the Other but in responding to the Other. Only these two deferrals give content to the notion of community: Like Husserl's transcendental ego, Spinoza's community of beings is as certain as it is empty.[21]

None of this is to deny that the hope that appears in a community might have universal scope. Even if the unity of all beings in one community remains a task, it still might correctly identify the proper order of things. It is, of course, a further step to claim that the life of a particular community expresses the life of God (for Spinoza, the *essentia actuosa*); such a claim would have to be articulated in whatever story identifies the community. It is clear, though, that the claim that individual entities express God's power and actuality can only come at the end of a work of interpretation and as a practical task in real communities. The community's ethical aim is a hope doubly deferred—in attestation (through a hermeneutics of detours) and in being (it is an ongoing task).[22] Ricoeur's reserve with respect to Spinoza should be taken as a warning against reducing the *conatus* to a community. Rather, we have to regard the *conatus* as, in some sense, precommunal. To assert the opposite would be to reduce the *conatus* to an empty space where the community's hope echoes. The precommunal self is only glimpsed where each asserts "mine" of a community's hope, and yet that hope only lives where it is put into action by actual selves. *Conatus* expresses this mutual dependence of self and community ontologically.

5.5.3 *Situating the Dialectic of the Same and the Other in Community*

Ricoeur puts into a dialectical relation an ontology of the Same (the dialectic of *ipse* and *idem* projected into a speculative discourse) and an ontology of the Other. That double dialectic now has to be sighted within the community as the self's correlate. To this end, I identify the community of inquirers presupposed in Ricoeur's hermeneutics of the self and show that within various brackets these inquirers describe phenomena in the life of a community.

By what right, though, may I speak of Ricoeur and his interlocutors as members of one community? Isn't it rather that the itinerary of *Oneself as Another* is an ad hoc conversation created by Ricoeur's choice of interlocutors? In the end, to assert that these inquirers share one community is no more ambitious than Ricoeur's project to construct an ontology of selfhood beneath their diverse discourses. His ontology of the self everywhere presupposes such a community. A reconfigured ontology of the self in community thus stands or falls with Ricoeur's project. Such a community is the background against which the ontology of the self appears and is the space in which we argue about an ontology of the self. But why construct an ontology of the self at all? Two considerations drive the project. First, an ontology of the self stands in for Husserl's transcendental ego, albeit with considerably less pretension.[23] Second, it articulates the real attested in a conversation across diverse discourses about selfhood.

First, in what sense can an ontology of the self stand in for the transcendental ego? Husserl sought to ground reference as a characteristic of an intentionality (a meaning or sense for the ego) that could be validated on appeal to a transcendental ego that constitutes the sense.[24] The transcendental ego is the pole where the world as meant is constituted for the ego. By *self* Ricoeur continues to denote a pole of constitution but one caught up in a dialectic of Same and Other. Validation is no longer referred to a solipsistic ego but to a self always already constituted in and through its relation to others. Thus although validation retains an immanent dimension, it is also public. In consequence of this publicness, assurance is no longer certainty (à la Descartes) but testimony that might be countered by other testimony. So Ricoeur's ontology of the self can be regarded as a deeply chastened stand-in for Husserl's transcendental ego. The focal point of attestation shifts from the subject to the self and other as correlates in some shared discursive space. But what is this shared discursive space? The second answer to "why posit an ontology of the self?" is that an ontology of the self articulates the real that appears in Ricoeur's itinerary of detours. Here it will be helpful to look more closely at the discursive space presupposed in those detours.

In the first nine studies, aporias attest to a self presupposed by analytic discourses. To honor the boundaries of these discourses do we have to settle for diverse accounts of the self without any underlying unity—a linguistic self, an acting self, a narrated self, a responsible self? To speak of a unified self that underlies these divergent discourse is to stake a claim, however qualified, that they investigate aspects of the same reality. Lest anyone suppose that here phenomenology cries "Aufgehoben!" to analytic philosophy, recall that phenomenology only gains content as reflection on analysis. Practitioners in each of these discourses rightfully claim their own field of objects; yet they can and often do converse across disciplines. And that is precisely what Ricoeur arranges in the first nine studies of *Oneself as Another*, namely, a many-sided conversation between Fregean semantics, speech act theory, pragmatics, studies of identity, narrative theory, and ethics. The claim that all of these discourses always already presuppose a reflexive self (and that each could make sense of what the others mean by *the self*) is not an *Aufgehoben* imposed from above but the presupposition of an actual conversation. Admittedly, Ricoeur sets up the order of this particular conversation; yet it involves public texts that any reader may rightly bring into conversation with each other. Indeed, by virtue of their public claims, these texts already participate in a public conversation that Ricoeur simply articulates as such. Nor is the conversation at issue just a rarified conversation among theorists. Instead, these theorists claim to describe, within various methodological brackets, what happens in their own lifeworld. In other words, the interpretand of Ricoeur's hermeneutics is not simply "the self of the Western analytic theorist" but the self glimpsed reflexively within the (admittedly Western) horizon shared by these theorists and the rest of us. The self is disclosed in the discursive space opened by this actual conversation.

So if an ontology of the self is possible, then there is a discursive space in which participants in these diverse discourses converse about aspects of the same reality, namely, a self that is a unity, even if only analogically. That the self is an *analogical* unity respects that the self is never glimpsed as a whole but in detours. This analogical unity does not ground these discourses (it always comes too late) but is disclosed retrospectively as something presupposed and (indirectly) talked about. Following the lead of the previous chapter, I am permitted to suggest that the discursive space of this conversation is a community that embraces the interlocutors.

Of course, this discursive space might not be a community after all but what Hans-Georg Gadamer calls a fusion of horizons.[25] In any particular case, though, that is an interpretation that can be tested, and it is by no means the only possible interpretation. As I suggested in the previous chapter, such conversations can be narrated in several ways: as a fusion of horizons, the assimilation of one community by another, or the retrospective recognition that one community has always already embraced all of the interlocutors. How such an encounter is eventually emplotted is the topic of an ongoing conversation. Yet the story is not arbitrary because the actions of each interlocutor will have been shaped by myriad prior involvements in a community, and the better stories will plot more of these involvements. Of course, such stories do not belong to phenomenology (which can, however, study them within the phenomenological bracket) but to the communities they identify. To examine one such story must therefore wait until the itinerary turns back from philosophy to theology. For now it is enough to observe that the community involved might exceed a simple fusion of horizons: The content of the word *community* is proportionate to the best narrative account of the encounter.

What gives credence to an ontology of the self? On the one hand, it is the testimony that emerges at the end of an itinerary of detours. Yet a community is the condition of testimony—it opens the discursive space where self and other meet; notwithstanding, in such meetings the self and other carry their communities into the future. The testimony that arises in a hermeneutics of the self is thus the testimony of a community of inquirers. The real that resists reinterpretation can only be articulated when one considers simultaneously the self, the other, and the community in which they meet—a community that correlatively appears in the encounter of self and other.

If something stands in for Husserl's transcendental subject it is not the self but the self in community, a community of selves. Ricoeur takes the first step in this direction by enclosing his ontology of the self within a dialectic of Same and Other. Yet he never takes as a theme the communal space in which the dialectic of Same and Other appears. In making this communal space a theme of reflection, I do not mean to posit the community as a kind of super subject. Instead, the locus before which reflection pauses is a self that appears always already related to another (Ricoeur's original point) in a shared community (my qualification). At the same time, community only ever appears in the meetings of actual persons, so the first-person perspective is not subservient to the community.

If the dialectic of Same and Other appears in a community, then what happens to the ontology that articulates this dialectic when the community's self-understanding shifts? In particular, what happens when the resolution of a conflict challenges a prior understanding of whose suffering matters? Or of who constitutes a genuine other? Or of whose voice calls in conscience? In all of these questions I presuppose the ontology of the self in community. My question is not, for example, whether in some conflict the very idea of an ontology of the flesh might become untenable. Rather, I stand within the community to ask what happens to the community when in reaching out to embrace others in their alterity, our self-understanding shifts in a way that challenges our prior understanding of being.

5.5.4 The Otherness of the Flesh and Other People in Community

First I consider the otherness of the flesh and the otherness of other people together. In a conflict over whether others deserve to be recognized as flesh, like us, I ask what cost might be borne by the self and its community. In the next section I ask what further cost there might be if such a conflict were to motivate a shift in the story that identifies how the self relates to itself in conscience.

Just as it was necessary to reinscribe the self in the public world through naming, so "it is necessary, as Husserl himself states, to *make* the flesh part of the world if it is to appear as a body among bodies" (Ricoeur, *Oneself as Another* 326). Such a reinscription is not optional but a constitutive moment of selfhood insofar as I am being-in-the-world: To share a public world with others belongs to the meaning of selfhood. For all that, to reinscribe my body in a world-with-others does not create the otherness of my body but presupposes it. Resources for reinscription circulate in a community. What can be blocked—by restraint, by torture, by murder, or more insidiously, by the withdrawal of the resources to narrate suffering—is my capacity to reinscribe in discourse how I relate to my body as other. In such instances I am wounded in the very capacity to bring my most intimate other into my public life with others. Because I am who I am in relation to others, such a wound diminishes my very power to exist (my *conatus*). So the community that provides me the resources to relate to my body as other, in a world with others, can also negatively impact my prior relation to my body: first by wounding my ability to live out that relatedness and second by wounding my ability to express my suffering when it denies me access to the community's narrative resources. That is not to say that the community has an obligation to tell the story of everyone who suffers. Rather, a wrong is perpetrated when the community denies the sufferer access to resources necessary to tell his or her own story. To deprive someone of these resources introduces a suffering that is concealed but nevertheless real if it appears against a background of the ontology of the flesh.

A conflict carried to an ontology of the flesh would involve a protest against some exclusionary practice that presupposes that others do not feel their own bodies as "we" do; or that their suffering is justified or necessary; or that they have no right to benefit from our world-with-others—whether due to physical characteristics or to other socially constructed boundary markers. At the end of such a conflict, an appeal to an ontology of the flesh might lead to something startlingly different, namely, a more encompassing community with bodies once excluded that now appear in an original synthetic grasp as flesh, like me. Following Husserl, Ricoeur names the original synthetic grasp of the other as flesh the *appresentation* of the other (Ricoeur, *Oneself as Another* 334). If there is a shift in the community's understanding of appresentation, I may now admit a likeness where I once represented another to myself as if his or her suffering did not matter. How are we, from this later perspective, to understand the self and the community that formerly denied this original grasp? Did the faculty of appresentation change in the transition, or did those members of the community, in its former misdirection, simply mischaracterize the faculty?

What would it mean for the faculty of appresentation to change? Suppose that some fundamental lack in the community is supplied by innovation or outside intervention. The degree to which this innovation or loan connects with the community's tradition determines whether the community can retell its story as assimilation by another community, as a fusion of horizons, or as one community that has always embraced the agent and sufferer in one community. In the first case, it is not that the faculty of appresentation changes, but that the other's community articulates it more originally. In the second case (fusion) the other's community may articulate it more originally, or something completely new could come about in the meeting of the two communities. Yet that this fusion would constitute a radically new mode of appresentation, unconnected to either tradition, seems highly unlikely. (Even what Moltmann designates novum is the *fulfillment* of a promise given to the community.) At any rate, in practice such an extraordinary claim would have to be judged against the actual connections between this new mode of appresentation and the two traditions put into play in the encounter. But when a community aims to embrace all others in their genuine alterity, there are limits to how it can retell its story if the community is to retain its identity: It cannot be assimilated to another community, and if there is a fusion or innovation, the community has to reconnect this new insight with its tradition. In short, to remain true to its aim such a community would have to admit culpability for having mischaracterized the faculty of appresentation, whatever the provenance of the insight that led to its reformulation.

In this event we could gesture and say, "*Those* people in the past did not represent our community in their actions." But unless historical continuity is to be utterly sacrificed, then we have to answer how the community persisted through the transition. We may be able to gesture toward some actual person or persons and assert, "*They* represented this community in their actions even though, by and large, other members of the community were misdirected." It could happen, however, that no one in the tradition escapes unscathed. In some conflicts, perhaps the most that can be said is that some recognized a principle without recognizing all of its consequences; or that some hoped for a solution that in retrospect redressed (or at least ought to have redressed) the wrong. The question is whether such anticipations would be enough to ground a non-trivial continuity of the community in its orientation to the ethical aim. Unless one appeals to something like Hegel's absolute Spirit, then the narrated continuity of the community has to be indexed to actual persons who enact the community's hope. Without a teleology such as Hegel's, though, are mere anticipations of this enactment enough to ground the community's continuity where real harm has been done?

In chapter 3, I argued that in interpreting the past we can assert one community with our forebears as we let their claims speak again in our interpretations. Drawing on this insight, we might find authorization to claim that insofar as we share one community through time with these figures from our past, then perhaps their halting solutions and hopes can be realized in us—just as our halting solutions and hopes might only be realized in a generation to follow. Community is maintained when we not only take up their hopes and solutions but also bear the consequences of their incompleteness. There are two possibilities. In speaking for the community one could accept responsibility for consequences of past actions without imputability, or one could acknowledge these actions as imputable to oneself and the community jointly. The question, however, is whether it makes sense to impute guilt to oneself—and to claim to speak for a community in doing so—where there is no personal guilt apart from one's connection to the community. Here St. Paul's account is suggestive (though my retrieval of Paul's self-understanding is not complete until the next chapter).

When Paul speaks for his community, he also imputes guilt to himself for the persecution that arose out of his own misdirected zeal (Gal. 1:13–14). Paul's self-imputed guilt, then, is equally connected to his personal acts. Yet that Paul understands Israel to have died in its Christ presupposes a much stronger identification between self and community in the person of Jesus. If Christ became a curse for Israel (Gal. 3:13) but is not himself the perpetrator of his own death, then Christ is somehow able to bear responsibility for his community without himself having participated in the act. So those who speak for the Church, the body of Christ, can hope to accept not only responsibility for consequences of past actions but even (albeit under extraordinary circumstances) imputed guilt where there is no shared personal guilt. From the theological perspective of the next chapter, this possibility belongs to the community of the living and dead in Christ. From the philosophical perspective of the present chapter, the possibility is intelligible only to the extent that one can plausibly claim that the other out of the community's past speaks again in the self.[26]

We thus embrace in one community both the other out of our own past who erred and the other who should have been recognized but who suffered through action, complicity, or inaction on the part of our community. Such an embrace is broken in two ways. First, it cannot heal the suffering inflicted in the past, though it can at least identify it as a wrong. Second, the present community stands under the same necessity as its former incarnation—to be open to signs of unarticulated alterity and new ways to articulate it. Paradigmatically, the alterity we fail to recognize is the suffering other who recedes beneath the community's discourse. The perennial problem, of course, is how to decide when otherness constitutes genuine alterity and when the community can rightly judge that some difference cannot be encompassed within its ethical aim. In forming such judgments, we are permitted to bear our considered convictions confidently in conversation with others who do not share those convictions. Yet we are never certain in Hegel's absolute sense but in hope: The hope that when we recognize alterity in a new way and it reopens a debate about convictions, we will be able to retell our community's story. If, as Levinas has it, the community is more primordial than the self, then we might conclude that the self was reconstituted by an encounter with radical exteriority. Or if, as Husserl has it, the self is more primordial than the community, we might conclude that a transcendental self spanned the gap between an old and a new community. But if the self and its community are correlates, then neither the self nor the community is more primordial. Instead, the two are at stake together in the conflict and can (at least potentially) be rearticulated together. Of course, there is no guarantee that such a joint rearticulation will always be possible—it remains a hope.

5.5.5 The Other of Conscience in Community

Having considered together the otherness of the flesh and the otherness of other people (in a conflict over whether others deserve to be recognized as flesh, like us), I now ask what further cost there might be if such a conflict were to motivate a shift in the story that identifies how the self relates to itself in conscience.

Ricoeur's account of conscience oscillates between two kinds of certainty that are suspect—the certainty of absolute Spirit and the certainty of the transcendental ego. Hegel's dialectic undermines the certainty of the transcendental ego, whereas Nietzsche's radical doubt undermines the certainty of absolute Spirit. As Ricoeur says, Hegel unduly stresses the "fulfilled achievement" of spirit over its "unfulfilled claim."[27] We should, of course, continue to affirm the real achievements of objective spirit, but we have to balance this affirmation by a healthy suspicion where spirit's promise remains unfulfilled. For all that, suspicion need not overwhelm attested achievements; rather, attestation and suspicion proceed dialectically. The dialectic of Same and Other in a community is thus a locus where reflection pauses before the real; notwithstanding, reflection does not come to a complete halt (as it would in a philosophy of absolute spirit) because in conflicts we might have to recede beneath this ontology. But recede back to what? Not to a nullity, but to the ethical aim, that is, to the desire to live well, with and for others, in just institutions.

What guides the return to the ethical aim is not absolute spirit but *phronēsis*—"the tie connecting conviction to its ethical ground, through the level of imperatives" (Ricouer, *Oneself as Another* 352).[28] I want to suggest that the locus of *phronēsis*, like the ethical aim itself, is conjointly the self and community as correlates. Admittedly, Ricoeur never takes this locus as a theme, but it is presupposed when he says that the wisest choice in a conflict "is all the less arbitrary as the decision maker . . . has taken the counsel of men and women reputed to be the most competent and the wisest" (Ricoeur, *Oneself as Another* 273). In asserting a conviction that emerges from practical wisdom along this dialectical route, one also claims to speak with the wise in his or her community. It would be incorrect to conclude that *phronēsis* mediates between the self and its community; rather, *phronēsis* belongs to the self and its community together. The *phronimos* (the self as wise) instantiates a *phronēsis* that belongs to the community, but *phronēsis* enters the world only as instantiated in the *phronimos*.

Yet if *phronēsis*, not absolute spirit, guides the dialectic, then what assurance is there that the ethical aim itself is intersubjectively real? The detour through ethics and morality, guided by *phronēsis*, is reinscribed in conscience as being-enjoined by an Other. So one crucial assurance that the self and its community approach an ethical aim that is intersubjectively real is the testimony to the Other in conscience. But then the story that articulates the ethical aim is at stake together with the story that articulates the relation of the self to itself in conscience.

What happens, then, if the articulation of the self's relation to itself in conscience shifts? When Ricoeur asks what philosophy is permitted to say in response to the question "who calls me?" he replies with characteristic modesty: The philosopher must "maintain a certain equivocalness of the status of the Other [of conscience] on the strictly philosophical plane, especially if the otherness of conscience is to be held irreducible to that of other people" (Ricoeur, *Oneself as Another* 355). What I want to add is that this equivocalness in the ontological status of the Other is nevertheless compatible with a certain ordering of the figures of the Other of conscience. Such an ordering is attested in a reflection on the self as the correlate of a community and can offer points of articulation to gauge the adequacy of various bids to tell a community's story.

The journey reinscribed in conscience is not guided by absolute Spirit but by *phronēsis*, and *phronēsis* appears conjointly in the self and its community as correlates. Thus to say that the call arrives at the self in the voice of a community does no damage to the transcendence of the Other who calls. Am I enjoined by God, living God, absent God? If I am, I am enjoined as the correlate of a community by a God who transcends the self and community in the call. The alternation of living God, absent God (or even more radically, empty place) in the Other of conscience memorializes the ambiguity of the joint dialectic of *ipse* and *idem*, Same and Other. "Living God" expresses the hope that we are enjoined by a real Other who transcends us toward an ethical aim that is not an epiphenomenon of discourse, a God with whom we celebrate the fulfilled achievements of spirit; "absent God" and "empty place" express the suspicion that we are alone and culpable for Spirit's unfulfilled claims. None of these figures should be ruled out of court on purely philosophical grounds, but none should be held to the exclusion of the others lest this beneficial equivocalness be sacrificed. Yet a different figure appears in Ricoeur's examples, namely, the other whose suffering cannot be articulated in the community's discourse (Ricoeur, *Oneself as Another* 352). It is in attending to this silently suffering other that the self and community uncover the unfulfilled claim. It is in attending to the suffering other that the self is open to what transcends the self and community. A proper ordering of the figures of the Other of conscience should thus recognize that the call arrives at the self in some actual other—paradigmatically, the other whose suffering cannot be articulated in the community's discourse. For all that, the figures "God—living God, absent God—or an empty place," which express transcendence, should not be reduced to other people or to a community.

In view of this ordering, I can now describe the sort of change that could radically challenge the community's understanding of the relation of the self to itself in conscience. In such a conflict, one or more of these figures would have been asserted to the exclusion of the others. Such one-sided construals may not be innocent of actual harm. If "living God" is asserted to the exclusion of "absent God," then humility in the face of the unfulfilled claim recedes behind the glory of the fulfilled achievement. If "empty place" is asserted to the exclusion of the dialectic of the living God and absent God, then no criteria can guide the choice of action (or at least, considered conviction has no more cachet than mere opinion). If the other person (or the ancestor) is asserted to the exclusion of what transcends the community, then there is no recourse for the one whose silent suffering falls beneath the community's discourse. This figure of the silent suffering other thus has a certain priority as the one who calls the self and community forward on their journey. It is this other who suffers if the community's stories misconstrue the Other of conscience, and in attending to this inarticulate pain such misdirection is uncovered. Yet conscience commands. For the silently suffering other to command the self, the figure must be maintained jointly with the figures of the transcendent (living God, absent God, or empty place). On the narrative plane, all of these figures are put into play together, and the adequacy of stories that relate the self to itself in conscience can be measured against their ability to sustain this play.

The detour to the self in community is now complete on the ontological level where philosophical inquiry ends. In preparing to move from philosophy to theology, we have to first consider faith not as belief but as a way of being in the world. Putting Ricoeur's biblical theology into conversation with Bultmann's, I propose that the kerygma is one public story among a plurality of stories that aim to identify the community we share.

5.5.6 Conclusion: Implications of an Ontology of the Self for Telling the Community's Story

Can an account of the proper ordering of these figures on the ontological plane help adjudicate between stories that claim to identify the community? I do not just ask whether the community can remain self-consistent in a larger, anonymous space where the self and other meet. Rather, I ask whether, in the face of the call from the silently suffering other, the self and other can embrace in their differences in one community—and narrate the space they meet in as the one community that has always already embraced them both. Can the adequacy of the story that identifies that community be judged against the proper ordering of these figures of the Other on the ontological plane? To answer that question, I engage some of Ricoeur's essays on biblical hermeneutics to see how Ricoeur relates his philosophical understanding of selfhood to the Christian story. In so doing, I move to the theological-narrative plane, that is, to the level of actual communities where self and community are narrated. From that perspective, I can examine in retrospect the relation between the figures of the Other on the ontological plane and the articulation of those figures on the narrative plane.

I am aware that Ricoeur tries to keep his theological concerns separate from his philosophical works. Yet the reverse is not true; that is, Ricoeur's philosophy does play a role in his writings on biblical hermeneutics.[29] In separating theology from philosophy in the way he does, Ricoeur refuses—even at the theological level—to let the Christian story narrate the space in which persons from different traditions engage in conversation. The ordering of the figures of conscience implies, however, that there are criteria to be met in telling the story of this shared space as a community. Does conscience in this community's story articulate a call from the community as the self's correlate? Can the story nevertheless articulate a call that transcends the self and community toward universality? Finally, does the transcendence of the call attune the self and its community to the suffering other who falls beneath the level of the community's discourse? These questions, which can be taken as criteria by which to measure bids to tell the community's story, are presupposed in Ricoeur's practice even if they never become a theme there.

Because I am not aware of any systematic treatment of "Church" in Ricoeur's work, I have to confront his biblical hermeneutics in a somewhat piecemeal fashion. To facilitate a comparison with Bultmann, I treat the same questions addressed in chapter 3 in the same order—the human question (that is, a theological account of the human being) followed by the God question (God disclosed as the one who calls the human being).

The way into Ricoeur's theological anthropology starts with his signature account of revelation: The truth of religious language is its reference to "the world in front of the text" (Ricoeur, "Philosophy and Religious Language" 41). The religious text refers to the world "not only at the level of manipulable objects but at the level Husserl designated by the expression *Lebenswelt* and which Heidegger calls being-in-the-world" (Ricoeur, "Philosophy and Religious Language" 42). What is disclosed in front of the reader is a possible way of being in the world. That is not to say that the world in front of the text is radically subjective; rather, the text takes up the world of the reader and refigures it (or it fails to be a revelatory text):

> The biblical world has aspects that are cosmic (it is a creation), that
> are communitarian (it speaks of a people), that are historical and
> cultural (it speaks of Israel and the kingdom of God), and that are
> personal. Humankind is reached through a multiplicity of dimen-
> sions that are as much cosmological and historical and worldly as

they are anthropological, ethical, and personal. (Ricoeur, "Philosophy and Religious Language" 44)

In the world in front of the biblical text, the reader confronts not just an existential decision but a decision as to whether this story articulates the cosmos in which she stands; articulates the community in which she esteems herself as another, the other as another self; and articulates the history and culture that her actions draw on and project into the future. Here Ricoeur appears to offer a rather full-bodied understanding of the communal nature of the kerygma. Moreover, Ricoeur's account surpasses Bultmann's because in refiguring the hearer's world, the kerygma has concrete consequences for the hearer's community, history, and culture. Finally, the signs of this refiguration are not simply evidenced in the immanent orientation of the hearer but are open to public scrutiny, specifically, questions about whether the hearer's actions are appropriate to the community's story.[30] It is worth noting that for all of this focus on action, Ricoeur never abandons hermeneutics for a political theology; rather, he says, the two are related in a "dialectic of poetics and politics" or a "poetics of politics" that offers "models for a partnership between God and God's people and the rest of humanity."[31]

Yet despite its robustness relative to Bultmann's account, Ricoeur's interpretation of the kerygma retains a certain individualism even while it situates the individual in a world-with-others. *With whom* should the reader offer concrete signs in the world according to the logic of Jesus?[32] *What community* empowers those actions and the way of being they instantiate? The community designated "God's people" appears to the hearer as a possible refiguration of her own community. More important, the kerygma does not narrate community in itself but as a dimension of the hearer's own humanity: Community appears as a dimension of selfhood rather than as a full-bodied correlate of the self. Without a doubt, Ricoeur's multidimensioned correlation of the self and kerygma far surpasses Bultmann's and ensures the connection between the kerygma and action. Yet Ricoeur continues to follow Bultmann in regarding the kerygma as a possible life story, not as the story of an actual community.

If the kerygma were the story of an actual community, would that mean that the hearer has to convert to some actual Christian social group to be transformed by the way of being in front of the text? The question does not occur for Ricoeur because his religious poetics enjoins hearers within their own communitarian dimensions. Their transformation by the kerygma is witnessed (or not) in concrete signs by which the kerygma can be seen to refigure their selves, communities, and cultures. But *who* confirms the adequacy of these signs of the kerygma? Insofar as they are the sacred texts of the Church, the Church must have some say; yet insofar as they are public texts that purport to narrate the self in dimensions that are cosmic, communitarian, and historical-cultural, the Church's claims enter a larger conversation.[33] It would appear that for Ricoeur, though, the discursive space of that larger conversation has no narrative identity as a community; it is anonymous—the intersection of a plurality of narratives.[34] But it is precisely in the kerygma's claim to narrate *that* community that the possibility arises that both interlocutors might embrace in one community.[35]

In narrating the identity of that larger community the ordering of the figures of the Other of conscience can help decide between stories. To reiterate, does the narrative preserve the equivocalness of the figures of the Other of conscience? Does it articulate a call from the community as the self's correlate? Can the story nevertheless articulate a call that transcends the self and community toward universality? Finally, does the transcendence of the call attune the self and its community to the suffering other who falls beneath the level of the community's discourse? I turn, then, to assess Ricoeur's own narration (in biblical hermeneutics) of the transcendence of the call of conscience, exploring his answer to what Gareth Jones calls the God question.

For Bultmann, theological language speaks of God by the only avenue open to the sort of being who stands before God as the light that reveals her own authentic self; christology articulates that event. Yet in focusing revelation so narrowly on the subject's experience of the eschatological event, Bultmann offers no help in identifying particular actions as rooted in that event. Like Bultmann, Ricoeur also focuses revelation on the subject's encounter, but he executes a detour through the public reinscription of that encounter in "the total context constituted by the whole space of gravitation of stories, prophecies, laws, hymns, and so forth."[36] What is revealed in the encounter is not simply Being-as-such but an Other—a *Oneself*—who confronts the self: "It is the function of the preaching of the cross and resurrection to give the word 'God' a *density* that the word 'being' does not possess. In its meaning is contained the notion of *its* relation to us as gracious and *our* relation to it as 'ultimately concerned' and as fully 'recognizant' of it" (Ricoeur, "Philosophy and Religious Language" 46). Moreover, the Other who confronts the hearer in the kerygma is identified in a dialectic of weakness and power: The Christ symbol articulates both "the celebration of total power" and "the confession of total weakness."[37]

This encounter imposes a dialectical labor on the hearer to articulate her own identity as being-enjoined by an Other who appears in the dialectic of weakness and power (Ricoeur, "Naming God" 232). Here the understanding of oneself is the correlate of an understanding of the other. In attending to the suffering other, the account memorializes the dialectic of the fulfilled achievement (actions in accord with the community's ethical aim) and the unfulfilled claim (failure to fulfill aspects of that aim in regard to the suffering other). This dialectical labor imposed on the hearer is not solitary. For example, the hearer is enjoined to participate in naming God: The "doctrine of the Trinity did this labor for one epoch of thought. A similar labor ought to be undertaken today, one that would take up the whole space of the naming of God and its discordant concordance" (Ricoeur, "Naming God" 232). Thus the self achieves its refiguration in the presence of third parties—a community. But does Ricoeur's account adequately preserve the insight that the call arrives at the self in the voice of a community? I suggest that this insight is better preserved in an account that draws on both Bultmann and Ricoeur.

From his hermeneutical perspective, Ricoeur focuses on the text and the world in front of the text; Bultmann gives a fuller account of an actual encounter between a self and other, namely, the hearer and the risen Lord in the proclaimer. Yet the cost for Bultmann was the genuine alterity of the other and the genre of the kerygma as the story that identifies a community. Ricoeur adds ontological density to Bultmann's bare encounter, which is to say that the certain (but empty) self gains a realist twist in reflection on the itinerary of detours. An ontology of self (which expresses this "real" in ontological language) can serve as a locus where worldly signs of the kerygma in action can be correlated with the encounter of self and other (here, the human self and divine Other). Thus in supplementing Bultmann with Ricoeur, we can hope to correlate signs of the kerygma with truth claims (attestations) concerning the presence of the risen Lord in the world.

Yet an ontology of the self is always an ontology of the self in community, a community of selves. So if we add to this correction of Bultmann by Ricoeur an additional correction of both thinkers by attention to the self and community as correlates, then to indicate the presence of the risen Lord in the world is to gesture toward a self in community, a community of selves: "*There* is the risen Lord in *this* person who speaks for *this* community." One particular story that identifies a community, the kerygma, articulates the Other of conscience as a suffering other, Jesus Christ, who is himself the symbol of the living God, absent God. Such a construal of the kerygma emplots all the points of articulation posed on the philosophical level: It preserves the equivocalness of the figures of the Other of conscience; it articulates a call that arrives at the self in a community, transcends the self and community yet preserves the first-person perspective; and it attunes the self and community to the suffering other who falls beneath the level of the community's discourse.

Of course, that philosophical insight is not innocent of the kerygma's influence. But why should it be? After all, an ontology is only reconstructed in retrospect after detours through analysis. I do not deny that the Bible is one book among many; nor do I claim, a priori, that we possess ready-to-hand criteria to decide between rival forms of life.[38] For all that, the kerygma can enter into an open conversation with other public stories in the hope that at the end of the day we will be able to affirm that the kerygma tells the story of a community that embraces all human beings in their genuine alterity. The question remains, of course, as to what constitutes genuine alterity and what characteristics the community may rightly exclude as not constitutive of self-hood. We cannot say ahead of time how all such conflicts will be decided. But there has to be a real dialogue open to the possibility that genuine modes of alterity might be occluded in our community's present self-understanding.

On the philosophical level, the last detour to the self in community is now complete in both hermeneutics and ontology. On the theological level, the turn to Ricoeur's biblical theology has lifted the itinerary out of philosophy into theology. Yet philosophy and theology are related insofar as the kerygma aims to narrate the community we share with others: There are points of articulation in the lifeworld that the community's story should be able to emplot. Some of these points of articulation are conveyed in an ontology of the self in community, and they can be discussed with others who tell different stories of the community. Ricoeur's concern is answered that the kerygma does not assume a "cryptophilosophical function" but continues to "assume its own insecurity"—in dialogue we join with others in putting at stake the story we claim identifies the community we share (Ricoeur, *Oneself as Another* 25). What remains is to correlate this ontology of the self in community with the communal self presupposed in Paul's letters.

6

Conclusion: The Crucified and Resurrected Self

6.1 Correlating Paul's Story with an Ontology of the Self in Community

To correlate the ontology of the self in community with Paul's communal self is to affirm what we share with Paul while acknowledging our real distance from him. This correlation responds to two interrelated questions. First, how can the ontology help us understand Paul? Second, how can the ontology help us let Paul address us again? In responding to these questions, I am guided in part by Bultmann's account of Paul's anthropology, adjusted to address issues of alterity and community. How is this correlation justified? In closing, I offer a theological account of interpretation in community: Paul can speak again in our interpretations because we live with him in the community of the living and dead in Christ and because the Spirit of Christ speaks in our conversation.

6.1.1 Reconfiguring Bultmann's Fundamental Structure of Human Existence

The problem that emerged in chapter 2 was whether Paul's communal understanding of the self should be demythologized, or if, instead, to understand Paul's meaning in our context called for a different understanding of the self. Bultmann collapses the temporal distance between Paul's self-understanding and ours by positing a shared formal structure of human existence. I raised three criticisms against this move. First, Bultmann's account loses the connection between the kerygma and social structures external to the self. Second, in Bultmann's decontextualized eschatology, the encounter between the hearer and the proclaimer loses the character of a genuine encounter between actual people. One of the casualties is the genuine alterity of Paul. Third, although Bultmann recognizes that social groups contribute to the plight of human beings, he never takes the community's contribution to the solution as a theme.

If Bultmann's demythologizing does not capture Paul's intent, then what does it do? Gareth Jones argues that Bultmann closes a window that looks out onto Paul's horizon when he substitutes for Paul's intent an analogy that expresses a modern interpretation (that the kerygma expresses the transcendental conditions of human existence in mythological dress).[1] In response to that criticism, I reappropriate Bultmann's formal structure of existence for what it actually is—an analogy for expressing an interpretation of Paul—but now corrected for its lack of attention to alterity and community. I follow Jones's steps to show how this reappropriation is accomplished.

To restore Paul as our dialogue partner first calls for a historical-critical exegesis of the text, then an interpretation of the dominant analogy at work in the text.[2] The dominant analogy at work in Paul's letters (chapter 2) is a story that identifies Israel: Israel as a community died and rose in its Christ, and the individual I locates its own identity when it dies and rises in that community. The interpreter is liable for two additional steps: a critique of the interpreter's context followed by the application of an analogy to express the interpretation in the present. The hermeneutics of the self in community (chapter 4) critiques selfhood in our context, and the ontology of the self in community (chapter 5) involves an analogy that can express the kerygma in our context: The kerygma is the story of a community where self and other meet in their genuine difference.

If the kerygma as the story that identifies our community is just one analogy among a plurality of analogies, then the choice of analogy guides what counts as essential to meaning and what can be put out of consideration (demythologized). It is true, of course, that a plurality of analogies might better express the richness of Paul's alterity. But unless we stake the further claim that some particular analogy aims at what Paul really meant (even if only as a regulative ideal), we could never claim that Paul addresses us again in his difference from us, no matter how many analogies we put into play. For all that, the claim that an analogy aims at what Paul really meant should be submitted to the most rigorous suspicion. Are we at an impasse? The root problem is that Jones, like Bultmann and Ricoeur, takes the space in which these analogies are put into play as itself anonymous. I submit, rather, that if we let the kerygma narrate this space as a community, then we can order the analogies within a regulative ideal of what Paul really meant—and still keep up a critical conversation to guard against ideology hijacking interpretation.

Bultmann might well object, though, to positing the self as a "being," out of concern that the horizon of the decision might cease to be revelatory, reduced to something chosen by a predialogical self. Yet the predialogical self is always grasped as the correlate of a community. So although the ontology of the self in community does mark one pole of constitution, it is always indexed to the self and community jointly. Bultmann's formal structure of existence performs a similar function, marking a pole of constitution where the self accepts responsibility for its orientation in a horizon it didn't choose: As *conscience*, the self is responsible in accepting a voice of authority; as *spirit* the self is responsible in its orientation to the divine will; as *body* the self is responsible in opening itself to the other. The telling difference between Bultmann's formal structure of existence and the ontology of the self in community is not that the former is existential and the latter is metaphysical; rather, in the former the transcendental conditions of selfhood are self-validating, whereas in the latter validation refers to an intersubjective process in a community.

6.1.2 A Contextual Appropriation of Paul's Soma

So it is possible in principle to correlate the ontology of the self in community with Paul's story using Bultmann as a mediating figure. First, Bultmann's proposal that by *soma* Paul intends the subject's ability to relate to herself reflexively can be correlated with Ricoeur's notion of flesh. (To avoid confusion with the Pauline *sarx* I use "the living body" to refer to Ricoeur's notion of "flesh."[3]) I am open to encounter with others as a body among bodies, yet in retrospect my experience of the other presupposes a prior relation to my own body—the living body as my most intimate other. What Ricoeur means by living body is not alien to Bultmann's use of *soma*. Yet the connection between living body and Paul's *soma* cannot be self-validating. In a shared community with Paul I could argue that we share an understanding of *soma*, but lest the exercise descend into vicious circularity I could never turn around and validate our shared community through the notion of *soma*. Rather, I have to interpret Paul, interpret my own horizon, and narrate the continuity between the two as one community through time. That story can then be tested within the community in an ongoing dialectic of attestation and suspicion. Within these limits, however, such a correlation can clarify the similarity between the sort of conflict Paul responds to and the general sort of conflict I described in chapter 5, namely, a shift in how one understands the suffering other as a living body like me.

Paul fails to recognize his community with Jesus because of a misdirection of the community's aim in Paul and others. In what Paul later articulates as an encounter with the risen Christ, he is confronted by a silent suffering other who cannot be articulated in his community's story. When he retells the community's story so that Jesus can appear as a living body like himself, Paul can finally represent Christ's suffering as his own ("I bear on my body the brand-marks of Jesus," Gal. 6:17).[4] In this reconfigured story, a more original community of persons is disclosed in which each person is a living body. Paul shifts from one who confidently addresses his world to one who is addressed by a new referent—the crucified and risen Christ.[5] That the referent is new does not mean that Paul's reconfiguration created it. Rather, in retrospect he can say that his community always bore witness to Christ and that the community is continuous in its embrace of this other despite its former misdirection. Paul narrates this concordant discordance as the community's dying and rising with Christ and locates his own dying and rising in the community.

6.1.3 A Contextual Appropriation of Paul's Syneidesis

Second, Bultmann interprets Paul's *syneidesis* as the condition of one's capacity to say "mine" of an authority that transcends the self. A transcendent authority speaks in conscience, yet I am responsible because the voice that calls is also my own. Yet Bultmann never offers an adequate account of the intersubjective tools the self uses to validate the authority of the voice, nor does he offer an account of the subjectivity of the one who calls (being-as-such is not a "self"). The dialectic of Self and Other, now resituated in community, reasserts inter-subjectivity while it preserves the mutual transcendence of the self and the Other of conscience. I am enjoined by an Other, irreducible to any one figure, who transcends the community and yet calls me in my community's voice. This dialectic can ground a correlation of our understanding of conscience with Paul's *syneidesis*.

In the shift that lets the crucified and resurrected Christ come into phrases, Paul's understanding of the Other who calls him in conscience also shifts. Israel's hope is that God's Spirit will be present in the world through God's gracious dealings with Israel. After his encounter with Christ, Paul associates this gift of the Spirit with Christ rather than with Torah observance. That does not mean that Israel lacked the Spirit before Christ. Rather, as Israel's story was fulfilled in Christ, the Spirit in Israel is discerned in retrospect by the

Spirit of Christ. This discernment exposes a deadly misdirection of the Spirit's gift of life in Paul and some of his contemporaries (Rom. 7). But now God's righteous community is manifest in the world because Paul can finally gesture unambiguously to Christ and say, "*There* is God's Spirit in the world" (Rom. 3:21–26). Christ is not alone in this community because all those of faith are in Christ (the people is included in its king). So the community in Christ no longer enjoins Paul in a general way as the Spirit in the Torah-observant community but rather as the Spirit of this particular man, Jesus Christ.

As a communal personality, Paul (before Christ) would have understood the call of conscience as arriving from his neighbor under Torah but transcending the neighbor as the call of God's Spirit in Israel. Paul failed to see, however, that the boundary of eschatological Israel was not Torah but the faithfulness of Abraham, so the suffering other who was not Torah-observant (by Paul's standards) fell outside the community. When Paul encounters Christ, he has to retell Israel's story. In Israel reconfigured, Paul hears the call of conscience as the call of his neighbor in Christ. Because Paul encounters Christ in his neighbor, this redefines the Other who calls in conscience, as Paul says, "Christ lives in me" (Gal. 2:19).

6.1.4 A Contextual Appropriation of Paul's Pneuma

The intertwining of spirit and conscience leads to the third component of Bultmann's formal structure of existence, namely, *pneuma* as the transcendental condition of orienting the human will to the divine will. Yet will, it has been noted, is too thin a notion to convey the relation between the divine Spirit and the human spirit. On the way to the self through community it became clear that the spirit in a community encompasses shared language, praxis, narrative, patterns of interpersonal relationships, and orientation to an ethical aim—the total itinerary of detours. Yet in contradistinction to Hegel's absolute Spirit, the spirit in a community is disclosed in an open conversation involving both attestation and suspicion. An open-ended *phronēsis* (wise deliberation) stands in for the closed Hegelian *Sittlichkeit* (the surpassing moment of objective spirit). *Phronēsis* is located neither in the self nor the community per se but in the self and community as correlates. This retrieval of Aristotle's *phronēsis* responds better to Paul's use of *pneuma* than Bultmann's reduction of spirit to the condition of will.

Paul refers spirit in his community to a particular suffering other, Christ, who comes into phrases only at the cost of retelling the community's story. In contrast, Bultmann never offers criteria whereby the proclamation of the kerygma could challenge the order of a community. Rather, his decontextualized eschatology abstracts from all such concrete criteria. If against Bultmann's advice we reinstate such criteria (that this or that concrete course of action does or does not represent the spirit in the community), we have to keep up a conversation about the rightness of the criteria. Here the dialectic of attestation and suspicion (on the philosophical plane) can be taken up into Paul's struggle of spirit and flesh (on the theological plane).

What can be said, then, of spirit as a social category? Bultmann's account can be helpful in correlating our understanding of the social world with Paul's understanding of spirit. For Paul the human world or *kosmos* grows up out of human selves until it "comes to constitute an independent super-self over all individual selves," that is, the "spirit of the world."[6] The *kosmos* is the domain of demonic spirits who exist *for us* in the sense that we exist in dependence on them in a way that properly belongs to God alone. Faith, as a new way of being, confronts the sinner with the possibility of having her life restored to its proper dependence on God but as a continuity within discontinuity. Her former existence as dependent on sin and the *kosmos* dies; she is crucified with Christ (Bultmann 1:257). At the same time, sin and the *kosmos* are defeated in her because they receive their power to exist from the human who has now been released from dependence. Thus Christ's victory over sin and death takes place in the moment of faith. All believers join with Paul in the eschatological moment, sharing the eschatological purpose of Jesus Christ—that is, faith as a new possibility of being, utter dependence on God.

All of this is advantageous except for one thing: the self-validating nature of the encounter with the risen Lord. Bultmann is certainly right that Christ's victory takes place in the individual encounter. Yet the encounter is transmitted, validated, empowered, and lived (it is a possible way of life) in a community. Thus where Bultmann sees conflict between the individual and the corporate, a better appropriation of Paul's intent is that in the eschatological moment the individual believer appropriates the aim of her community more originally. She asserts, for example, that her action to embrace another in one community embodies the community's ethical aim more originally than to deny that embrace. It is true, as Bultmann says, that in the decision of faith an individual can exert the right to find for herself what is properly Torah (Bultmann 1:342). But that is a public act, and it makes her liable in principle to identify how an action that accords with what is properly Torah also accords with the wisest decisions in the tradition. It makes her liable, that is, to retell her community's story.

6.1.5 A Contextual Appropriation of Paul's "I Have Been Crucified with Christ"

Can we then repeat, without hyperbole, Paul's "I have been crucified with Christ?" "Dying and rising with Christ" is the narrative shape Paul gives to the shift in his understanding of self and community. Does such a shift permit one to say that the community or the self died in an ontological sense? I have to reject this possibility. It is true that to exist in the later horizon presupposes much more than an existential choice: Rather, it presupposes a tremendous work in retelling the community's story and retelling one's own story within its ambit. My own life is continuous and intelligible only at the cost of a concordant discordance in my community. But that is exactly what the dialectic of Same and Other aims to articulate, namely, a concordant discordance. Concordance would be overwhelmed by discordance if the self or the community ceased to exist in the transition. Thus taking the ontology of the self in community as a starting place, one cannot interpret this death ontologically.

Is that limitation adequate to what Paul intends? On one side stand Paul's affirmations of newness, for example, the newness of Spirit (Rom. 7:6), the new covenant (1 Cor. 11:25, 2 Cor. 3:6), and a new creation (2 Cor. 5:17, Gal. 6: 15). On the other side stand Paul's affirmations that the new continues the old, for example, that his Gentile converts are grafted into Israel (Rom. 11:17–24); that the blessing they have received is as those who are "blessed with Abraham, the believer" (Gal. 3:9); and that "all Israel" ultimately includes those who are now "enemies for your sake, but from the standpoint of election are beloved for the sake of the fathers" (Rom. 11:28). This pattern of continuity within discontinuity, both at the level of the self and the community, can be redescribed as a concordant discordance. Paul articulates this concordant discordance as the community's participation in the death and the resurrection of Christ (Rom. 6:4). "Resurrection" expresses in part the newness on the other side of the retold story where the suffering Christ has come into phrases. What dies in the shift from the old telling to the new is not just the story itself but a way of being. The transition certainly marks a profound shift in Paul's way of being—Paul who had once persecuted those he now regards as righteous. But it also puts on offer a new way of being for Paul's fellow Jews who may now, in Christ, share table fellowship with Gentiles of faith. Finally, it marks a shift in the way of being of the Gentile of faith who dies in historic Israel because Israel, in its aim, encompasses all those of faith. Of course, the Gentile's actual community is not historic Israel, and not all those of faith presently participate in the actual community that is the body of Christ. But eschatologically we can hope that all people of faith will be able (in principle) to see how their communities have passed through Israel's death in Christ and are ordered more originally to the risen Christ. That is a theological way to express the hope that the community will embrace all peoples in their genuine alterity. Robert Jenson is surely right that we cannot speculate on the circumstances of the "eschatological address of the gospel."[7] Yet in a dialectic of attestation and suspicion, it is not just the other whose worldview is challenged: We only come to know who the eschatological Christ is, and who we ourselves are, in dialogue with other communities.

The kerygma thus puts to the test a way of being disclosed in some community, and insofar as God's Spirit is present in the community, the kerygma orients the hearer more originally to that divine Spirit. Such ways of being exist only as they are practiced; they cease to exist as such when those who practice them embrace a different way of being—a way of being that is new (discordant) and yet more original (concordant).

We have already seen that to be crucified and raised with Christ is not hyperbolic in Paul's context. I am now prepared to give a nonhyperbolic interpretation in our context. To be crucified and raised with Christ articulates a concordant discordance of the self and its community. A believer who dies and rises rejects a misdirected way of being and sets out on a way of being directed more originally to the community's aim. The community dies and rises because the misdirected way of being passes out of being in the believer's decision while a new way of being comes into being. Self and community are a concordant discordance, yet to say that the self and community die and rise is not hyperbole. An actual way of being ceases to be, and a formerly unrealized way of being becomes actual practice—a way of being that is at once new (it could not be practiced before Christ) and yet more original (in retrospect we see that the community always aimed at it, though brokenly).

Can we make sense, finally, of Christ as one particular person in whom our community dies and rises? N. T. Wright makes a convincing case that this interpretation is possible for Paul because he understands "in Christ" to convey the people included in its king.[8] I doubt, though, that as a citizen of a democracy I can really grasp what it means for a people to be included in its king the way Paul intends. One way to recognize but transcend our difference from Paul on this point is to focus on a different but related Pauline theme: "The Christ" means the king of Israel, but it also means "the anointed of God." The better metaphor to apply in our context is not Christ the king but Christ as the one anointed with God's Spirit.

6.2 The Spirit of Christ in the Community of the Living and Dead in Christ

Bultmann's account of Paul's anthropology has now been corrected by the ontology of the self in community, securing the original goal to retrieve, without hyperbole, "I have been crucified with Christ" and "Christ lives in me." As a last step, to ground this correlation theologically calls for a theological account of interpretation in community. Paul can address us again in our interpretations because we live with him in the community of the living and dead in Christ, and because the Spirit of Christ speaks in our community's conversation.

6.2.1 Jürgen Moltmann and the Community of the Living and Dead in Christ

How might we today, like Paul, understand ourselves as a community that dies and rises in Christ? Here my thinking about community has been guided by Jürgen Moltmann's interpretation of Romans 14:9 ("For this end Christ died and lived again, that he might be Lord both of the dead and of the living"):

> In dying, Christ became the brother of the dying. In death, he be-
> came the brother of the dead. In his resurrection—as the one risen—
> he embraces the dead and the living, and takes them with him on
> his way to the consummation of God's kingdom. If I understand it
> rightly, this means that the dead are dead and not yet risen, but they
> are already "in Christ" and are with him on the way to his future.[9]

The community that dies and rises with Christ is a community of the living and the dead in Christ. The future this community testifies to, in witness to the resurrection, embraces the living, the suffering, and the dead. First, as the community of the living and dead in Christ, we are called to embrace our neighbor in Christ and all those of faith who—though not part of this community in present practice—are oriented in hope to this eschatological community in their own communities' stories. Second, we are called to attend especially to those suffering and dying others whose pain might be concealed by our present conversation. Finally, we are called to community with the dead. Surely we are one community with our own dead in Christ, that is, those who belong to our historical community; yet we are also one community in hope with all those "dead of faith." Thus one mark by which the eschatological community can be known is the embrace of all those of faith—the living, the dying, and the dead.

The traditional doctrine of purgatory seems to lead in this direction. What Moltmann finds commendable in the doctrine is "the idea of an enduring communion between the living and the dead in Christ, and of the community of Christ as a communion of the living and dead" (Moltmann, *Coming of God* 98). What he finds objectionable is that purgatory should be conceived as an expiatory community where the living intercede on behalf of the dead for sins that separate them from God. That separation, Moltmann worries, can only be healed by God's unconditional love. Yet elsewhere Moltmann acknowledges that expiation or atonement has three different human dimensions: toward the victim, the perpetrator, and the community.[10] Unless the Church is also an expiating community, how can these human dimensions of expiation enter the world so that the Church can say it bears the Spirit of Christ? In Moltmann's own terms, how is the Spirit of Christ to appear in the Church as at once "*the presence of Christ* among and in the victims of violence" and "*the atoning power* of Christ's substitution among and in the perpetrators" (Moltmann, *Coming of God* 143)? Elizabeth Johnson offers an example of a soul laboring after death, not for its own salvation but to mend the specific harms done in life. But where can the dead perform this labor except in a community of the living and the dead? Johnson says, "the community of sinful yet redeemed people of God extends not only across spatial boundaries to include those living in different lands at the present moment, but also extends across time boundaries to include those living in different historical periods."[11]

Thus a different way to understand expiatory community is that present members of the community accept responsibility for the consequences of actions initiated by past members; we can also accept imputed guilt if we can assert intelligibly that the dead speak in us again. As one community in Christ, we affirm and bring forward the attestations of spirit in our forebears; we also accept responsibility for and expiate the consequences of their misdirection. Such an act is partial in two ways. First, past suffering can never be made right without reestablishing the first-person perspective of the victim; second, the present community, like its former incarnation, does not escape the suspicion that the suffering other might continue to recede beneath the story we tell.

These two limits provide the protection Moltmann seeks from misunderstandings of expiation but do not eliminate expiation entirely from our relation to the dead. On one hand, no act of the present community can establish God's righteousness, which remains utter gift. On the other hand, in striving to let the community's dead and their victims speak in the present, members of the community do practice a kind of expiation—not with respect to the offense against the divine but with respect to the offense against other created beings. In these expiating individuals the community does not earn the healing of the divine love; but the community does make that healing love present in the world as the mark of the righteous community. Finally, an expiating community can assert the continuity of the community through potentially disastrous failures in practice by embracing, in retrospect, the perpetrator and victim in one community.

Yet perhaps in this retrieval the resurrection comes to look more like a practice among the living than a hope for the dead. What of the resurrected body? If selfhood appears against a ground at once potential and actual, then for the dead to be embodied in the eschatological future they must continue to have bodies now. Moltmann offers a suggestion:

> Death has to be seen as a transformation of the person's spirit, that is to say his or her Gestalt and life history; and this means the whole person. . . . The dead are no longer there as temporally limited and spatially restricted "contact persons," but we sense their presence whenever we become aware that we are living "before God"; and wherever we sense their presence, we feel the divine "wide space" which binds us together. (Moltmann, *Coming of God* 76–77)

I take this to mean that the dead are embodied at death in the eschatological body of Christ, and that the eschatological body of Christ is present in the world in the Church as the body of Christ. Yet I fear that Moltmann's thought comes dangerously close to collapsing the first-person perspective (at least in the case of the dead) into the community. Still, Paul seems to move in this direction in 2 Corinthians when he speaks of his own resurrection body in terms reminiscent of building the church (2 Cor. 5:1–5; see also 10:8, 12:19, 13: 10). At any rate, Moltmann does grant that hope of the resurrection is fulfilled only when each can affirm (first-person), "I shall again come back to my life, and in the light of God's grace and in the power of his mercy put right what has gone awry, finish what was begun, pick up what was neglected, forgive the trespasses, heal the hurts, and be permitted to gather up the moments of happiness and to transform mourning into joy" (Moltmann, *Coming of God* 117). We must preserve the first-person perspective and never reduce the resurrection to the community's practice. Most specifically, we experience community with the dead in worship, especially in the Eucharist and prayer. When we try to express this community with the dead outside the worship experience, perhaps the best we can do is to honor the regulative ideal to participate with the dead in our praxis.

6.2.2 Robert Jenson and the Spirit of Christ as the Subject of the Church's Conversation

The self in community journeys from the ethical aim to decisions in practice and back again where no norm guides certainly; the call of conscience testifies to an Other who calls the self forward on this journey. I am enjoined by other people (each a living body like me), by the community we all share and (so the story goes) by an Other who transcends the self and community.[12] I can follow Bultmann in characterizing this call as the encounter with the risen Lord, though I cannot agree that it is self-validating. But if the encounter is not self-validating, we must insist that genuine encounters with the risen Lord are borne in our community in an unbroken stream. As responsible members of this community, we assert that the Other who calls us on this journey is the world's one God and creator, identified in the story of the crucified and resurrected Christ of Israel. If the Christ event is God's decisive act to reveal God and the true human aim, then we bear the true human aim in our tradition and lived experience. Paul can address us again in the shared community of the living and dead in Christ, and we can assert that Paul's claims about the self are normative to the extent that this community realizes its goal to embrace others in their genuine alterity. It would be an understatement to remark that such claims, however well attested, are also subject to the most strenuous suspicion. Yet this suspicion is not imposed on the community from outside but arises out of its own ethical aim. Because we are perpetually on the way to embrace others who are unlike us in one community, we never fully grasp the eschatological Christ as who he is, nor do we fully know who we are—that is, who we will be at the end of our next encounter.

For Paul to address us again, one requirement is that we share one community, which is the community of the living and dead in Christ. But the notion of community cannot in itself ground an unbroken stream of encounters through time. So the claim that Paul speaks again because we share one community with him needs a supplement, namely, that the Spirit of Christ speaks in our community's conversation. The Spirit of Christ, as the subject of the community's conversation, is the unity of the community's experiences. Yet the Spirit of Christ, like the self, is disclosed in a dialectic of Same and Other. I survey this dialectic from two perspectives: a philosophical account of dialogue (Paul Ricoeur and Charles Taylor) and a theological account of Spirit (Robert Jenson).

By way of introducing the philosophical perspective, first I ask what could possibly decide between the Church's claim to represent the eschatological community and its interlocutors who reject that claim. Insofar as the claim is articulated within the Church's horizon, it might seem impossible to adjudicate the dispute because the interlocutors do not share the same background story. The problem is acute, however, not only when Christians encounter non-Christians but even when we try to join Paul's framework to ours. It is, of course, a commonplace that Christians live in a horizon where Paul's letters contribute to our understanding of community and self. But that is not enough to guarantee that our interpretations engage Paul in his alterity. First, how do we deal with readings of Paul that render his concerns alien to ours? If Paul's concerns are so different, are we truly in communion with him in our interpretations? Second, how can Scripture continue to challenge the Church in ways that might undermine our present understanding of community and self? That, recall, is the task Paul himself accepted on behalf of Israel demarcated by Torah. Both questions testify that we can and do become alienated from the historical conversation in our own community. Not only missionaries need to worry about how to justify the Church's ambition to apply its story normatively; the same problem faces us at the very core of our community and selves as historical.

Ricoeur and Taylor both agree that these differences cannot be adjudicated on appeal to a transcendental ego.[13] What they both press instead is open and uncoerced dialogue. But then is "true," as Richard Rorty says, just a compliment we pay to statements that meet our community's criteria?[14] Even if some variant of Paul's vision of the eschatological community "wins" at the end of a dialogue, acute problems remain. First, was it right that Paul's vision won? Or did raw power predetermine the outcome? Second, the original problem was that criteria appeared to be relative to communities. Has a sleight of hand now overcome this relativity by obliterating the other community and absorbing it into our own?

Ricoeur and Taylor redirect such general skeptical questions onto more concrete objections: Who has been overpowered? What is their claim on us? Although no closure can meet the most abstract skeptical challenges, we can always continue to affirm what is already disclosed and yet remain open to the next concrete challenge. Paradigmatically, what calls the community forward is its aim to embrace the suffering other who, as Jean-François Lyotard says, cannot come into phrases.[15] Yet the community disclosed in the itinerary of detours does not just throw a "new idiom" over the suffering other but struggles to embrace the other in one community, even at the cost of retelling its own story. Thus the ultimate criterion of suspicion is not the right to aesthetic play (the invention of a new idiom), but the desire to embrace in one community the suffering other who is systematically excluded from discourse. An ontology of the self in community attributes ontological density to what can only be glimpsed in retrospect at the end of such conflicts, that is, the self and other together in one community.

If the self revealed in Christ and carried in the community in Christ is in any sense normative, then this normativeness can only be known proleptically, partially, and under the sign of the cross. "Under the sign of the cross" means that its normativeness is asserted, yet what counts as satisfying that norm is always placed at risk in dialogue. The normative self is a reality only where the community's story is retold, over and over again, to embrace new forms of alterity. That does not mean that the continuity of the normative self is a narrative construction; rather, its continuity (which is real) can only be expressed in a story that is always up for discussion. Narrative expresses the real. As a community, we engage in an ongoing dialogue comparing reconstructions of the self in our own early strata with contemporary accounts of who we are as selves. At the same time, these accounts are put into dialogue with non-Christian understandings of the self.[16] The attempt to adjudicate these accounts within an appropriate story is the ongoing task we have inherited from Paul. In so doing, we gain a more authentic understanding of ourselves as historical and communal. At the same time, the story lends plausibility to the assertion that we approach the other (in this case, Paul) in his or her genuine alterity.

Thus far I have considered the continuity of experience from a philosophical perspective. How does this continuity appear from a theological perspective? The short answer is that the Church understands the Spirit of Christ to be the subject of its imaginative act to understand others in Christ, that is, to understand others in their genuine alterity as members of one eschatological community. As Jenson says,

> Every individual person has and is a spirit: this is his or her personal liveliness, as a "wind" that stirs that to which he or she directs personal energies. But also every community has a spirit, which is not a mere aggregate of members' spirits. . . . A community's spirit is the liveliness that blows through it, the freedom in which it is more than the sum of its parts because each member moves in the liberating impetus from all the others. . . . It is the church's founding miracle that her communal spirit is identically the Spirit that the personal God is and has.[17]

The subjectivity of the Spirit in the Church is "the Son's personal subjectivity as one who identifies himself to his people" (Jenson 175). If the Spirit of Christ is the subject of the Church's conversation, then the risen Lord is present in the Church for the world. Consequently, what the one who hears the kerygma meets is not just an authentic individual but a community, the body of Christ, in the proclaimer. That the Church is the body of Christ is *true* because truth is disclosed in a conversation that already participates in the eschatological future, and such a conversation is possible only where the divine Spirit is: Christ, the *logos*, gives the divine Spirit to the Church to enable its union with this eschatological person (Jenson 182). Because the risen Christ gives the divine Spirit to a historical community rooted in the life of the historical Jesus, there is no conflict between Spirit and historical structures: The Spirit of Christ is the subject of a community that lives in those very structures.

Here, then, is the theological account of the community's hope expressed in the self's journey from the ethical aim, through conflict, and back again where no norm guides certainly. Of course, Jenson might well object to matching his theology with an ontology of the self, as he says in one place,

> The transcendental viewpoint of those whose community is finally the church and only in the meantime other "public things" and that of those whose community is the latter only have the same abstract structure. To avoid God, modernity and its precursors posited a focus of consciousness that was itself this abstraction, the same for all by virtue of its pure formality. No such thing subsists. My life has originating focus either within the community of the church and the communities of the *libido dominandi* or within the latter communities only. (Jenson 2:99)

Yet in putting the ontology of the self at stake with the community's story, I express a similar reserve with respect to metaphysics: Any ontological account of selfhood must remain the correlate of a community. For all that, if the true aim of all human beings has been revealed in the risen Christ, then the community that lives by the Spirit of Christ can plausibly claim that the structure of the human disclosed in it exerts a normative claim. There is a danger in Jenson's account (though I do not claim he succumbs to it), namely, that if the self as the constituting pole of meaning should disappear altogether, then the community's story or the community itself (rather than the transcendental ego) might be taken as self-validating. But a community can only be held responsible in the selves it comprises. The assertion "the spirit lives *here*" can gesture to institutions, but only if it also gestures to actual persons in whom spirit is manifest. An ontology of the self in community memorializes this insight. Properly limited, such an ontology does not pose the opposite danger that worries Jenson, namely, that a predialogical self would be cut loose from its communal setting. Rather, the self and its community as correlates journey together from the ethical aim to conflicts in practice and back to the ethical aim where no norm guides certainly.

The assurance that the ethical aim expressed in our community is the true aim of all human beings can only be attested in the community's practice: Can our community embrace other peoples in their genuine alterity in one community without violence? We can never escape the possibility that we might be misguided (even radically so) in practices that we say instantiate this ethical aim. But we can hope that as a community and as individuals we are called forward by an Other who transcends the community toward universality. Because that call cannot be self-validating, we always have to gesture toward another in whom the Other appears. That was Paul's experience when he encountered the crucified and resurrected Christ; it is the experience he hoped his little communities would share as a portion of the Spirit of Christ; and it is our experience today of Christ and the Spirit in the ongoing life of the Church, historically instituted and enlivened by the Spirit of Christ.

When Paul retells his community's story, he recognizes that life this side of the eschaton is necessarily a struggle of flesh and spirit—there is no unambiguously righteous community. In spite of that, the divine Spirit has appeared in the world in a man, Jesus of Nazareth, who fulfills Israel's hope: He is the risen Christ. As the spirit of the risen Christ, the divine Spirit lives in our community, its structures, and our very selves. This Spirit brings the eschatological future into time. As the spirit of the crucified Christ, the Spirit enjoins us to put at risk our stories about that reality to embrace the silently suffering faithful who fall beneath our present understanding of "neighbor." The kerygma thus invites the proclaimer and hearer to each recognize the community disclosed the kerygma as her own community understood more originally and the Spirit of Christ as the true aim of the spirit in her community.

But who is the eschatological Christ? His story narrates the space where bids to tell the community's story are debated, yet his story is at stake in the debate. So we can never fully know what it means for the other of faith to be embraced by the eschatological Christ, for we do not finally know the eschatological Christ, nor can we even foresee how we ourselves might be changed by our encounters with others. We can hope that at the end of such encounters we will be able to retell the community's story. In so doing we let the kerygma be in our context what it was for Paul—namely, a story that identifies the self and its community as correlates but as the story of a particular man, Jesus, the crucified and risen Christ of Israel.

In proclaiming the story of this particular man, and in acting by his spirit, the Church can hope to claim that the aim disclosed in our community is the true human aim. Yet what we proclaim and how we act never escapes suspicion. For all that, the church exercises its own mode of suspicion, not predicated on the destruction of the cogito but on a more original grasp of the ethical aim to embrace the suffering other. The kerygma identifies the community in which the self and other meet in their genuine alterity in one community, but the community identified in the kerygma puts its own self-understanding at risk to let the suffering other come into phrases. Yet that risk never assumes the character of a radical skepticism because it is guided by actual encounters with genuine alterity. Such encounters are only possible in a community, but the identity of the community may be at stake in articulating the encounter. Theology so understood is mindful of Ricoeur's warning not to stand in where philosophy can no longer stand as a fundamental ground of selfhood. Here theology risks its own uncertainty, which St. Paul identifies as the struggle of flesh and Spirit.

Notes

CHAPTER I

1. All of these studies presuppose E. P. Sanders's *Paul and Palestinian Judaism: A Comparison of Patterns of Religion* (Minneapolis: Fortress Press, 1977). Dunn coins the phrase "new perspective" in "The New Perspective on Paul," *Bulletin of the John Rylands University Library of Manchester* 65 no. 2 (Spring 1983): 95–122. The three main figures I engage in the new perspective are James D. G. Dunn, N. T. Wright, and Terence Donaldson. For their respective positions see James D. G. Dunn, *The Theology of Paul the Apostle* (Grand Rapids: Eerdmans, 1998), 1–27 and 334–90; N. T. Wright, *The Climax of the Covenant: Christ and the Law in Pauline Theology* (Minneapolis: Fortress Press, 1993), 137–57 and 258–66; and Terence Donaldson, *Paul and the Gentiles: Remapping the Apostle's Convictional World* (Minneapolis: Fortress Press, 1997), 3–29. Wright's *What St. Paul Really Said: Was Paul of Tarsus the Real Founder of Christianity?* (Grand Rapids: Eerdmans, 1997) expresses his position in a less scholarly mode. Stephen Westerholm's *Perspectives Old and New on Paul: The "Lutheran" Paul and His Critics* (Grand Rapids: Eerdmans, 2004) is arguably one of the finest reviews to date of the positions for and against the new perspective and a penetrating critique in its own right. Westerholm's bibliography and summaries of the various positions have been invaluable to me. Among the authors Westerholm classes as alternatives to the new perspective, I have frequently consulted Frank Thielman, *Paul and the Law: A Contextual Approach* (Downers Grove: Intervarsity Press, 1994), and J. Louis Martyn, *Galatians: A New Translation with Introduction and Commentary* (New York: Doubleday, 1997).

2. Douglas Harink, *Paul among the Postliberals: Pauline Theology beyond Christendom and Modernity* (Grand Rapids: Brazos Press, 2003).

3. Paul Ricoeur, *Oneself as Another*, trans. Kathleen Blamey (Chicago: University of Chicago Press, 1992); originally published as *Soi-même comme un Autre* (Paris: Éditions du Seuil, 1990).

4. Martin Luther, *Galatians—1535*, trans. Jaroslav Pelikan, in *Luther's Works*, vol. 26 (Saint Louis: Concordia, 1963), 287.

5. See especially Wright, "*Christos* as 'Messiah' in Paul: Philemon 6," in *Climax*, 41–55. On the community of the living and dead in Christ see Jürgen Moltmann, *The Coming of God: Christian Eschatology*, trans. Margaret Kohl (London: SCM, 1996), 105.

6. Robert Jenson, *Systematic Theology*, 2 vols. (New York: Oxford University Press, 1997–99), 2:181.

7. Stephen Westerholm, *Israel's Law and the Church's Faith: Paul and his Recent Interpreters* (Grand Rapids: Eerdmans, 1988).

8. Sanders, *Paul and Palestinian Judaism*, 422.

9. Heiki Räisänen, *Paul and the Law* (Philadelphia: Fortress Press, 1983), 268.

10. See, for example, D. A. Carson, P. O'Brien, and M. Seifrid, eds., *Justification and Variegated Nomism*, 2 vols. (Grand Rapids: Baker Academic, 2001, 2004). Volume 1, *The Complexities of Second Temple Judaism* (2001) revisits the evidence for patterns of religion in Second Temple Judaism. Volume 2, *The Paradoxes of Paul* (2004), reexamines the letters of Paul. Other contributions in this vein include Mark A. Elliott, *The Survivors of Israel: A Reconsideration of the Theology of Pre-Christian Judaism* (Grand Rapids: Eerdmans, 2000); A. Andrew Das, *Paul, the Law and the Covenant* (Peabody, Mass.: Hendrickson, 2001); and Thomas R. Schreiner, *The Law and Its Fulfillment: A Pauline Theology of Law* (Grand Rapids: Baker, 1993).

11. Wright, *What St. Paul Really Said*, 125. See also Donaldson, *Paul and the Gentiles*, 165–86; Dunn, *Theology of Paul the Apostle*, 354–85.

12. Westerholm, *Perspectives*, 240.

13. See, for example, David Tracy, *The Analogical Imagination: Christian Theology and the Culture of Pluralism* (New York: Crossroad, 1981), 3–79.

14. Wright, *Climax*, 242; Dunn, *Theology of Paul the Apostle*, 355.

15. Dunn, *Theology of Paul the Apostle*, 143–50.

16. Thielman, *Paul and the Law*, 239–41.

17. Dunn, *Theology of Paul the Apostle*, 528.

18. Several authors have suggested that Paul's formulation of justification in Christ was intended for Gentiles while Jews continued to enjoy the benefits of the covenant with Abraham. See John Gager, *The Origins of Anti-Semitism: Attitudes toward Judaism in Pagan and Christian Antiquity* (New York: Oxford University Press, 1983); Lloyd Gaston, *Paul and the Torah* (Vancouver: University of British Columbia Press, 1987); and Stanley Stowers, *A Rereading of Romans: Justice, Jews and Gentiles* (New Haven, Conn.: Yale University Press, 1994).

19. Dunn is quite clear about the benefits of righteousness for the individual (see in particular *Theology of Paul the Apostle*, 385–89). I doubt Wright would deny any of this, though his rhetoric can sometimes seem reductive (see, e.g., *What St. Paul Really Said*, 124–25).

20. Westerholm, *Perspectives*, 286–96.

21. N. T. Wright, *Letter to the Romans*, in *The New Interpreter's Bible*, vol. 10 (Nashville: Abingdon Press, 2002), 473.

22. Richard Hays, *The Faith of Jesus Christ: An Investigation of the Narrative Substructure of Galatians 3:1–4:11* (Missoula: Scholars Press, 1983). For Dunn's dissent see Dunn, *Theology of Paul the Apostle*, 379–85, which includes relevant bibliography on both sides of the question.

23. Dunn, *Theology of Paul the Apostle*, 196, 383.

24. Sam K. Williams, *Jesus' Death as Saving Event: The Background and Origin of a Concept* (Missoula: Scholars Press, 1975), 54, 37–38; Wright, *Letter to the Romans*, 465–66, 473–74.

25. Martin Luther, "The Freedom of a Christian," trans. W. A. Lambert and Harold J. Grimm, in *Luther's Works*, vol. 31 (Philadelphia: Muhlenberg Press, 1957), 351, 368.

26. Martin Luther, "Two Kinds of Righteousness," trans. Lowell J. Satre, in *Luther's Works*, vol. 31, 293–306.

27. "Just as a bridegroom possesses all that is his bride's and she all that is his—for the two have all things in common because they are one flesh—so Christ and the Church are one spirit" (Luther, "Two Kinds of Righteousness," 297).

28. Luther, "Two Kinds of Righteousness," 305–306.

29. Luther, *Galatians—1535*, 289–90.

30. Martin Luther, "The Magnificat," trans. Jaroslav Pelikan and A. T. W. Steinhaeuser, in *Luther's Works*, vol. 21 (Philadelphia: Fortress Press, 1956), 339–42.

31. Martin Luther, "The Sacrament of the Body and Blood—Against the Fanatics," in *Martin Luther's Basic Theological Writings*, ed. Timothy F. Lull (Minneapolis: Fortress Press, 1989), 327–28.

32. Martin Luther, "Temporal Authority: To What Extent It Should Be Obeyed," in *Basic Theological Writings*, 665.

33. Luther, "Temporal Authority," 663.

34. Luther, *Galatians—1535*, 285.

35. Jean-François Lyotard characterizes the postmodern condition as "incredulity toward metanarratives," which are narratives that attempt to usher all discourses to their places in dialogue (Jean-François Lyotard, *The Postmodern Condition: A Report on Knowledge*, trans. Geoff Bennington and Brian Massumi [Minneapolis: University of Minnesota Press, 1984], xiii–xxv). The metanarrative that has most famously come into dispute is, of course, Enlightenment rationalism. Ricoeur describes the failure of the Cartesian cogito as a foundation for knowledge in *Oneself as Another*, 1–16. For a discussion of the self in postmodernity see Calvin O. Schrag, *The Self after Postmodernity* (New Haven, Conn.: Yale University Press, 1997), 1–9.

36. Fergus Kerr, *Theology after Wittgenstein*, 2nd ed. (London: SPCK, 1997), 3–27.

37. Stanley Hauerwas, "Agency: Going Forward by Looking Back," in *Christian Ethics: Problems and Prospects*, ed. Lisa S. Cahill and James F. Childress (Cleveland: Pilgrim Press, 1996), 189.

38. David Tracy, "Literary Theory and Return of the Forms for Naming and Thinking God in Theology," *Journal of Religion* 74, no. 3 (1994): 316.

39. Paul Ricoeur, "Heidegger and the Question of the Subject," in *The Conflict of Interpretations: Essays in Hermeneutics*, ed. Don Ihde (Evanston: Northwestern University Press, 1974), 223–35. Martin Heidegger, *Being and Time*, trans. John Macquarrie and Edward Robinson (San Francisco: Harper and Row, 1962). Don Ihde offers a clear discussion of the issues involved in joining hermeneutics and phenomenology in *Hermeneutic Phenomenology: The Philosophy of Paul Ricoeur* (Evanston: Northwestern University Press, 1971), 3–25. See also Henry Isaac Venema, *Identifying Selfhood: Imagination, Narrative, and Hermeneutics in the Thought of Paul Ricoeur* (New York: State University of New York Press, 2000), 28–37.

40. On Ricoeur's shift from ego to self, see Kathleen Blamey, "From the Ego to the Self: A Philosophical Itinerary," in *The Philosophy of Paul Ricoeur*, ed. Lewis Edwin Hahn (Chicago: Open Court, 1995), 571–603, esp. 591–600. For Ricoeur's account of Husserl's phenomenology, see *Husserl: An Analysis of his Phenomenology*, trans. Edward G. Ballard and Lester E. Embree (Evanston: Northwestern University Press, 1987), especially chapter 1, "Introduction: Husserl (1859–1938)," 3–13.

41. Blamey, "From the Ego to the Self," 590–91.

42. William Richardson suggests that Heidegger's later works undergo a reversal or *Kehre* (William J. Richardson, *Heidegger: From Phenomenology to Thought* [The Hague: Martinus Nijhoff, 1963], 209–99). It is a reversal from a more subjective perspective in *Being and Time* (a questioning from Dasein to Being) to an inquiry that starts from Being and can only reflect retrospectively about the being who inquires. Ricoeur emphasizes the continuity in Heidegger's work when it is conceived in terms of a hermeneutics of the "I am" (Ricoeur, "Heidegger and the Question of the Subject," 224, 234–35).

43. Ricoeur gives an account of Nietzsche's rejection of the cogito in *Oneself as Another*, 11–16.

44. Heidegger says that "a word, the forming of a name [establishes] in its Being a being that is opening itself up and preserves it in this open-ness, constriction, and constance" (Ricoeur's translation in "Heidegger and the Question of the Subject," 233; see Martin Heidegger, *An Introduction to Metaphysics*, trans. Ralph Manheim [New Haven, Conn.: Yale University Press, 1959], 172). Ricoeur takes this to mean that the being who speaks comes into existence with the same word in which Being enters language: The human being and Being are disclosed together. One may ask, then, "who" is called into being with the emergence of the word. No longer a first truth, the "I am" appears only at the end of the detour through analysis, namely, a hermeneutics of the "I am." Thus a "hermeneutics of the I am," Ricoeur concludes, "is not fundamentally changed from *Being and Time* to the last essays of Heidegger" ("Heidegger and the Question of the Subject," 234).

45. The term is a translation of Husserl's *Lebenswelt* (Ricoeur, *Husserl*, 138; see also Edmund Husserl, *Cartesian Meditations: An Introduction to Phenomenology*, trans. Dorion Cairns [Dordrecht: Kluwer Academic, 1995], especially chapter 5, "Fifth Meditation," 89–151).

46. The etymology of *aporia* is the Greek *a-* (privation) plus *poros* (passage). The concept appears frequently in Aristotle and is translated nicely as "impasse" by Joe Sachs, who offers the following explanation: "The word is often translated as 'diffi-

culty' or 'perplexity,' which are much too weak; it is only the inability to get past an impasse with one's initial presuppositions that forces the revision of a whole way of looking at things" (Joe Sachs, glossary in *Aristotle's Physics: A Guided Study* [New Brunswick, N.J.: Rutgers University Press, 1995], 248). An aporia is not an antinomy wherein two arguments of reason face one another but an impasse beyond which a given discourse cannot pass. At each such impasse, Ricoeur appeals to a new discourse to articulate the aporia (from linguistics to action theory, from action theory to narrative, from narrative to ethics). The new discourse does not replace the old, but the two proceed dialectically—the one leading into the aporia, and the other articulating it and then in turn, meeting its own aporias. Aporias thus promote the sort of open dialectic that characterizes Ricoeur's work (open, that is, in contrast to the sort of closed synthesis that characterizes the Hegelian dialectic).

47. Paul Ricoeur, *Freud and Philosophy: An Essay on Interpretation*, trans. Denis Savage (New Haven, Conn.: Yale University Press, 1970), 43.

48. Ricoeur, *Oneself as Another*, 3.

49. See Husserl, *Cartesian Meditations*, 83–88.

50. Ricoeur, *Oneself as Another*, 21.

51. Two other recent books that develop a theological understanding of selfhood in dialogue with Ricoeur's *Oneself as Another* have been especially helpful to me. Anthony C. Thiselton undertakes a postmodern reinterpretation of selfhood in dialogue with Ricoeur and Jürgen Moltmann (*Interpreting God and the Postmodern Self: On Meaning, Manipulation, and Promise* [Grand Rapids: Eerdmans, 1995]). On analogy with Trinitarian *perichoresis*, Thiselton offers an account of a self that transcends its facticity yet persists in relation to others (155–56). In David F. Ford's *Self and Salvation: Being Transformed* (Cambridge: Cambridge University Press, 1999), Ricoeur's *Oneself as Another* frames one discussion in a multisided conversation on selfhood involving Ricoeur, Emmanuel Levinas, and Eberhard Jüngel. The book develops Levinas's metaphor of the face to redescribe salvation. Ford's book is a deep and beautiful reflection on selfhood in a multidimensional Christian practice—in singing and liturgical life, in political engagement, and in Eucharistic feasting. The salvation that transforms the self is a communal salvation—participation in Christ is "the creation of a new place of love which is infinitely capacious" (119).

52. On correlates as mutually constituting conditions see Husserl, *Cartesian Meditations*, 91, and Ricoeur, *Husserl*, 138. On the method of correlation see David Tracy, *The Analogical Imagination: Christian Theology and the Culture of Pluralism* (New York: Crossroad, 1981), 79–81.

53. Such a genealogy might take as its starting point Charles Taylor's *Sources of the Self: The Making of the Modern Identity* (Cambridge, Mass.: Harvard University Press, 1989). Taylor's itinerary, however, travels from Plato to Augustine without reference to St. Paul.

CHAPTER 2

1. N. T. Wright, *The Climax of the Covenant: Christ and the Law in Pauline Theology* (Minneapolis: Fortress Press, 1993), 23.

2. Terence Donaldson, *Paul and the Gentiles: Remapping the Apostle's Convictional World* (Minneapolis: Fortress Press, 1997), 172.

3. Bruce J. Malina, *The New Testament World: Insights from Cultural Anthropology* (Louisville: Westminster/John Knox Press, 1993), 67.

4. Wright, *Climax*, 26.

5. N. T. Wright, *What St. Paul Really Said: Was Paul of Tarsus the Real Founder of Christianity?* (Grand Rapids: Eerdmans, 1997), 74.

6. See E. P. Sanders's *Paul and Palestinian Judaism: A Comparison of Patterns of Religion* (Minneapolis: Fortress Press, 1977), 221, 223. The Shekinah reference is from A. M. Goldberg, *Untersuchungen über die Vorstellung von der Schekhinah in der Frühen Rabbinischen Literatur, Studia Judaica; Forschungen zur Wissenschaft des Judentums*, vol. 5 (Berlin: De Gruyter, 1969), 385–99. As to Torah observance making one worthy to receive the Spirit, one second-century text says, "Heedfulness leads to cleanliness, and cleanliness leads to purity, and purity to abstinence, and abstinence leads to holiness, and holiness leads to humility, and humility leads to the shunning of sin, and the shunning of sin leads to saintliness, and saintliness leads to [the gift of] the Holy Spirit, and the Holy Spirit leads to the resurrection of the dead" (Mishna Sota 9:15; cited in John R. Levison, *The Spirit in First Century Judaism* [Leiden: Brill, 1997], 55).

7. Levison, *Spirit in First Century Judaism*, 79.

8. Robert W. Kvalvaag, "The Spirit in Human Beings in Some Qumran Non-Biblical Texts," in *Qumran between the Old and New Testaments*, ed. F. H. Cryer and T. L. Thompson (Sheffield: Sheffield Academic Press, 1998), 171.

9. See also Gordon Fee, *God's Empowering Presence: The Holy Spirit in the Letters of Paul* (Peabody, Mass.: Hendrickson Publishers, 1994), 914.

10. On the role of the Spirit in Paul's reading of the scripture, see Carol Kern Stockhausen, *Moses' Veil and the Glory of the New Covenant: The Exegetical Substructure of II Cor. 3,1–4, 6* (Rome: Editrice Pontificio Istituto Biblico, 1989), 146–50.

11. Donaldson, *Paul and the Gentiles*, 207, 211.

12. Wright, *Climax*, 25.

13. Donaldson, *Paul and the Gentiles*, 243.

14. Ibid., 284–92; Wright, *What St. Paul Really Said*, 26; and James D. G. Dunn, *The Theology of Paul the Apostle* (Grand Rapids: Eerdmans, 1998), 346–54. Although I find the arguments of Dunn, Wright, and Donaldson compelling, the hypothesis that Paul belonged to such a sect remains disputed among biblical scholars. For a contrary position see Sanders, *Paul and Palestinian Judaism*, 138.

15. Donaldson, *Paul and the Gentiles*, 286.

16. Donaldson enumerates the models as (1) Gentiles as aliens and strangers without hope, (2) natural law proselytes, (3) righteous Gentiles, and (4) the proselyte model (Donaldson, *Paul and the Gentiles*, 51–78). By elimination he argues that convictions presupposed in Paul's letters conflict on a fundamental level with each of the other models, leaving the proselyte model (293–307).

17. See Dunn, *Theology of Paul the Apostle*, 528.

18. Donaldson, *Paul and the Gentiles*, 295.

19. James D. G. Dunn, *Jesus and the Spirit: A Study of the Religious and Charis-*

matic Experience of Jesus and the First Christians as Reflected in the New Testament (London: SCM Press, 1975), 108.

20. Donaldson, *Paul and the Gentiles*, 91.

21. Dunn, *Theology of Paul the Apostle*, 722; Wright, *Climax*, 40; Donaldson, *Paul and the Gentiles*, 248.

22. Jean-François Lyotard, *The Differend: Phrases in Dispute*, trans. Georges Van Den Abbeele (Minneapolis: University of Minnesota Press, 1988), §23, 13.

23. Dunn, *Theology of Paul the Apostle*, 211. The Barth citation is from G. C. Berkouwer, *The Triumph of Grace in the Theology of Karl Barth* (Grand Rapids: Eerdmans, 1956), 135.

24. When he observes, for example, that "the sacrificial act was, as it were, God's legal justification for remitting due penalty" (Dunn, *Theology of Paul the Apostle*, 215).

25. The "man who rebels against his relation of creaturely dependence on God (which is what faith is) becomes subject to degenerative processes" (James D. G. Dunn, *Romans 1–8* [Dallas: Word Books, 1988], 55).

26. Dunn cites Pauline passages that convey the communal aspects of participation in Christ in *Theology of Paul the Apostle*, 402. The list is too large to reproduce here. These phrases encompass "the common privilege, experience and task of believers" (e.g., Rom. 15:30; Phil. 2:25) and "sharing in Christ's death and life" (e.g., Phil. 3:10).

27. See, for example, Donaldson, *Paul and the Gentiles*, 244–48.

28. Donaldson, *Paul and the Gentiles*, 245.

29. Wright, *Climax*, 141, 152.

30. See Dunn, *Theology of Paul the Apostle*, 362.

31. See Wright, *Climax*, 212.

32. Fee, *God's Empowering Presence*, 374.

33. Malina, *New Testament World*, 67.

34. Dunn, *Jesus and the Spirit*, 325.

35. Here I follow Wright's interpretation in *Climax*, 183–92.

36. Dunn argues in an earlier article that 2 Cor. 3:17 is an exegesis of Exodus 34:34 and that "Lord" (*kyrios*) refers to Yahweh (James D. G. Dunn, "The Lord Is the Spirit," *Journal of Theological Studies* 21 [1970]: 309–20; cited in Stockhausen, *Moses' Veil*, 130). Dunn's article is intended to rebut the identification of Christ and the Spirit in 2 Cor. 3:17.

37. Wright, *Climax*, 185.

38. Jesus was conceived through the power of the Spirit (Matt. 1:20; Luke 1:35), and the Spirit descends on him at his baptism (Matt. 3:13–17; Mark 1:9–11; Luke 3:21–22; John 1:33).

39. Dunn, *Romans 1–8*, 15.

40. Dunn, *Theology of Paul the Apostle*, 263. There is, for example, the Spirit's cry "Abba! Father!" (Rom. 8:14–17), which is probably a dominical saying. And the mark of the Spirit's inspiration is the confession "Jesus is Lord" (1 Cor. 12:3). Finally, Paul identifies the Spirit as "the Spirit of Christ" (Rom. 8:9) and "the Spirit of God's Son" (Gal. 4:6).

41. Dunn, *Theology of Paul the Apostle,* 263.

42. Of course, one must beware of reading Paul's position off what is apparently an early creedal formula; yet here Paul is certainly not citing a formula he disagrees with. At any rate, the formula is not incompatible with the claim that Jesus went to the cross anointed with the Spirit. See Dunn, *Romans 1–8,* 22–23.

43. Sam K. Williams, *Jesus' Death as Saving Event: The Background and Origin of a Concept* (Missoula: Scholars Press, 1975), 54, 37–38; N. T. Wright, *Letter to the Romans in the New Interpreter's Bible,* vol. 10 (Nashville: Abingdon Press, 2002), 465–66, 473–74.

44. Dunn, *Romans 1–8,* 170.

45. Stanislas Lyonnet and Léopold Sabourin, *Sin, Redemption, and Sacrifice: A Biblical and Patristic Study* (Rome: Editrice Pontificio Istituto Biblico, 1998), 165.

46. Wright, *What St. Paul Really Said,* 107.

47. Wright, *Letter to the Romans,* 475.

48. See Wright, *Climax,* 196–200, 217–19. Douglas Moo argues a similar point in his commentary, *The Epistle to the Romans* (Grand Rapids: Eerdmans, 1996), 423–31, esp. 430–31.

49. Dunn, *Romans 1–8,* 380–81.

50. Charles Taylor, "The Importance of Herder," in *Philosophical Arguments* (Cambridge, Mass.: Harvard University Press, 1995), 98.

51. See Dunn, *Theology of Paul the Apostle,* 224–25 and 502, for a brief introduction to the problem and relevant bibliography.

52. One scholar interprets Rom. 8:32 as an allusion to 2 Sam. 21:1–14. Whereas David does not spare the sons of Saul in making expiation for the Gibeonites killed by Saul, God does not spare his own son in making expiation for us. See Daniel R. Schwartz, "Two Pauline Allusions to the Redemption Mechanism of the Crucifixion," *Journal of Biblical Literature* 102, no. 2 (1983): 259–68. Schwartz admits that Paul could not possibly have hoped such an allusion would be recognized by his readers, but he counters that the alleged allusion to the Aqedah would also be difficult for a reader to pick up (267). Difficult, yes, but with Rom. 4 in the background at least possible. If Schwartz is right, Paul then crafts a statement in which the rhetorical force of the scriptural allusion is almost nil. That seems unlikely. It seems more likely, rather, that in both Rom. 4 and 8:32 Paul is reworking the Abraham story in telling Israel's story.

53. On the identification of the death in v. 4 and 9, see Dunn, *Romans 1–8,* 401.

54. Dunn argues that Paul's readers (and of course, Paul himself) would have been well aware of the extreme expressions of Jewish zeal (James D. G. Dunn, *Romans 9–16* [Dallas: Word Books, 1988], 595).

55. Although some have argued that the passage is inauthentic, it is present in all the early extant manuscripts, and a majority of scholars accept it as genuine. For a recent defense of its authenticity and relevant bibliography see Raymond Brown, *Death of the Messiah,* 2 vols. (New York: Doubleday, 1994), 1:378.

56. C. E. B. Cranfield, *A Critical and Exegetical Commentary on the Epistle to the Romans,* 2 vols. (London: T and T Clark, 1975), 2:556. Cranfield is citing Karl Barth,

Church Dogmatics, vol. 2, part 2, trans. G. T. Thomson (Edinburgh: T and T Clark, 1957), 278–79.

57. Moo, *Romans*, 437.

58. See Richard Hays, *The Faith of Jesus Christ: An Investigation of the Narrative Substructure of Galatians 3:1–4:11* (Missoula: Scholars Press, 1983), 249.

59. Katekrino, "condemn sinners to death or destruction" in Walter Bauer, William F. Arndt, F. Wilbur Gingrich, and Frederick Danker, *A Greek-English Lexicon of the New Testament and Other Early Christian Literature*, 2nd ed. rev. and aug. (Chicago: University of Chicago Press, 1979).

60. J. Louis Martyn, *Galatians: A New Translation with Introduction and Commentary* (New York: Doubleday, 1997), 325.

61. In Gal. 3:11 and 12 "Paul uses a midrashic rule that when two texts of Scripture contradict each other, a third text can resolve them" (Luke Timothy Johnson, *The Writings of the New Testament: An Interpretation* [Philadelphia: Fortress Press, 1986], 311).

62. Jürgen Moltmann, *The Coming of God: Christian Eschatology*, trans. Margaret Kohl (London: SCM, 1996), 93–96.

63. See Dunn, *Theology of Paul the Apostle*, 528.

64. Wright, *What St. Paul Really Said*, 146; Dunn, *Theology of Paul the Apostle*, 143.

65. Dunn, *Theology of Paul the Apostle*, 211.

66. Robert Jewett, *Paul's Anthropological Terms: A Study of their Use in Conflict Settings* (Leiden: E. J. Brill, 1971), 194.

67. Fee, *God's Empowering Presence*, 568 and 66.

68. Emphasis added. As "component" and "place of intersection," see Fee, *God's Empowering Presence*, 66; as "place of Spirit's habitation" see ibid., 338. Dunn, I think, is closer to Fee than Jewett in that although Dunn acknowledges that the human spirit may refer to the apportioned divine spirit (Dunn, *Theology of Paul the Apostle*, 77), Dunn's portrayal of the spirit as a "dimension of the person" and "the depths of the individual" seem closer to Fee's more individual interpretation.

69. Fee, *God's Empowering Presence*, 568 n. 285. Although Jewett's position gives difficulty with Rom. 8:16, it seems to me that Fee's position runs afoul of 1 Cor. 5:4. The idea of spirit as the apportioned divine spirit lends a certain realism to Paul's "when you and my spirit are assembled." Clearly Fee wants to affirm this realism (124–25). But if the spirit is a "component" of the ego (or a "place" within it), it is difficult to see how Paul's usage here is anything other than a figure of speech.

70. Judith Plaskow offers an account of what she calls communal personhood that joins feminist and Jewish understandings of personhood: "The knowledge that human beings are located in community is, of course, not limited to women; shared by many cultures, it is central to both Jewish theology and the Jewish social experience. If to be a woman is to absorb and wrestle with a cultural understanding of femaleness, so to be a Jew is to absorb the history of the Jewish people" (*Standing Again at Sinai: Judaism from a Feminist Perspective* [San Francisco: Harper and Row, 1990], 79).

71. Malina, *New Testament World*, 64.

72. James D. G. Dunn, *The Epistle to the Galatians* (Peabody, Mass.: Hendrickson, 1993), 145; Dunn, *Theology of Paul the Apostle*, 262; Wright, *Climax*, 45; Fee, *God's Empowering Presence*, 374.

73. Dunn, *Theology of Paul the Apostle*, 77; Fee, *God's Empowering Presence*, 66, 338; Wright, *Climax*, 45.

74. Dunn, *Theology of Paul the Apostle*, 410.

75. Bernd Jochen Hilberath suggests that to understand the Spirit as person we must appeal to a different sense of person, namely, "the ability of the one to be in or with the other" ("Identity through Self-Transcendence: The Holy Spirit and the Fellowship of Free Persons," in *Advents of the Spirit: An Introduction to the Current Study of Pneumatology*, eds. Bradford E. Hinze and D. Lyle Dabney [Milwaukee: Marquette University Press, 2001], 282).

76. Dunn, *Galatians*, 213.

77. Lyotard, *Differend*, §23, 13.

78. Alan F. Segal, *Paul the Convert: The Apostolate and Apostasy of Saul the Pharisee* (New Haven, Conn.: Yale University Press, 1990), 202.

79. Wright, *Climax*, 157–74.

CHAPTER 3

1. Charles Taylor, *Sources of the Self: The Making of the Modern Identity* (Cambridge, Mass.: Harvard University Press, 1989), see especially pp. 3–111 and 495–523.

2. Gareth Jones, *Bultmann: Towards a Critical Theology* (Cambridge: Blackwell, 1991).

3. Rudolf Bultmann, *Theology of the New Testament*, 2 vols., trans. Kendrick Grobel (New York: Charles Scribner and Sons, 1951).

4. Martin Heidegger, *Being and Time*, trans. John Macquarrie and Edward Robinson (San Francisco: Harper and Row, 1962).

5. The quote is from Albert Schweitzer, *The Quest of the Historical Jesus: A Critical Study of its Progress from Reimarus to Wrede* (Baltimore, Md.: Johns Hopkins University Press, 1998), 399.

6. I agree, rather, with New Testament scholars N. T. Wright and John J. Collins that apocalypse has as its referent the transcendent dimension of occurrences in space-time, not the destruction of space-time. See, for example, N. T. Wright, *The New Testament and the People of God* (Minneapolis: Fortress Press, 1992), 280–99 and *Jesus and the Victory of God* (Minneapolis: Fortress Press, 1996), 207–10. Wright's dialogue partner is Collins, for which see Collins, *The Apocalyptic Imagination: An Introduction to Jewish Apocalyptic Literature* (Grand Rapids: Eerdmans, 1998), 1–43, 256–80.

7. In *Being and Time* the existentiales are to Dasein as the categories are to being as substance. See *Being and Time* §9, 70.

8. See, for example, Martin Heidegger, *An Introduction to Metaphysics*, trans. Ralph Manheim (New Haven, Conn.: Yale University Press, 1959), 199–206.

9. The lecture that leads Bultmann to the God question "through phenomenol-

ogy to faith" (Jones, 101) is Heidegger's 1928 lecture "Phenomenology and Theology," in *Wegmarken*, Gesamtausgabe, vol. 9 (Frankfurt am Main: Klostermann, 1976).

10. See, for example, Martin Heidegger, "The Origin of the Work of Art," in *Martin Heidegger: Basic Writings*, ed. David Farrell Krell (New York: Harper and Row, 1977), 143–89.

11. See David Fergusson, *Bultmann* (London: Geoffrey Chapman, 1992), 115–16, 126–30.

12. For Jones's interpretation of Bultmann on sin, see his reference to "the willful turning in on oneself" (77) and his account of myth as inauthentic discourse (118–22).

13. Paul Ricoeur, *Oneself as Another*, trans. Kathleen Blamey (Chicago: University of Chicago Press, 1992), 341–56.

14. I acknowledge that I may well share Bultmann's Lutheranism on this point. See, for example, Martin Luther on Gal. 3:13 in *Galatians—1535*, trans. Jaroslav Pelikan, in *Luther's Works*, vol. 26 (Saint Louis: Concordia, 1963), 276–91. Ian Siggins rightly sees that the purpose of Luther's victory motif is "the assertion of Christ's all sufficiency" *in us*, not a "cosmic dualism" (Ian Siggins, *Martin Luther's Doctrine of Christ* [New Haven, Conn.: Yale University Press, 1970], 140).

15. On the translation of *das Man* as the They, see Heidegger, *Being and Time*, 149, note 1. Heidegger's attitude toward the They is expressed in *Being and Time*, §27, 163–68.

16. Bultmann observes that Paul employs various Jewish and Hellenistic categories to this end, namely, propitiatory sacrifice (Rom. 3:25), vicarious sacrifice (2 Cor. 15: 21; Rom. 8:3), redemption (Gal. 3:13), the death of the divinity in the mystery religions (Rom. 6:10), and gnostic myth (Phil. 2:6–11).

17. Rudolf Bultmann, "The Significance of the Historical Jesus for the Theology of Paul" (1929), in *Faith and Understanding*, trans. Robert W. Funk (London: SCM, 1969), 236.

18. Jürgen Moltmann, *The Coming of God: Christian Eschatology*, trans. Margaret Kohl (London: SCM, 1996), 7.

19. Rudolf Bultmann, *Jesus Christ and Mythology* (New York: Scribner's, 1958), 69.

20. Here I follow the critique in Fergusson, *Bultmann*, 116 and 126–30. See also James F. Kay, *Christus Praesens: A Reconsideration of Rudolf Bultmann's Christology* (Grand Rapids: Eerdmans, 1994), 125–73.

21. Robert Jenson, *Systematic Theology*, 2 vols. (New York: Oxford University Press, 1997–99), 1:169.

22. Kathleen Blamey, "From the Ego to the Self: A Philosophical Itinerary," in *The Philosophy of Paul Ricoeur*, ed. Lewis Edwin Hahn (Chicago: Open Court, 1995), 587.

23. N. T. Wright, *What St. Paul Really Said: Was Paul of Tarsus the Real Founder of Christianity?* (Grand Rapids: Eerdmans, 1997).

24. Hans-Georg Gadamer, *Truth and Method*, 2nd ed. (New York: Continuum Publishing, 1989), 300–307.

25. In the following remarks I am indebted to conversations with Professor Pol Vandevelde at Marquette University. See Pol Vandevelde, "A Pragmatic Critique of Pluralism in Text Interpretation," *Metaphilosophy* 36, no. 4 (2005): 501–21. See also Kevin Vanhoozer, *Is There a Meaning in this Text: The Bible, the Reader, and the Morality of Literary Knowledge* (Grand Rapids: Zondervan, 1998), especially chapter 5, "Resurrecting the Author: Meaning as Communicative Action," 201–81. I take Vanhoozer's notion of resurrecting the author quite seriously here and in chapter 6. Vanhoozer analyzes the public communicative action of the author to ask "Is anybody there?" (230). Vanhoozer offers, on analogy with the mediation of Christ's presence spiritually in the Lord's Supper, that the "author's 'spirit' and thoughts are really 'exhibited' by the text, considered as a kind of 'sacrament'" (240). Though I agree with Vanhoozer that we can and must assert the truth of our claims against a shared background, I attempt to bring to thematic clarity, through a study of Paul's encounter with Christ, the enormous cost a community may bear when such a background is called into question.

26. Terence Donaldson, *Paul and the Gentiles:Remapping the Apostle's Convictional World* (Minneapolis: Fortress Press, 1997).

27. Jürgen Habermas, "What Is Universal Pragmatics?" in *Communication and the Evolution of Society*, trans. Thomas McCarthy (Boston: Beacon Press, 1979), 1–68. Also see Jürgen Habermas, "Discourse Ethics," in *Moral Consciousness and Communicative Action*, trans. Christian Lenhardt and Shierry Weber Nicholsen (Cambridge, Mass.: MIT Press, 1990), 43–115, esp. 58–60.

28. Habermas's strong claim is tied to a complex empirical research program. For a cogent exposition and critique of this empirical program see Thomas McCarthy, "Reason and Rationalization: Habermas's 'Overcoming' of Hermeneutics," in *Ideals and Illusions: On Reconstruction and Deconstruction in Contemporary Critical Theory* (Cambridge, Mass.: MIT Press, 1993), 127–51.

29. David Tracy, *The Analogical Imagination: Christian Theology and the Culture of Pluralism* (New York: Crossroad, 1981), 3–47.

30. Ricoeur notes a number of ways in which the self is structured by its social encounters. There are social structures that enable the self to become human (*Oneself as Another*, 254); the universals come about in actual communities and yet transcend their origins (287–90); the morality to which autonomy corresponds is sedimented on analogy with court law (276–80). In all of these dimensions, the I exists as a human self only within structures that are given to it. Similarly, Johann Baptist Metz points out that Kant's autonomous I presupposes certain empowering social structures that render autonomy an unrealized goal in much of the world. See Metz, *Faith and History in Society: Toward a Practical Fundamental Theology*, trans. David Smith (New York: Seabury Press, 1980), 54. That these realities are relative to social structures does not a priori rule out their normativeness, which case Ricoeur makes in *Oneself as Another* 287–90.

31. See, for example, Jenson, *Systematic Theology*, 2:181. I explore the connection between my account of the self in community and Jenson's pneumatology in chapter 6.

32. Ricoeur, *Oneself as Another*, 23.

33. Paul Ricoeur, "Preface to Bultmann," in *Essays on Biblical Interpretation*, ed. Lewis S. Mudge (Philadelphia: Fortress, 1980), 49–73.

34. Paul Ricoeur, "Heidegger and the Question of the Subject," in *Conflict of Interpretations: Essays in Hermeneutics*, ed. Don Ihde (Evanston, Ill.: Northwestern University Press, 1974), 234.

CHAPTER 4

1. Paul Ricoeur, *Oneself as Another*, trans. Kathleen Blamey (Chicago: University of Chicago Press, 1992).

2. Ricoeur characterizes *body* and *person* as two sorts of basic particulars with reference to Peter Strawson, *Individuals* (London: Methuen, 1957). See Ricoeur, *Oneself as Another*, 30–33.

3. Ricoeur interacts here with Donald Davidson, *Essays on Actions and Events* (Oxford: Clarendon Press, 1980).

4. On Kant's third antinomy, see Immanuel Kant, *Critique of Pure Reason*, trans. Norman Kemp Smith (New York: St. Martin's Press, 1965), 409–15.

5. As something attested, Ricoeur compares this power to act to Kant's fact of reason, or the consciousness of freedom. That is not to say that Ricoeur follows Kant in positing some sort of noumenal realm. Rather, for Ricoeur, the consciousness of freedom, and the even more basic power to act, testify to the self. On Kant's fact of reason, see Immanuel Kant, *Critique of Practical Reason*, trans. Lewis White Beck (New York: Macmillan, 1993), 43–52.

6. Derek Parfit, *Reasons and Persons* (Oxford: Oxford University Press, 1986).

7. My discussion follows the account in Ricoeur, *Oneself as Another*, 125–39. Ricoeur refers there to John Locke, *An Essay Concerning Human Understanding* (New York: World Publishing, 1964) and David Hume, *A Treatise on Human Nature* (New York: Penguin Books, 1969).

8. Parfit, *Reasons and Persons*, 211.

9. Ricoeur, *Oneself as Another*, 142. *Emplotment* is a neologism used by Ricoeur's translators to translate the French *mise en intrigue*. *Emplotment* means, quite literally, to put into plot discordant events such that the plot discloses these events, retrospectively, as a discordant concordance. See Paul Ricoeur, "Emplotment: A Reading of Aristotle's Poetics," chapter 2 in *Time and Narrative*, vol. 1, trans. K. McLaughlin and D. Pellauer (Chicago: University of Chicago Press, 1984), 1:31–51. In *Oneself as Another* Ricoeur transfers the notion of emplotment from events to characters.

10. Ricoeur, *Time and Narrative*, 1:52–87. For an analysis of Ricoeur's use of these terms in theological hermeneutics, see Mark I. Wallace, *The Second Naiveté: Barth, Ricoeur, and the New Yale Theology*, 2nd ed. (Macon, Ga.: Mercer University Press, 1995), 56, 69.

11. Alasdair MacIntyre, *After Virtue: A Study in Moral Theory* (Notre Dame, Ind.: University of Notre Dame Press, 1984), 190–209.

12. Here Ricoeur acknowledges his debt to Hannah Arendt's distinction between

power in common and domination in Hannah Arendt, *Crisis of the Republic* (New York: Harcourt Brace Jovanovich, 1972), 143.

13. For Kant's deduction of the feeling of respect for the moral law see Kant, *Critique of Practical Reason*, 75–92. Kant is at great pains to show how the feeling of respect can arise out of reason alone, giving rise to a fault line through the subject's faculty of desiring that parallels the fault line through the subject's faculty of self-rule.

14. See Immanuel Kant, *Religion within the Limits of Reason Alone*, trans. Theodore M. Greene and Hoyt H. Hudson (New York: Harper and Row, 1960), 15–39.

15. On Hegel's *Sittlichkeit* see Charles Taylor, *Hegel* (Cambridge: Cambridge University Press, 1997), 376–78.

16. Here I summarize Ricoeur's discussion of imputability, responsibility and recognition in Ricoeur, *Oneself as Another*, 291–96.

17. In *Time and Narrative* Ricoeur says that "every speech act (or every act of discourse) commits the speaker and does so in the present" (3:232). He adds that "if every-speech act implicitly commits its speaker, some types do so explicitly. This is the case with 'commissives,' for which the promise is the model" (3:233). Here Ricoeur speaks of commitment to an interlocutor rather than involvement in a community as is my focus. "Speech act" and "discourse" used in the way Ricoeur does here may invite an overly linguistic sense of action. Rather, I would include under the rubric of "involvements" more mundane actions like the example given in the text (eating with a fork). At any rate, here Ricoeur allows that one is made responsible by acts that do not attain the explicit level of commitment characteristic of promising.

18. Ricoeur, *Time and Narrative*, 1:74–75.

19. Jean-François Lyotard, *The Postmodern Condition: A Report on Knowledge*, trans. Geoff Bennington and Brian Massumi (Minneapolis: University of Minnesota Press, 1984), xxiii–xxv, 66.

20. Ricoeur acknowledges elsewhere that communities, like selves, are identified in narratives (Ricoeur, *Time and Narrative*, 3:246). Moreover, he says that "it was in telling these [biblical] narratives taken to be testimony about the founding events of its history that biblical Israel became the historic community that bears this name" (3:248). Yet while allowing that a community and a self are both identified in a narrative, Ricoeur never takes as a theme the relation between these two sorts of narrative. Might the individual's story be at stake in retelling the story of the community? Might the community's narrative be at stake in retelling the individual's story?

21. Ricoeur, *Oneself as Another*, 320; Jean-François Lyotard, *The Differend: Phrases in Dispute*, trans. Georges Van Den Abbeele (Minneapolis: University of Minnesota Press, 1988), 13. Also worth noting in this context is Ricoeur's notion of a "social imagination" that redeploys elements of the social world (Paul Ricoeur, "Ideology and Utopia," in *From Text to Action*, trans. Kathleen Blamey and John B. Thompson [Evanston, Ill.: Northwestern University Press, 1991], 308–25). Ricoeur thus accounts for the possibility of reconfiguring the social world, yet without taking narratives that identify communities as a theme, he does not adequately account for the potential cost of such a reconfiguration as a shift in the identity of a community.

22. Ricoeur links the desire of the individual to the spirit in a community in a

provocative way in an earlier article when he says that "the task of a philosophical anthropology after Freud is to pose this problem in ever more rigourous terms and to resolve it in a synthesis which satisfies both the Freudian *economics* of desire and the Hegelian *teleology* of spirit" (Paul Ricoeur, "The Question of the Subject: The Challenge of Semiotics," in *The Conflict of Interpretations: Essays in Hermeneutics*, ed. Don Ihde [Evanston, Ill.: Northwestern University Press, 1974], 245).

23. Hans-Georg Gadamer, *Truth and Method*, 2nd ed. (New York: Continuum, 1989), 300–307.

24. What I say here is presupposed in Ricoeur's mediation between universalism and contextualism (*Oneself as Another*, 283–91). Perhaps in drawing primarily on Habermas rather than Karl-Otto Apel for an account of communicative reason, Ricoeur may underplay the connection between communication and a community of discourse. Consider, for example, his observation that "only a real discussion, in which convictions are permitted to be elevated above conventions, will be able to state, at the end of a long history yet to come, which alleged universals will become universals recognized by 'all the persons concerned' (Habermas), that is, by the 'representative persons' (Rawls) of all cultures" (290). Insofar as such a discussion recognizes the "representative persons of all cultures," does it not itself appear in a space between cultures that implies some sort of shared community? For Apel's account of the communication community see Karl-Otto Apel, "Transcendental Semiotics and the Paradigms of First Philosophy," in *From a Transcendental-Semiotic Point of View*, ed. Marianna Papastephanou (Manchester: Manchester University Press, 1998), 43–63.

CHAPTER 5

1. Paul Ricoeur, *Oneself as Another*, trans. Kathleen Blamey (Chicago: University of Chicago Press, 1992), 297–99.

2. The benefits of placing the self under the traditional heading of *ousia* are not altogether lost insofar as for Aristotle the distance appears to collapse between the *dunamis-energeia* pair and being as *ousia*. That is, "nothing can be said to be potential without reference to something said to be real, in the sense of actual, completed" (Ricoeur, *Oneself as Another* 305). Ricoeur never considers the self as substance, perhaps presupposing the critique in Heidegger's *Being and Time* (Martin Heidegger, *Being and Time*, trans. John Macquarrie and Edward Robinson [San Francisco: Harper and Row, 1962], §25, 149–53). The question remains to what extent an ontology of substance could support the double dialectic of *idem* and *ipse*, the same and the other. On the possibility of an ontology of the self as substance that admits relationality into the constitution of selfhood see W. Norris Clarke, *Person and Being* (Milwaukee: Marquette University Press, 1993). Certainly we are allowed to regard substance (Clarke) and potentiality-in-act (Ricoeur) as alternative models of selfhood. One can compare what is concealed and what is disclosed in each model. Note that Ricoeur is not opposed to an appropriation of Aristotelian *ousia* so much as the "substantialism of the tradition" (305).

3. Ricoeur, *Oneself as Another*, 316; Benedict Spinoza, *Ethics* in *The Collected Works of Spinoza*, vol. 1, trans. and ed. Edwin Curley (Princeton, N.J.: Princeton University Press, 1985), IIIP6, 498.

4. "Welcome indeed the thinker who would be able to carry the 'Spinozist' reappropriation of Aristotelian *energeia* to a level comparable to that now held by the 'Heideggerian' reappropriations of Aristotelian ontology" (Ricoeur, *Oneself as Another* 317).

5. Here I follow Ricoeur's analysis of Husserl in *Oneself as Another*, 322–29 and 331–35. For Husserl's own account of the flesh, see Edmund Husserl, "Fifth Meditation," in *Cartesian Meditations: An Introduction to Phenomenology*, trans. Dorion Cairns (Dordrecht: Kluwer Academic, 1995), 89–151. For a more detailed account by Ricoeur, see his *Husserl: An Analysis of his Phenomenology*, trans. Edward G. Ballard and Lester E. Embree (Evanston, Ill.: Northwestern University Press, 1987), especially chapter 5, "Husserl's Fifth Meditation," 115–43, and chapter 7, "Kant and Husserl," 175–202.

6. For a contrary opinion, see Lyotard's rejection of the possibility of making sense of the events at Auschwitz (Jean-François Lyotard, *The Differend: Phrases in Dispute*, trans. Georges Van Den Abbeele [Minneapolis: University of Minnesota Press, 1988], §§155–60, 97–106).

7. Ricoeur brings the two accounts into conversation in *Oneself as Another*, 329–41. For Husserl's account, see the works already referenced, namely, Husserl, "Fifth Meditation," and Ricoeur, "Husserl's Fifth Meditation" and "Kant and Husserl." For Levinas's account see Emmanuel Levinas, "The Face Speaks," in *Totality and Infinity: An Essay on Exteriority*, trans. Alphonso Lingis (Pittsburgh: Duquesne University Press, 1969); *Time and the Other*, trans. Richard A. Cohen (Pittsburgh: Duquesne University Press, 1987); and *Otherwise than Being, or, Beyond Essence*, trans. Alphonso Lingis (Pittsburgh: Duquesne University Press, 1998).

8. Friedrich Nietzsche, *On the Genealogy of Morals*, trans. Walter Kaufmann and R. J. Hollingdale (New York: Vintage Books, 1967).

9. Heidegger, *Being and Time*, §§57–60, 319–48.

10. For Heidegger the call of conscience issues *from* Dasein *to* Dasein and yet *says* nothing—it is a silence (*Being and Time*, §57, 319–25). Notwithstanding, the call evinces a certain superiority insofar as it "comes *from* me and yet *from beyond me and over me*" (Ricoeur, *Oneself as Another*, 348).

11. For Heidegger, the human is Dasein (literally "being there," or "the there being") insofar as an analysis of Dasein, who is characterized by an unthematized understanding of Being, prepares the way for an analysis of Being as such (*Being and Time* §5, 39).

12. Nor, Ricoeur concludes, is there any help from Heidegger's link between conscience and resoluteness, namely, that as intending to be-a-whole in the face of my own inevitable death I "want to have a conscience." Resoluteness appears in an analysis of the phenomenon of Dasein's intention to be-a-whole played out against the backdrop of its certain death: "This reticent self-projection upon one's ownmost Being-guilty, in which one is ready for anxiety—we call 'resoluteness' " (Heidegger, *Being and Time*, §60, 343; Ricoeur, *Oneself as Another*, 350). Ricoeur observes that "cut off from the demands of others and from any properly moral determination, resolute-

ness remains just as indeterminate as the call to which it seems to reply" (*Oneself as Another* 350).

13. The notion of conscience as a dialogue of the self with itself is perhaps clearer in a companion piece to the unpublished theological reflections that were part of the Gifford lectures but not part of *Oneself as Another*. (Ricoeur accounts for this deliberate omission in *Oneself as Another* 23–25.) This companion piece was published as "The Summoned Subject in the School of the Narratives of the Prophetic Vocation," in Paul Ricoeur, *Figuring the Sacred: Religion, Narrative, and Imagination*, ed. Mark I. Wallace, trans. David Pellauer (Minneapolis: Fortress Press, 1995), 262–75. Where Ricoeur speaks in *Oneself as Another* of the receptiveness of the self to the voice of the master of justice, here he says, with respect to the particular Christian paradigm, that the "christomorphic self is grafted" onto conscience as "the dialogue of the self with itself" (271). Ricoeur concludes: "In this graft, the two living organs are changed into each other: on the one side, the call of the self to itself is intensified and transformed by the figure that serves as its model and archetype; on the other side, the transcendent figure is internalized by the moment of transformation that transmutes it into an inner voice" (271).

14. Ricoeur, "The Summoned Subject," 274.

15. See Paul Ricoeur, "Hope and the Structure of Philosophical Systems," in *Figuring the Sacred*, 203–17.

16. For an account of Spinoza's notion of *conatus* see Edwin Curley, *Behind the Geometrical Method: A Reading of Spinoza's* Ethics (Princeton, N.J.: Princeton University Press, 1988), 107–16.

17. Philip Clayton offers a critique of Spinoza's *Ethics* considered as a pantheistic articulation of God's being in *The Problem of God in Modern Thought* (Grand Rapids: Eerdmans, 2000), 387–441.

18. "For singular things are modes by which God's attributes are expressed in a certain and determinate way (by IP25C), i.e., (by IP34), things that express, in a certain and determinate way, God's power, by which God is and acts" (Spinoza, *Ethics*, IIIP6, demonstration, 499).

19. Spinoza "identified God with Nature, not conceived as the totality of things, but conceived as the most general principles of order exemplified by things" (Curley, *Behind the Geometrical Method*, 42). See also Clayton, *The Problem of God*, 438–39.

20. Clayton, *The Problem of God*, 397–99, 425.

21. Clayton argues (or rather, adduces Friedrich Jacobi's argument) that Spinoza's concept of an absolutely transcendent unity of all things is empty (*The Problem of God* 420–22).

22. On Ricoeur's recommendation of Kantian hope over Hegelian absolute knowledge, see Ricoeur, "Hope and the Structure of Philosophical Systems."

23. For an account of the role of the transcendental ego in phenomenology, see Husserl, "Second Meditation," in *Cartesian Meditations*, §12, 27–29. See also Paul Ricoeur, "A Study of Husserl's *Cartesian Meditations*, I–IV," in *Husserl*, 82–115.

24. Ricoeur, *Oneself as Another*, 322–29 and 331–35. For Husserl's own account of the constitution of the alter ego in the ego see Husserl, "Fifth Meditation"; see also Ricoeur, "Husserl's Fifth Meditation," and "Kant and Husserl."

25. Hans-Georg Gadamer, *Truth and Method*, 2nd ed. (New York: Continuum, 1989), 300–307.

26. For Ricoeur's perspective on our relation to persons in the community's past see Paul Ricoeur, *Time and Narrative*, vol. 3, trans. K. McLaughlin and D. Pellauer (Chicago: University of Chicago Press, 1988), 3:228–29.

27. Ricoeur, "Hope and the Structure of Philosophical Systems," 210.

28. Ricoeur states explicitly that he has shifted the focus of Hegel's *Sittlichkeit* back to Aristotelian *phronēsis* (*Oneself as Another*, 257, 259, 261, 273, 285, and 290).

29. The following quotes are from Ricoeur, "Philosophy and Religious Language," in *Figuring the Sacred*, 35–47.

30. See, for example, Paul Ricoeur, "The Logic of Jesus, the Logic of God," in *Figuring the Sacred*, 279–83. "Perhaps you will ask how it is possible for us, in our day, to live according to this logic of superabundance . . . what we can do is give some signs of this new economy" (283). Ricoeur offers as examples efforts to reconfigure the penal system and the market economy. These would be, Ricoeur says, "concrete signs that it is asked of us to give today according to the logic of Jesus" (283).

31. Ricoeur, "Naming God," in *Figuring the Sacred*, 235.

32. Ricoeur, "The Logic of Jesus," 283.

33. On interpretation in the church see Paul Ricoeur, "The 'Sacred' Text and the Community," in *Figuring the Sacred*, 68–72. On the relation of a general and particular hermeneutics, see Ricoeur, "Philosophy and Religious Language," 46–47.

34. Thus Ricoeur says that "it is only in listening to this book to the very end, *as one book among many*, that we can encounter it as the word of God" (Ricoeur, "Philosophy and Religious Language," 45, emphasis added). Or again, "the Christian life is a wage and a destiny, and those who take it up are not led by their confession either to assume a defensive position or to presume a superiority in relation to every other form of life, because *we lack criteria of comparison capable of dividing among rival claims*" (Ricoeur, "The Summoned Subject," 263, emphasis added).

35. Bernard Dauenhauer cautions that in Ricoeur's political thought "there is no vanguard position or group that can legitimately claim the right to pick out which putative human rights are genuine and to specify just what they entail" (Bernard P. Dauenhauer, *Paul Ricoeur: The Promise and Risk of Politics* [Lanham, Md.: Rowman and Littlefield Publishers, 1998], 289). Dauenhauer continues, "to practice responsible politics, one must commit oneself to the historical community to which one belongs as a community that is positively worthwhile. But at the same time, one must be prepared to criticize it in the name of a peace that is global and lasting rather than merely local and self-serving" (289–90). Once again, though, the space in which the self and other meet is anonymous. What both Dauenhauer and Ricoeur miss by not acknowledging a community's legitimate ambition to narrate this space is the potential cost of such a conversation for the community's identity. I acknowledge the opposite danger, namely, that such a narration might mask an attempt to dominate others (the community as vanguard of the future). Yet in Paul's perspective, embracing the other (the crucified and resurrected Christ) in one community called his own community's story into question. The lesson of Paul's experience is that the community in

Christ must regard simultaneously its ambition to tell its story as the one true story of the world and its repeated failures to embrace others in their genuine alterity.

36. Ricoeur, "Philosophy and Religious Language," 45–46.

37. Ricoeur, "Naming God," 231.

38. See Ricoeur, "Philosophy and Religious Language," 45, and Ricoeur, "The Summoned Subject," 263.

CHAPTER 6

1. See Gareth Jones, *Bultmann: Towards a Critical Theology* (Cambridge: Blackwell, 1991), 163–75.

2. Ibid., 168 and 174.

3. In *Soi-même comme un Autre* (*Oneself as Another*) Ricoeur translates *Körper* as *le corps* (body) and *Leib* as *le chair* (flesh) (Paul Ricoeur, *Oneself as Another*, trans. Kathleen Blamey [Chicago: University of Chicago Press, 1992]; originally published as *Soi-même comme un Autre* [Paris: Éditions du Seuil, 1992]). To avoid confusion with the Pauline "flesh" (*sarx*) I have chosen in this chapter to follow David Carr's translation of *Leib* as "living body" (see, for example, Edmund Husserl, *The Crisis of the European Sciences and Transcendental Phenomenology*, trans. David Carr [Evanston, Ill.: Northwestern University Press, 1970], 106).

4. See also, for example, Gal. 2:20; Gal. 6:11–12; 2 Cor. 4:7–12; Phil. 3:10.

5. See Jean-François Lyotard, *The Differend: Phrases in Dispute*, trans. Georges Van Den Abbeele (Minneapolis: University of Minnesota Press, 1988), §§47–58, 32–40.

6. Rudolf Bultmann, *Theology of the New Testament*, 2 vols., trans. Kendrick Grobel (New York: Charles Scribner and Sons, 1951), 1:256–57.

7. "If a partial or complete *apokatastasis* of those outside the people of God is to take place, it can only be by an eschatological address of the gospel, about the circumstances of which it would be entirely useless to make guesses" (Robert Jenson, *Systematic Theology*, 2 vols. [New York: Oxford University Press, 1997–99], 2:364). For a more thorough account of the this-worldly orientation of all peoples to this telos, see J. A. DiNoia, *The Diversity of Religions: A Christian Perspective* (Washington, D.C.: Catholic University of America Press, 1992), 65–109. I recommend a greater emphasis on the transformation that may appear in our own community through dialogue: We come to know better who Christ is in dialogue with others, and this can potentially transform our own understanding of the community that comes to embrace self and other.

8. See chapter 2 of this book and N. T. Wright, "Christos as 'Messiah' in Paul: Philemon 6," in *Climax of the Covenant: Christ and the Law in Pauline Theology* (Minneapolis: Fortress Press, 1993), 41–56.

9. Jürgen Moltmann, *The Coming of God: Christian Eschatology*, trans. Margaret Kohl (London: SCM, 1996), 105.

10. Jürgen Moltmann, *The Spirit of Life: A Universal Affirmation*, trans. Margaret Kohl (Minneapolis: Fortress Press, 1993), 133.

11. Elizabeth A. Johnson, *Friends of God and Prophets: A Feminist Theological Reading of the Communion of Saints* (New York: Continuum, 1998), 65.

12. I say this without denying the possibility that this Other can enjoin us in other created beings as well. Johnson, for example, hopes that the communion of saints can be amplified "to include other living creatures, ecosystems, and the whole natural world to itself" (Johnson, *Friends of God and Prophets*, 240).

13. See, for example, Ricoeur, *Oneself as Another*, 286–90, or Charles Taylor, "Explanation and Practical Reason," in *Philosophical Arguments* (Cambridge, Mass.: Harvard University Press, 1995), 34–61.

14. Richard Rorty, "Pragmatism and Philosophy," in *After Philosophy: End or Transformation*, ed. Kenneth Baynes et al. (Cambridge, Mass.: MIT Press, 1989), 31.

15. Lyotard, *Differend*, §23, 13.

16. See, for example, J. A. DiNoia, "The Providential Diversity of Religions," chapter 3 in *The Diversity of Religions*, 65–109. On the whole I agree with DiNoia's project to shift Karl Rahner's anonymous Christianity into an eschatological key, which he calls a "prospective rather than hidden affiliation with the Christian community" (106). I wonder, though, if DiNoia's account is sufficiently sensitive to the sort of events that might transform our own articulations of the human aim. What is vital to the identity of the Church as a concordant discordance is that in retrospect we should be able to affirm that the Spirit was always already present in our actions and beliefs, directing us toward that aim, in a dialectic of attestation and suspicion. In an expiatory community, such continuity might be articulated even through almost complete failures in practice. DiNoia's affirmation that the Church bears witness to the true aim of life should be balanced, then, by an account of this community's innerly posited obligation (as the community of the crucified Christ) to entertain suspicion of articulations of its own aim and to perhaps transform those articulations when seeking to embrace the other in her concrete alterity.

17. Jenson, *Systematic Theology*, 2:181.

Selected Bibliography

Apel, Karl-Otto. "Transcendental Semiotics and the Paradigms of First Philosophy." In *From a Transcendental-Semiotic Point of View*, ed. Marianna
Papastephanou. Manchester: Manchester University Press, 1998.

Arendt, Hannah. *Crisis of the Republic*. New York: Harcourt Brace Jovanovich, 1972.

Barth, Karl. *Church Dogmatics*. Vol. 2, part 2. Trans. G. T. Thomson. Edinburgh: T and T Clark, 1957.

Bauer, Walter, William F. Arndt, F. Wilbur Gingrich, and Frederick Danker.
*A Greek-English Lexicon of the New Testament and Other Early Christian
Literature*, 2nd ed. rev. and aug. Chicago: University of Chicago Press,
1979.

Berkouwer, G. C. *The Triumph of Grace in the Theology of Karl Barth*. Grand
Rapids: Eerdmans, 1956.

Blamey, Kathleen. "From the Ego to the Self: A Philosophical Itinerary." In
The Philosophy of Paul Ricoeur, ed. Lewis Edwin Hahn. Chicago: Open
Court, 1995.

Brown, Raymond. *Death of the Messiah*. 2 vols. New York: Doubleday, 1994.

Bultmann, Rudolf. *Theology of the New Testament*. 2 vols. Trans. Kendrick
Grobel. New York: Scribner's, 1951.

———. *Jesus Christ and Mythology*. New York: Scribner's, 1958.

———. *Faith and Understanding*. Trans. Robert W. Funk. London: SCM,
1969.

———. "Liberal Theology and the Latest Theological Movement" (1924). In
Faith and Understanding, 1969.

———. "The Significance of the Historical Jesus for the Theology of Paul"
(1929). In *Faith and Understanding*, 1969.

———. "On the Problem of Demythologizing" (1961). In *New Testament and*

Mythology and Other Basic Writings, ed. and trans. Schubert M. Ogden. Philadelphia: Fortress Press, 1984.

Carson, D. A., P. O'Brien, and M. Seifrid, eds. *Justification and Variegated Nomism*. 2 vols. Grand Rapids: Baker Academic, 2001–2004.

Clarke, W. Norris. *Person and Being*. Milwaukee: Marquette University Press, 1993.

Clayton, Philip. *The Problem of God in Modern Thought*. Grand Rapids: Eerdmans, 2000.

Collins, John J. *The Apocalyptic Imagination: An Introduction to Jewish Apocalyptic Literature*. Grand Rapids: Eerdmans, 1998.

Cranfield, C. E. B. *A Critical and Exegetical Commentary on the Epistle to the Romans*. 2 vols. London: T and T Clark, 1975.

Curley, Edwin. *Behind the Geometrical Method: A Reading of Spinoza's* Ethics. Princeton, N.J.: Princeton University Press, 1988.

Das, A. Andrew. *Paul, the Law and the Covenant*. Peabody, Mass.: Hendrickson, 2001.

Dauenhauer, Bernard P. *Paul Ricoeur: The Promise and Risk of Politics*. Lanham, Md.: Rowman and Littlefield, 1998.

Davidson, Donald. *Essays on Actions and Events*. Oxford: Clarendon Press, 1980.

DiNoia, J. A. *The Diversity of Religions: A Christian Perspective*. Washington, D.C.: Catholic University of America Press, 1992.

Donaldson, Terence L. *Paul and the Gentiles: Remapping the Apostle's Convictional World*. Minneapolis: Fortress Press, 1997.

Dunn, James D. G. "The Lord Is the Spirit." *Journal of Theological Studies* 21 (1970): 309–20.

———. *Jesus and the Spirit: A Study of the Religious and Charismatic Experience of Jesus and the First Christians as Reflected in the New Testament*. London: SCM Press, 1975.

———. *Romans 1–8*. Dallas: Word Books, 1988.

———. *Romans 9–16*. Dallas: Word Books, 1988.

———. *The Epistle to the Galatians*. Peabody, Mass.: Hendrickson, 1993.

———. *The Theology of Paul the Apostle*. Grand Rapids: Eerdmans, 1998.

Elliott, Mark A. *The Survivors of Israel: A Reconsideration of the Theology of Pre-Christian Judaism*. Grand Rapids: Eerdmans, 2000.

Fee, Gordon. *God's Empowering Presence: The Holy Spirit in the Letters of Paul*. Peabody, Mass.: Hendrickson, 1994.

———. "Paul's Conversion as Key to His Understanding of the Spirit." In *The Road from Damascus: The Impact of Paul's Conversion on His Life, Thought, and Ministry*, ed. Richard N. Longenecker. Grand Rapids: Eerdmans, 1997.

Fergusson, David. *Bultmann*. London: Geoffrey Chapman, 1992.

Fitzmyer, Joseph. "Pauline Theology." In *The New Jerome Biblical Commentary*, ed. Raymond E. Brown, Joseph A. Fitzmyer, and Roland E. Murphy, 1382–1416. Englewood Cliffs, N.J.: Prentice Hall, 1990.

Ford, David F. *Self and Salvation: Being Transformed*. Cambridge: Cambridge University Press, 1999.

Gadamer, Hans-Georg. *Truth and Method*, 2nd ed., rev. New York: Continuum, 1989.

Gager, John G. *The Origins of Anti-Semitism: Attitudes toward Judaism in Pagan and Christian Antiquity*. New York: Oxford University Press, 1983.

———. *Reinventing Paul*. Oxford: Oxford University Press, 2000.

Gaston, Lloyd. *Paul and the Torah*. Vancouver: University of British Columbia Press, 1987.

Habermas, Jürgen. "What Is Universal Pragmatics?" In *Communication and the Evolution of Society*, trans. Thomas McCarthy. Boston: Beacon Press, 1979.

———. "Discourse Ethics." In *Moral Consciousness and Communicative Action*, trans. Christian Lenhardt and Shierry Weber Nicholsen. Cambridge, Mass.: MIT Press, 1990.

Harink, Douglas. *Paul among the Postliberals: Pauline Theology beyond Christendom and Modernity*. Grand Rapids: Brazos Press, 2003.

Hauerwas, Stanley. "Agency: Going Forward by Looking Back." In *Christian Ethics: Problems and Prospects*, ed. Lisa S. Cahill and James F. Childress. Cleveland: Pilgrim Press, 1996.

Hays, Richard. *The Faith of Jesus Christ: An Investigation of the Narrative Substructure of Galatians 3:1–4:11*. Missoula: Scholars Press, 1983.

———. *First Corinthians*. Louisville: John Knox Press, 1997.

Heidegger, Martin. *An Introduction to Metaphysics*. Trans. Ralph Manheim. New Haven, Conn.: Yale University Press, 1959.

———. *Being and Time*. Trans. John Macquarrie and Edward Robinson. San Francisco: Harper and Row, 1962.

———. "Phenomenology and Theology." In *Wegmarken*, Gesamtausgabe, vol. 9. Frankfurt am Main: Klostermann, 1976.

———. "The Origin of the Work of Art." In *Martin Heidegger: Basic Writings*, ed. David Farrell Krell. New York: Harper and Row, 1977.

Hilberath, Bernd Jochen. "Identity through Self-Transcendence: The Holy Spirit and the Fellowship of Free Persons." In *Advents of the Spirit: An Introduction to the Current Study of Pneumatology*, eds. Bradford E. Hinze and D. Lyle Dabney. Milwaukee: Marquette University Press, 2001.

Hume, David. *A Treatise on Human Nature*. New York: Penguin Books, 1969.

Husserl, Edmund. *Crisis of the European Sciences and Transcendental Phenomenology*. Trans. David Carr. Evanston, Ill.: Northwestern University Press, 1970.

———. *Cartesian Meditations: An Introduction to Phenomenology*. Trans. Dorion Cairns. Dordrecht: Kluwer Academic, 1995.

Ihde, Don. *Hermeneutic Phenomenology: The Philosophy of Paul Ricoeur*. Evanston, Ill.: Northwestern University Press, 1971.

Jaspert, Bernd, and Geoffrey Bromiley, eds. *Karl Barth/Rudolf Bultmann: Letters 1922–1966*. Grand Rapids: Eerdmans, 1981.

Jenson, Robert. *Systematic Theology*. 2 vols. New York: Oxford University Press, 1997–99.

Jewett, Robert. *Paul's Anthropological Terms: A Study of their Use in Conflict Settings*. Leiden: Brill, 1971.

Johnson, Elizabeth A. *Friends of God and Prophets: A Feminist Theological Reading of the Communion of Saints*. New York: Continuum, 1998.

Johnson, Luke Timothy. *The Writings of the New Testament: An Interpretation*. Philadelphia: Fortress Press, 1986.

Jones, Gareth. *Bultmann: Towards a Critical Theology.* Cambridge: Blackwell, 1991.

Kant, Immanuel. *Religion within the Limits of Reason Alone.* Trans. Theodore M. Greene and Hoyt H. Hudson. New York: Harper and Row, 1960.

———. *Critique of Pure Reason.* Trans. Norman Kemp Smith. New York: St. Martin's Press, 1965.

———. *Critique of Practical Reason.* Trans. Lewis White Beck. New York: Macmillan, 1993.

Kay, James F. *Christus Praesens: A Reconsideration of Rudolf Bultmann's Christology.* Grand Rapids: Eerdmans, 1994.

Kerr, Fergus. *Theology after Wittgenstein,* 2nd ed. London: SPCK, 1997.

Kvalvaag, Robert W. "The Spirit in Human Beings in Some Qumran Non-Biblical Texts." In *Qumran between the Old and New Testaments,* ed. F. H. Cryer and T. L. Thompson. Sheffield: Sheffield Academic Press, 1998.

Levinas, Emmanuel. "The Face Speaks." In *Totality and Infinity: An Essay on Exteriority.* Trans. Alphonso Lingis. Pittsburgh: Duquesne University Press, 1969.

———. *Time and the Other.* Trans. Richard A. Cohen. Pittsburgh: Duquesne University Press, 1987.

———. *Otherwise than Being, or, Beyond Essence.* Trans. Alphonso Lingis. Pittsburgh: Duquesne University Press, 1998.

Levison, John R. *The Spirit in First Century Judaism.* Leiden: Brill, 1997.

Locke, John. *An Essay Concerning Human Understanding.* New York: World Publishing, 1964.

Lyonnet, Stanislas, and Léopold Sabourin. *Sin, Redemption, and Sacrifice: A Biblical and Patristic Study.* Rome: Editrice Pontifico Istituto Biblico, 1998.

Luther, Martin. "The Magnificat." Trans. Jaroslav Pelikan and A. T. W. Steinhaeuser. In *Luther's Works.* Vol. 21. Philadelphia: Fortress Press, 1956.

———. "The Freedom of a Christian." Trans. W. A. Lambert and Harold J. Grimm. In *Luther's Works.* Vol. 31. Philadelphia: Muhlenberg Press, 1957.

———. "Two Kinds of Righteousness." Trans. Lowell J. Satre. In *Luther's Works.* Vol. 31. Philadelphia: Muhlenberg Press, 1957.

———. *Galatians—1535.* Trans. Jaroslav Pelikan. In *Luther's Works.* Vol. 26. Saint Louis: Concordia, 1963.

———. "The Sacrament of the Body and Blood—Against the Fanatics." In *Martin Luther's Basic Theological Writings,* ed. Timothy F. Lull. Minneapolis: Fortress Press, 1989.

———. "Temporal Authority: To What Extent It Should Be Obeyed." In *Martin Luther's Basic Theological Writings,* ed. Timothy F. Lull. Minneapolis: Fortress Press, 1989.

Lyotard, Jean-François. *The Postmodern Condition: A Report on Knowledge.* Trans. Geoff Bennington and Brian Massumi. Minneapolis: University of Minnesota Press, 1984.

———. *The Differend: Phrases in Dispute.* Trans. Georges Van Den Abbeele. Minneapolis: University of Minnesota Press, 1988.

MacIntyre, Alasdair. *After Virtue: A Study in Moral Theory.* Notre Dame, Ind.: University of Notre Dame Press, 1984.

Malina, Bruce J. *The New Testament World: Insights from Cultural Anthropology*. Louisville: Westminster/John Knox Press, 1993.

Martyn, J. Louis. *Galatians: A New Translation with Introduction and Commentary*.
New York: Doubleday, 1997.

McCarthy, Thomas. "Reason and Rationalization: Habermas's 'Overcoming' of Hermeneutics." In *Ideals and Illusions: On Reconstruction and Deconstruction in Contemporary Critical Theory*. Cambridge, Mass.: MIT Press, 1993.

Metz, Johann Baptist. *Faith and History in Society: Toward a Practical Fundamental
Theology*. Trans. David Smith. New York: Seabury Press, 1980.

Moltmann, Jürgen. *The Spirit of Life: A Universal Affirmation*. Trans. Margaret Kohl.
Minneapolis: Fortress Press, 1993.

———. *The Coming of God: Christian Eschatology*. Trans. Margaret Kohl. London:
SCM, 1996.

Moo, Douglas. *The Epistle to the Romans*. Grand Rapids: Eerdmans, 1996.

Nietzsche, Friedrich. *On the Genealogy of Morals*. Trans. Walter Kaufmann and R. J.
Hollingdale. New York: Vintage Books, 1967.

Parfit, Derek. *Reasons and Persons*. Oxford: Oxford University Press, 1986.

Plaskow, Judith. *Standing Again at Sinai: Judaism from a Feminist Perspective*. San
Francisco: Harper and Row, 1990.

Räisänen, Heiki. *Paul and the Law*. Philadelphia: Fortress Press, 1983.

Richardson, William J. *Heidegger: From Phenomenology to Thought*. The Hague: Martinus Nijhoff, 1963.

Ricoeur, Paul. *Freud and Philosophy: An Essay on Interpretation*. Trans. Denis Savage.
New Haven, Conn.: Yale University Press, 1970. Originally published as *De
L'Interprétation: Essai sur Freud* (Paris: Éditions du Seuil, 1965).

———. *The Conflict of Interpretations: Essays in Hermeneutics*. Ed. Don Ihde. Evanston,
Ill.: Northwestern University Press, 1974. Originally published as *Le Conflit des
Interprétations: Essais d'Hermeneutique* (Paris: Éditions du Seuil, 1969).

———. "Heidegger and the Question of the Subject." In *The Conflict of Interpretations:
Essays in Hermeneutics*, 1974.

———. "The Question of the Subject: The Challenge of Semiotics." In *The Conflict of
Interpretations: Essays in Hermeneutics*, 1974.

———. "Preface to Bultmann." In *Essays on Biblical Interpretation*, ed. Lewis S.
Mudge. Philadelphia: Fortress Press, 1980.

———. *Time and Narrative*. Vol. 1. Trans. K. McLaughlin and D. Pellauer. Chicago:
University of Chicago Press, 1984. Originally published as *Temps et Récit, Tome 1*
(Paris: Éditions du Seuil, 1983).

———. *Time and Narrative*. Vol. 2. Trans. K. McLaughlin and D. Pellauer. Chicago:
University of Chicago Press, 1985. Originally published as *Temps et Récit, Tome 2:
La Configuration Dans Le Récit De Fiction* (Paris: Éditions du Seuil, 1984).

———. *Time and Narrative*. Vol. 3. Trans. K. McLaughlin and D. Pellauer. Chicago:
University of Chicago Press, 1988. Originally published as *Temps et Récit, Tome 3:
Le Temps Raconté* (Paris: Éditions du Seuil, 1985).

———. *Husserl: An Analysis of his Phenomenology*. Trans. Edward G. Ballard and Lester E. Embree. Evanston, Ill.: Northwestern University Press, 1987.

————. "Humans as the Subject Matter of Philosophy." In *The Narrative Path: The Later Works of Paul Ricoeur,* ed. T. Peter Kemp and David Rasmussen. Cambridge, Mass.: MIT Press, 1989.

————. *Oneself as Another.* Trans. Kathleen Blamey. Chicago: University of Chicago Press, 1992. Originally published as *Soi-même comme un Autre* (Paris: Éditions du Seuil, 1990).

————. "Ideology and Utopia." In *From Text to Action,* trans. Kathleen Blamey and John B. Thompson. Evanston, Ill.: Northwestern University Press, 1991.

————. "Intellectual Autobiography." In *The Philosophy of Paul Ricoeur,* ed. Lewis Hahn. Chicago: Open Court, 1995.

————. *Figuring the Sacred: Religion, Narrative, and Imagination.* Ed. Mark I. Wallace. Trans. David Pellauer. Minneapolis: Fortress Press, 1995.

————. "Naming God." In *Figuring the Sacred: Religion, Narrative, and Imagination,* 1995.

————. "Hope and the Structure of Philosophical Systems." In *Figuring the Sacred: Religion, Narrative, and Imagination,* 1995.

————. "Philosophy and Religious Language." In *Figuring the Sacred: Religion, Narrative, and Imagination,* 1995.

————. "The Summoned Subject in the School of the Narratives of the Prophetic Vocation." In *Figuring the Sacred: Religion, Narrative, and Imagination,* 1995.

————. "The 'Sacred' Text and the Community." In *Figuring the Sacred: Religion, Narrative, and Imagination,* 1995.

————. "The Logic of Jesus, the Logic of God." In *Figuring the Sacred: Religion, Narrative, and Imagination,* 1995.

Rorty, Richard. "Pragmatism and Philosophy." In *After Philosophy: End or Transformation?* ed. Kenneth Baynes et al. Cambridge, Mass.: MIT Press, 1989.

Sanders, E. P. *Paul and Palestinian Judaism.* Minneapolis: Fortress Press, 1977.

Schrag, Calvin O. *The Self after Postmodernity.* New Haven, Conn.: Yale University Press, 1997.

Schreiner, Thomas R. *The Law and Its Fulfillment: A Pauline Theology of Law.* Grand Rapids: Baker, 1993.

Schwartz, Daniel R. "Two Pauline Allusions to the Redemption Mechanism of the Crucifixion." *Journal of Biblical Literature* 102, no. 2 (1983): 259–68.

Schweitzer, Albert. *The Quest of the Historical Jesus: A Critical Study of its Progress from Reimarus to Wrede.* Baltimore, Md.: Johns Hopkins University Press, 1998.

Segal, Alan F. *Paul the Convert: The Apostolate and Apostasy of Saul the Pharisee.* New Haven, Conn.: Yale University Press, 1990.

Sheehan, Thomas. "Heidegger's Introduction to the Phenomenology of Religion, 1920–1921." *Personalist* 60, no. 3 (1979): 312–24.

Siggins, Ian. *Martin Luther's Doctrine of Christ.* New Haven, Conn.: Yale University Press, 1970.

Spinoza, Benedict. *Ethics.* In vol. 1 of *The Collected Works of Spinoza,* trans. and ed. Edwin Curley. Princeton, N.J.: Princeton University Press, 1985.

Stockhausen, Carol Kern. *Moses' Veil and the Glory of the New Covenant: The Exeget-*

ical Substructure of II Cor. 3,1–4,6. Rome: Editrice Pontificio Istituto Biblico, 1989.

Stowers, Stanley K. "*Ek Pisteōs* and *Dia Tēs Pisteōs* in Romans 3:30." *Journal of Biblical Literature* 108, no. 4 (1989): 665–74.

———. *A Rereading of Romans: Justice, Jews and Gentiles.* New Haven, Conn.: Yale University Press, 1994.

Strawson, Peter. *Individuals.* London: Methuen, 1957.

Taylor, Charles. *Sources of the Self: The Making of the Modern Identity.* Cambridge, Mass.: Harvard University Press, 1989.

———. *Philosophical Arguments.* Cambridge, Mass.: Harvard University Press, 1995.

———. "Explanation and Practical Reason." In *Philosophical Arguments*, 1995.

———. "The Importance of Herder." In *Philosophical Arguments*, 1995.

———. *Hegel.* Cambridge: Cambridge University Press, 1997.

Thielman, Frank. *Paul and the Law: A Contextual Approach.* Downers Grove: Intervarsity Press, 1994.

Thiselton, Anthony C. *Interpreting God and the Postmodern Self: On Meaning, Manipulation, and Promise.* Grand Rapids: Eerdmans, 1995.

Tracy, David. *Blessed Rage for Order: The New Pluralism in Theology.* New York: Seabury Press, 1975. Reprint, Chicago: University of Chicago Press, 1996.

———. *The Analogical Imagination: Christian Theology and the Culture of Pluralism.* New York: Crossroad, 1981.

———. "Literary Theory and Return of the Forms for Naming and Thinking God in Theology." *Journal of Religion* 74, no. 3 (1994): 302–19.

Vandevelde, Pol. "Karl-Otto Apel's Critique of Heidegger." *Southern Journal of Philosophy* 38, no. 4 (2000): 651–75.

———. "A Pragmatic Critique of Pluralism in Text Interpretation." *Metaphilosophy* 36, no. 4 (2005): 501–21.

Vanhoozer, Kevin. *Is There a Meaning in this Text? The Bible, the Reader, and the Morality of Literary Knowledge.* Grand Rapids: Zondervan Publishing House, 1998.

Venema, Henry Isaac. *Identifying Selfhood: Imagination, Narrative, and Hermeneutics in the Thought of Paul Ricoeur.* New York: State University of New York Press, 2000.

Wallace, Mark I. *The Second Naiveté: Barth, Ricoeur, and the New Yale Theology*, 2nd ed. Macon, Ga.: Mercer University Press, 1995.

Westerholm, Stephen. *Israel's Law and the Church's Faith: Paul and his Recent Interpreters.* Grand Rapids: Eerdmans, 1988.

———. *Perspectives Old and New on Paul: The "Lutheran" Paul and His Critics.* Grand Rapids: Eerdmans, 2004.

Williams, Sam K. *Jesus' Death as Saving Event: The Background and Origin of a Concept.* Missoula: Scholars Press, 1975.

Wright, N. T. *The New Testament and the People of God.* Minneapolis: Fortress Press, 1992.

———. *The Climax of the Covenant: Christ and the Law in Pauline Theology.* Minneapolis: Fortress Press, 1993.

———. "Christos as 'Messiah' in Paul: Philemon 6." In *Climax of the Covenant*, 1993.

————. *Jesus and the Victory of God*. Minneapolis: Fortress Press, 1996.

————. *What St. Paul Really Said: Was Paul of Tarsus the Real Founder of Christianity?* Grand Rapids: Eerdmans, 1997.

————. *Letter to the Romans*. In *The New Interpreter's Bible*. Vol. 10. Nashville: Abingdon Press, 2002.

Author and Subject Index

Abraham, 8–9, 17, 20–21, 32–33, 36–
  38, 45, 70, 133, 135, 154 n. 52
  See also Aqedah
Adam, 8, 17–18, 24, 31, 34, 43, 54
Apel, Karl-Otto, 161 n. 24
apocalypse, 156 n. 6
apokatastasis, 165 n. 7
aporia, 90–91, 97, 150 n. 46
Aqedah, 32, 154 n. 52
Arendt, Hannah, 159 n. 12
atonement, 6, 19, 37, 138
autonomy, 39, 83, 86, 92, 95, 97,
  158 n. 30

Barth, Karl, 4, 24, 59, 154 n. 56
Blamey, Kathleen, 150 n. 40
body. *See* flesh, phenomenon of;
  living body; *soma*
Brown, Raymond, 154 n. 55
Bultmann, Rudolf, 3, 4, 5, 10, 15,
  75, 98, 109, 137, 140, 157
  n. 14
  and Ricoeur's "Preface to
    Bultmann," 72–73
  and Ricoeur's biblical
    hermeneutics, 123–128
  demythologizing and community,
    64–72
  kerygma and alterity, 61–63

kerygma and community, 63–64
relation of phenomenology to
  theology, 46–51
structure of human existence, 51–
  53, 129–134
the human situation, 53–55
the person under faith, 55–58
time and eschatology, 58–61
See also demythologizing

Carson, D. A., 148 n. 10
Christ
  anointed with the Spirit at the
    cross, 5, 28–30, 34, 36, 38
  as sacrifice (*see* Christ, death of
    Israel in)
  death of Israel in, 7, 17, 24–26,
    28, 31–37, 54
  death of self in (*see* self, death in
    Christ)
  incorporation into, 7, 13, 19, 25,
    27, 29, 31–44, 133, 135–140, 151
    n. 51, 153 n. 26
  marriage to, 11, 31
  resurrection of self in (*see* self,
    resurrection in Christ)
  Spirit of, 26–30, 39
Christianity and Judaism. *See*
  Judaism and Christianity

Scripture Index